The Islamic Development Bank

The Islamic Development Bank

A case study of Islamic co-operation

S. A. Meenai

Foreword by H. E. Mohammed Abalkhail
Minister of Finance and National Economy
Kingdom of Saudi Arabia

Kegan Paul International
London and New York

First published in 1989 by Kegan Paul International Limited
PO Box 256, London WC1B 3SW

Distributed by
John Wiley & Sons Ltd
Southern Cross Trading Estate
1 Oldlands Way, Bognor Regis
W. Sussex, PO22 9SA, England

Routledge, Chapman and Hall Inc
29 West 35th Street
New York, NY 10001
USA

The Canterbury Press Pty Ltd
2/71 Rushdale Street
Scoresby, Victoria 3179
Australia

A CIP catalogue record for this book is available
from the British Library

Library of Congress Cataloging in Publication Data
Applied For

Produced by Worts-Power Associates

Set in Times New Roman
by Wessex Typesetters, Frome
and printed in Great Britain
by Dotesios Printers Ltd
Bradford-on-Avon

ISBN 07103 0329–7

Contents

Foreword

I came to know Dr. S. A. Meenai, the author of this study, in the course of the early stages of the establishment of the Islamic Development Bank, the IDB. At that time, and during the discussions of the idea of establishing the Bank, my colleague finance ministers representing some other Islamic countries and myself had full realisation that we were handling an entirely new project. There has been no precedent that a group of developing countries alone has come together for undertaking such a unique project. What made the effort for establishing IDB much more difficult was the fact that the Bank was to be founded on Islamic principles and ideals, which, of course, are quite different from those practised in similar development financing institutions. IDB needed to be designed to operate in conformity with the Islamic Shariah.

As a result, the new project inspired the participants to come up with an influx of different views and suggestions, which required, in turn, the holding of a series of meetings, and necessitated lengthy deliberations.

Ever since Dr. Meenai participated in the preparatory work for establishing IDB, he has always shown his keen interest in the establishment of the Islamic Development Bank. Those who happened to have a working acquaintance with Dr. Meenai in the project, are, I believe, of the view that he has contributed substantially to the success of the Bank. Every time I attended annual meetings of the Board of Governors, I found Dr. Meenai energetic and enthusiastic – as he has always been over the years.

Dr. Meenai was able to pursue further the work he has associated himself with from the beginning until the idea materialised and IDB became a reality.

What I wish to indicate by these words is that, in view of his long association with the Bank, Dr. Meenai is in a unique position to undertake the study on the evaluation of the IDB. Indeed Dr. Meenai's involvement with the project, as a head of the Secretariat Team under the Chairman of the Preparatory Committee, as Secretary in the Inauguration Meeting of the IDB, then a member of the first Board of Executive Directors and as the Bank's first Vice President, has given him the privilege of being a well-equipped person, and placed him in a position to review and analyse the activities of the Bank.

Finally, it gives me great pleasure to be able to contribute these words to this valuable study; and I am very delighted to have witnessed for more than ten years the development of IDB as a premier Islamic financing institution for development. I am particularly pleased to see that it plays a wide-ranging, growing and increasingly important role in the development process of its member countries individually as well as the Muslim Ummah as a whole.

Mohammed Abalkhail
Minister of Finance
and National Economy
Kingdom of Saudi Arabia

Preface

It is not unusual to have the activities of international development banks reviewed and analysed after they have been in operation for a certain period. A study entitled *The World Bank since Bretton Woods* by Edward S. Mason and Robert E. Asher published in 1973 is an instance in point.

The Islamic Development Bank has now been in business for over twelve years and this is the first analysis of its activities.

The approach adopted by the author may perhaps appear excessively comprehensive. This is for the reason that the study is designed to serve several purposes. On the one hand, it seeks to trace the history of the Bank since the time that the proposal was first mooted to its emergence as the premier Islamic financing institution and on the other it aims at projecting the image of the Bank and its role since its establishment. The primary aim is to promote interest in its development. At the same time, an attempt is made to evaluate the institution – its performance and prospects – in two ways: first the past performance of the institution is critically evaluated and secondly an effort is made to use the past performance in a diagnostic sense to prescribe what the Bank should do in future. Not only its achievements but also its difficulties and need for improvement are depicted. Furthermore, an effort has been made to highlight the uniqueness of the institution by portraying how it differs from other multilateral institutions.

The IDB, as an international financial institution, has the distinction of being an association of developing countries alone which differs in character from other multilateral institutions. Its donor countries though they have a high per capita income, are less advanced industrially than some of the recipient countries. The task of the Bank has been made more difficult by the preponderance of the least-developed countries in its membership.

Apart from the cardinal requirement of conformity to a Shariah, it has an Ummah-wide approach in that the mission assigned to it embraces the Muslim Ummah as a whole including the Muslim communities in non-member countries and is not confined to the member countries alone. As an association of developing countries alone, the donor countries do not enjoy the benefits of procurement and increased export earnings and it is the Islamic principle of mutual help and co-operation which binds the donors and recipients together. Its task is much more wide-ranging than that of other multilateral institutions, in that apart from its financing role it is entrusted with the functions of promoting foreign trade and economic co-operation among Muslim countries, as well as undertaking research to enable the economic, financial and banking activities in Muslim countries to conform to Shariah. The IDB has over the years added some new dimensions to its activities, such as refugee assistance and running a project for the utilisation of sacrificial meat during Haj.

There are a number of other features of the IDB which provide a contrast with conventional international development banks. As far as objectives are concerned, there is much greater emphasis on social progress and economic co-operation among member countries. The aim is to promote complementarity in the economies of Islamic countries through regional projects and joint ventures. There is special emphasis on meeting the needs fo the least-developed member countries and the provision of technical assistance.

While in the case of traditional international development banks, loans are the sole means of resource transfer, in the case of the IDB loans are not accorded the pride of place as they inherently involve interest. Loans attract only a modest service fee to cover administrative expenses. In the case of certain multilateral institutions, there was a prohibition on equity financing in the initial years. True, the International Finance Corporation (IFC), an affiliate of the World Bank, undertakes equity financing. However, by far the bulk of its financing has taken the form of loans while equity financing has been undertaken in combination with a loan operation, whereby its interests as an equity holder in the project are also partly safeguarded. In sharp contrast, equity financing is supposed to be one of the principal modes of financing by the IDB. Another important characteristic of the IDB is that it undertakes lease financing and instalment sales which is not the case with conventional multilateral institutions. Again, unlike traditional international development banks, large scale foreign trade financing is undertaken by the IDB with a view to promoting foreign trade among member countries and also as a means of placing short-term funds which are not immediately needed in project financing. The relationship with national development banks is organised on a different basis than is the case with conventional international development banking. In the latter case, international development banks can provide direct loans to national development banks, which utilise them in their operations whereas in the case of the IDB the national development banks, act, so to speak, as agencies authorised to identify, appraise and forward suitable projects for financing by the IDB in accordance with its own policies and procedures. This relationship which is designed to reach small enterprises in member countries through the medium of national development banks is conducted under what are known as line of equity, line of leasing, line of instalment sale and line of foreign trade financing arrangements. The national development banks are granted a line of amount of funding within which they identify, appraise and commend projects for financing.

Another distinguishing feature of the IDB is its relatively greater dependence on its capital. This is for the reason that because of the interest prohibition the IDB cannot raise resources from the market in the way traditional international banks do. At the same time, on account of equity financing and foreign trade financing the tempo of disbursement is faster in Islamic development banking compared to traditional international banking. This intensifies the need for resource replenishment. Here mention may be made of two other features which distinguish the IDB from conventional international development banks: first the acceptance of deposits from investors and second, the placement of short-term surplus funds in ways other than those followed by conventional multilateral institutions which place their surplus funds in government securities, government guaranteed securities, time deposits and certificates of deposits with banks.

While the IDB is designed to assist Muslim countries and communities, its activities are by no means devoid of interest for other developmental organisations and developing countries generally. In many ways, its work and operations have significant implications for the development financing process and its conceptual framework. For one thing, the Bank undertakes interest-free financing from its ordinary resources which represents a big stride in the field of concessional financing. Moreover, the Bank focuses on equity financing – an area which has remained generally neglected by the international banks. Its lease financing, foreign trade financing, system of instalment sales, modes of placement of surplus funds, the lines of equity and leasing arrangements, methods of resource mobilisation and its role in promoting economic co-operation among member countries are likely to be of special interest.

This book represents an effort to combine historical narrative with an analysis of the Bank's performance and future role. Having been associated with the Bank, first as Secretary of the Preparatory Committee, then as a member of the first Board of Executive Directors and finally as the Bank's first Vice President, I feel particularly well-equipped to undertake this task. I would like to acknowledge with thanks the assistance I have received from the Bank and its President, Dr. Ahmad Mohamed Ali, in regard to writing this book. My thanks are also due to His Excellency Sheikh Mohammed

Abalkhail, Minister of Finance and National Economy, Kingdom of Saudi Arabia, for contributing a foreword introducing the book.

S. A. Meenai
June 1988

Chapter 1

Origin of the Bank

It would be fitting, perhaps, to begin with a word about the overall economic and political perspective in which the idea of an Islamic Bank was conceived. True, the need for closer collaboration and greater solidarity among Muslim countries had been recognised much earlier. It had found expression in the establishment of an Islamic League and the convening of an Islamic Conference in Mecca. The events of the sixties, however, provided the real stimulus in this direction leading to the creation of a Permanent Secretariat in Jeddah in 1969 known as the Organisation of Islamic Conference.

The international economic scene at the time was characterised by serious difficulties. The developed countries, faced as they were with low levels of employment and huge balance of payments problems, were adopting policies clearly inimical to the economic interest of the relatively poorer countries. The economic prospects of developing countries were seriously jeopardised by budgetary and capital shortage constraints, lagging food production, rising levels of debt service payments,* slow growth in export earnings, a rising import bill due to higher capital goods prices, and the high interest rates, which made the cost of capital to the poor borrowing countries unbearable. At a time when the need for larger external financing had become urgent it

* The Pearson Commission on International Development described the debt situation as explosive.

was feared that the flow of concessional assistance to developing countries would decline in real terms. The Second and Third United Nations Conferences on Trade and Development (UNCTADs), having discussed the situation, had utterly failed to find any satisfactory solutions to the gigantic problems of more aid and freer trade.

However, perhaps, the most crucial single factor conditioning the entire atmosphere was the spectacular rise in oil prices and related developments. With the prosperity which followed, the oil exporting Muslim countries acquired a new importance and status. At the same time, the sharply rising oil price brought in its wake, serious economic hardship for the non-oil producing Muslim countries. On the whole, the oil boom gave a new hope and sense of confidence to the Islamic world engendering the expectation that the oil producing Islamic nations would be willing to share their God-given wealth with other Muslim countries. Again, as the western banking system became over-strained by massive financial surpluses and as the political risks attached to entrusting the capital surpluses to the west became apparent, it was but natural that the capital-rich Muslim countries should look for investment opportunities in the capital-scarce Islamic countries. While the non-oil producing Islamic countries needed assistance by way of capital resources from the oil exporting Muslim countries, the latter being under pressure from the west, soon realised that they were in dire need of support from their Muslim brethren.

The events connected with the Ramzan war of October 1973 with Israel, particularly the total lack of support and sympathy from the west and its massive and open assistance to the adversary, vividly brought home the paramount need for mutual assistance and co-operation to the Muslim nations. What appeared first as the need to promote Arab solidarity expanded into a case for co-operation based on Islam. Slowly, the entire atmosphere became charged with this sentiment, in turn preparing the ground for a new institution in the economic field, which could foster the development of Muslim countries by bringing them together. As the whole edifice was based on Islam, it was in the fitness of things that it did not remain confined to the need for setting up an international Bank for the Muslim countries but became transformed into a plea for the establishment of a bank operating in total conformity with the Islamic Shariah.

The idea of an Islamic Bank was first mooted at the Second Conference of Foreign Ministers of Muslim Countries held at Karachi in December 1970. The Conference had on its Agenda relating to "Economic, Cultural and Social Co-operation among participating States" an item entitled "International Muslim Bank for Trade and Development". The proposal which had been submitted by Pakistan came under discussion first at the Committee stage and the verbatim record of the Conference shows that the Arab Republic of Egypt volunteered to conduct the initial study. The delegate of the UAR submitted a detailed proposal for this purpose, which was supported by the delegates from Libya and Morocco. The delegates of Saudi Arabia and Tunisia, while supporting the proposal, argued that priority should be accorded to the creation of the Islamic Secretariat and that the preparation of the necessary documents for the establishment of the Bank should follow it. The delegate of Guinea proposed the establishment of an ad hoc committee composed of experts who would thoroughly study the entire matter. He suggested that after the study by experts had been completed, it should be sent to the member governments for their consideration. This view was supported by the delegate of Lebanon, who argued that just as a committee had been set up to examine the problems relating to the establishment of the Islamic Secretariat, another committee of experts be established to study the proposal for a Bank. The delegate of Kuwait took the position that the question of the establishment of an Islamic Bank called for comprehensive examination and study and until this was completed, it was difficult for his government even to approve in principle the establishment of such a bank. The delegate of Algeria expressed a similar view.

The Conference of Foreign Ministers, therefore, resolved that the Arab Republic of Egypt be entrusted with the study pertaining to the proposed bank for submission within a period of six months. The final resolution by the Conference read as follows:

> The Conference having examined a proposal submitted by Pakistan and the proposal made by the United Arab Republic relating to undertaking a study of the idea of establishing either an Islamic bank or an Islamic Federation of banks, recommends the following:
>
> (a) The UAR should be charged with the responsibility of making a comprehensive study of this project in the light of its own proposals and in the light of the discussions that took place in the Conference. The UAR shall submit the result of this study to the Secretary General in six months time;
>
> (b) The Secretary General shall forward his study to member states with a view to obtaining their written comments on it before submitting it to the next Conference for discussion and decision;
>
> (c) Any member state of the Conference may participate in the study, provided it sends to the Secretary General the names of specialists and experts nominated to participate in the work of this commission. These names will be communicated within a month by the Secretary General to the UAR so as to enable it to make its own study as early as possible.
>
> (d) This study, suggestions and recommendations shall not commit member states before the decision of the Conference.*

In accordance with this resolution, the UAR prepared a study entitled *The*

* Article 16 of the joint communique of the Second Islamic Conference held in Karachi in December 1970.

Egyptian Study on the Establishment of the Islamic Banking System (Economics and Islamic Doctrine), signed by Mr. Hassan Mohamed Al Tuhamy, who mentioned that he was submitting the study with the collaboration of Mr. Hassan Bolbol, Mr. Mohamed Samir Ibrahim, Dr. Gahreb El Gammal, Dr. Ahmed El Naggar, Dr. Shawki Ismail, Mr. Salah El Din Awad and Mr. Mahmoud Noaman El Ansary. The study started with a description of the Islamic economic system and proceeded to discuss the "cornerstones" or main principles of Islamic banking at local and international levels. It observed that it was time for the "Moslem Nation" to use its "modern thought" to find an "Islamic method" for the investment of "Moslem capital". It also dealt with the guarantees required for the sound use of funds of Islamic banks and the deposits held in trust by them. The focus of the study was primarily on commercial and trade transactions rather than development financing, though it suggested that the proposed institution could finance "the institutions of investment and development" existing in each Islamic state. The Bank was also to be entrusted with the task of administering the funds of the Baitul Maal and Auqaf as also the surplus liquid money of the "central institutions" of each Muslim country. The Bank was to have a board of trustees and a board of directors. In addition to the Bank, the study proposed the setting up of what it called "the Investment and Development Body of Islamic Countries and the consultative organ of economic and Islamic banks". The study also contained a supplementary note dealing with the permissibility of interest received by a Muslim from a non-Muslim debtor or on his deposits in non-Islamic banks. It pleaded that there could be absolutely no doubt that Muslims should collect the interest due to them from foreign banks, which could in turn be used to help Muslim countries to develop. In fact, the study argued that the forgoing of such interest would harm the interest of Islam, as the left-over interest could be used for preaching against Islam.*

The Egyptian study was discussed comprehensively at a meeting held in Al-Zehraa Hall, Cairo, between 7 and 9 February 1972. The meeting was attended by the Secretary General of the OIC, together with a delegation from the General Secretariat and also representatives from Afghanistan, Algeria, Egypt, Guinea, Indonesia, Iran, Jordan, Libya, Malaysia, Mali, Morocco, Pakistan, Saudi Arabia, Senegal, Somalia, the Sudan, Turkey and Yemen Arab Republic. The press release after the meeting stated that the Arab Republic of Egypt had submitted to the meeting a working paper containing the general Islamic approach to the investment of "Moslem money", and also a research paper on the setting up of Islamic banks on the basis of Islamic jurisprudence. This research paper included a practical application of how to develop banking on an Islamic basis and how to set up international Islamic banks and a Federation of Islamic Banks with necessary

* *The Egyptian Study on the Establishment of the Islamic Banking System* (pp. 51–52).

affiliated, consultative and executive organs. The committee in its meetings dealt with many Shariah aspects, with the aim of finding out the alternative Shariah ways as regards money dealing, deposits, and the gist of Islamic legislation concerning the employment of Islamic capital in the Islamic world or that deposited in non-Islamic countries.

While not clearly set out in the press release, it was evident that the study* undertaken by the Arab Republic of Egypt was considered to be highly generalised, focusing somewhat hazily on the creation of an Islamic banking and financial system rather than the establishment of an international development bank. It was finally decided that the discussion on the study be resumed in the Islamic Conference of Foreign Ministers to be held in Jeddah later in the year. Following this decision, the Egyptian study appears to have undergone some revision and was forwarded to the Secretary General of the OIC with the request that it be circulated for discussion at the ensuing Conference of Foreign Ministers. The Study was thus placed before the Conference of Foreign Ministers in Jeddah in 1972 which in turn decided that it be examined further by the Islamic Secretariat. The Secretariat was also required to ascertain the views of the member states concerning the establishment of the International Islamic Bank.

As directed by the Conference of Foreign Ministers, Tunku Abdul Rahman Putra, the Secretary General of the OIC, pursued the idea of an Islamic bank further. It seems that there was a discussion between him and Mr. Hassan Al-Tohaimi and it was proposed that a commission of banking and legal experts should visit firstly Libya and Morocco, secondly Indonesia, Pakistan, Afghanistan and Iran and finally some other Middle Eastern countries, in order to explain the concept of Islamic banks. It appears that it was contemplated that, at the initial stage, the member countries which accepted the concept of an Islamic bank would establish such a bank in their own country and that subsequently an association of Islamic banks would be formed. It was also envisaged that the financial and economic department of the OIC would co-ordinate their activities and advise these banks. Meanwhile, it was thought that a committee might be formed in Cairo to look into all the religious aspects of the matter. However, the Commission which was to start work in April 1972 could not do so until August 1972. Meanwhile, a paper was prepared by the Islamic Secretariat arguing that, as it would take some time to consult each individual member state as a condition prior to the establishment of the International Islamic Bank, it would be advisable to establish what was termed a "Development Islamic Bank" which would expand investment opportunities for the surplus funds available with the oil

* Though the Egyptian study did not help much in the framing of the IDB charter, it seems to have had one important consequence, namely the directing of attention toward the need and case for making the institution work on Islamic principles. The study itself did not shed adequate light on this matter but certainly helped to focus attention on this aspect.

producing Islamic countries and would assist in the implementation of the development plans in the developing Islamic states. The paper made references to the Asian Development Bank, the Inter-American Development Bank and the African Development Bank. The main objective of the proposed bank was to establish a "direct link between funds from oil exporting countries which seek a profitable and secure investment field and the development projects in Islamic world" without the intermediation of foreign banks. It was visualised that the bank "should serve as an additional source for financing development projects in Islamic countries, the fulfilment of which would benefit both lender and the borrower". The Bank was to be governed by two boards: (1) the Board of Trustees and (2) the Board of Directors. As for the technical management of the Bank, it was proposed that it should be entrusted "to a consortium of banks of international repute". As regards its resources, it was proposed that funds be raised "by borrowing in international markets or in financial markets in Islamic countries".

At this stage, the Secretary General of the OIC decided to obtain "a second opinion" on the proposal and for this he turned to some Malaysian experts. This resulted in a new draft closely patterned on the Articles of Agreement of the Asian Development Bank. The objectives of the proposed Bank were described as "encouraging and promoting in the true spirit of Islam, economic co-operation and collaboration in accordance with the tenets of Islam, to promote the development of Islamic countries and to foster their economic growth and economic co-operation and to seek and promote investment of the funds of the Bank based on sound banking principles to ensure a fair return to the Bank and benefits to the participants." The main functions of the Bank were proposed as "utilising its resources for profitable investment in addition to financing development projects in member countries and other regions or areas, promotion of investment of public and private capital for development of Islamic countries and communities, issuing of participating certificates, acceptance of deposits, granting loans and providing guarantees and other facilities, mobilising money and providing managerial and strategy development thereto, to assist Islamic countries in the co-ordination of their development policies and plans and the provision of technical assistance." The draft proposed that the authorised capital of the Bank be one billion units of account divided equally into paid-in shares and callable shares.

This working paper was considered at a meeting attended by Qatar, Bahrain, UAE, Oman, Libya, Malaysia and Morocco on 21 July 1973. It appears that, after a special approach to King Faisal, the great champion of Islamic solidarity, by the Secretary General, the Saudi representatives also joined this meeting. After examining the paper, the meeting decided that a draft agreement be prepared for the purpose of establishing the Islamic Development Bank, and that a conference of the Finance Ministers of Islamic countries should be convened to consider it.

A Conference of Finance Ministers was held in Jeddah, at the Jeddah

Palace Hotel on 15 and 16 December, 1973, under the chairmanship of Sheikh Mohammed Abalkhail, at that time the Minister of State for Finance and National Economy, Kingdom of Saudi Arabia. It was inaugurated by HRH Prince Fahad bin Abdulaziz and was attended by 25 Islamic countries. The Conference held wide-ranging discussions based on the documents submitted to it and issued a declaration of intent which read as follows:

> RECALLING one of the objectives specified in the Charter of the Islamic Conference which emphasises the need for closer co-operation among member countries for the economic, social and other fields:
>
> CONSIDERING the importance of closer co-operation as a means for achieving the most efficient utilisation of resources and for accelerating the economic development of member states of the Islamic Conference:
>
> RECOGNISING the significance of making available additional financing for development of Islamic states and investment through mobilisation of funds and other resources both from within and outside the Islamic countries and by seeking to grow and foster conditions conducive to increase domestic savings and investments and greater flow of development funds into these countries:
>
> REALISING the desirability of promoting the harmonious development of the economies of the Islamic states and communities and the establishment of an Islamic financial institution for development and investment of funds on Islamic principles and ideals:
>
> CONVINCED that the establishment of such financing institution will serve these needs:
>
> WE THE MEMBER COUNTRIES OF THE ISLAMIC CONFERENCE HAVE HEREBY DECLARED our intention to establish an Islamic Development Bank located in Jeddah.

This declaration of intent was signed by Algeria, Chad, Egypt, Guinea, Jordan, Kuwait, Lebanon, Libya, Malaysia, Mali, Mauritania, Morocco, Niger, Oman, Pakistan, Qatar, Saudi Arabia, Senegal, Somalia, Sudan, Tunisia, UAE and Yemen Arab Republic.

The Conference of Finance Ministers decided that the task of establishing the Bank be undertaken afresh and systematically. For this purpose, it established a Preparatory Committee under the chairmanship of Tunku Abdul Rahman Putra, who had by then retired as Secretary General of the OIC. The Preparatory Committee was required, taking into account other studies already presented and proposals and remarks of delegations of member states attending the Conference, to:

(1) Study and draft the necessary documents for the establishment of Islamic Development Bank including
  (a) The Articles of Agreement
  (b) The Bye-Laws
  (c) The Rules of Procedure of the Board of Directors

(d) The Headquarters Agreement with the Host Government.

(2) Study and recommend the structure and organisation of the Bank.

(3) Suggest such arrangements as will be required to give effect to the Declaration of Intent.

The Preparatory Committee was authorised to devise its own rules of procedure and it was laid down that the recommendations of the Committee should be presented to the Islamic Conference of Finance Ministers for consideration and approval. To meet the expenses of the Preparatory Committee, the Conference approved an amount not exceeding US$250,000 chargeable to the capital of the Bank.

Chapter 2

Preparatory Work

The first meeting of the Preparatory Committee for the establishment of the Islamic Development Bank was held at the Islamic Secretariat on 18 December, 1973, under its Chairman, Tunku Abdul Rahman Putra. The meeting elected Saudi Arabia as Vice Chairman and Pakistan as the Secretary of the Preparatory Committee. It was resolved that a special secretariat for the Chairman should be set up and that the Preparatory Committee could seek assistance from the Islamic Secretariat* or from any other organ as might be required. It was decided to hold the next meeting of the Preparatory Committee in Jeddah on 9 February, 1974.

In accordance with the resolution of the Preparatory Committee, the Government of Saudi Arabia nominated the late Mr. Anwar Ali, Governor, Saudi Arabian Monetary Agency, as the Vice Chairman, and the Government of Pakistan nominated Dr. Saeed Ahmad Meenai, Deputy Governor, State Bank of Pakistan, as the Secretary of the Preparatory Committee.

In view of the fact that the sum of money sanctioned at the meeting of the Finance Ministers in Jeddah in December, 1973, to meet the expenses of the Preparatory Committee had not been subscribed, the Chairman of the

* The Chairman, however, decided to be fairly self-sufficient – so that after the former's retirement from the OIC, the Islamic Secretariat remained totally dissociated from the preparatory work for the establishment of the Bank.

Preparatory Committee requested the Government of Malaysia to advance US$250,000 for the expenses of the Preparatory Committee. The Government of Malaysia not only agreed to make the advance but deputed an official, Mr. Mohammed Noor Rahim, from its Finance Ministry to control the expenditure and to maintain detailed accounts. With the help of this money, an office for the Committee was rented in the Dewan Bahasa Building in Kuala Lumpur and a skeleton staff was appointed. Two legal experts, Tan Sri Abdul Aziz Zain and Dr. Tawfiq Shawi, were invited to help with the legal aspects of the Committee's work and some part-time help from Dr. Rais Saniman of the Bank Bhumi Putra was also obtained as he had been associated with the earlier Malaysian study.

The first task was to identify and list the main issues involved in the establishment of the IDB and to formulate a general approach to the various problems. In this process, the statutes of the various international development banks, including the World Bank, the Asian Development Bank, the African Development Bank, the Inter-American Development Bank, the European Investment Bank, International Finance Corporation and the International Development Association were studied. Attention was also directed to institutions such as the Central American Bank for Economic Integration, East African Development Bank, Andean Development Corporation and the Caribbean Development Bank. The latest trends and developments in the international economic, financial and monetary system were also taken into account to serve as a background. Finally, an effort was made to derive a pattern and a model for the institution from the economic facts relating to the Muslim countries and their requirements and characteristics, as well as the principles and ideals of Islam.

At this stage, it was found necessary to review the issues collectively and also to involve the representative of Saudi Arabia in the deliberations. Therefore, the Chairman of the Preparatory Committee decided that he, along with the Secretary of the Committee and the members of his technical staff, should visit Jeddah, for purposes of consultation with the Vice Chairman from Saudi Arabia. They arrived in Jeddah on 7 March, 1974, with the list of issues, approach to the problem and other relevant documents. On reaching Jeddah, the Chairman was informed by the Vice Chairman that in view of the fact that the Preparatory Committee at its first meeting had decided to meet again in Jeddah on 9 February, 1974, some members of the Committee had arrived in Jeddah and a meeting had taken place in the Ministry of Foreign Affairs on 10 February, 1974, under his chairmanship. At this meeting, the Egyptian delegation circulated a paper entitled Draft Agreement and Statutes of the Islamic International Organisation for Development and Investment. The paper suggested that the authorised capital should be one billion SDRs* and the subscribed capital 500 million SDRs. Of the subscribed

* SDR is the abbreviation for Special Drawing Rights of the International Monetary

capital, 400 million SDRs was proposed to be subscribed by governments and 100 million SDRs by individuals and groups. The institution was to be given the power of accepting deposits and borrowing in the form of participation bonds. The Chairman felt that the earlier meeting was not in order as it had not been convened in the proper manner and he as Chairman had no knowledge of it.

At any rate, the issues were carefully examined and discussed with the Vice Chairman. In these discussions Dr. Umar Chapra and Mr. Misbahuddin Farooqi of the Saudi Monetary Agency also participated. As a result of the discussions, it was agreed not to include balance of payments financing among the functions of the Bank. This was on account of the feeling that alternative sources for balance of payments assistance were emerging and that the large donors might shy away if the range of the Bank's functions was extended to cover balance of payments financing also. It was also decided that there should be no provision for callable capital and local currency subscriptions and that, to start with, the Bank should not aim at too high a level of authorised and subscribed capital. Similarly, in regard to the voting power, the Vice Chairman's suggestion that it should fully reflect the respective capital subscriptions and that the basic votes should not exceed 500, was incorporated.

The preamble and articles relating to purpose, functions, capital structure and voting rights were then drafted as this constituted the most important part of the draft agreement. The draft which emerged was again discussed with the Vice Chairman who called attention to the need for spelling out the operating principles in the Articles of Agreement. It was explained to him that in the interest of flexibility, the operating principles had deliberately not been incorporated in the draft and that it was proposed to frame them outside the charter. The Vice Chairman, however, felt that it would be desirable to incorporate the operating principles in the Draft Articles also. A copy of the entire draft was taken by the Vice Chairman for purposes of consultation with the International Monetary Fund experts, particularly in regard to questions relating to the maintenance of value and the use of currencies. In this connection, Dr. Aziz Ali F. Mohammed of the Fund paid two visits to Jeddah at the invitation of the Vice Chairman, to provide advice. At the suggestion of the Vice Chairman, the idea of a round of visits to member countries was abandoned as it was felt that technical discussions with individual countries could create problems and lead to disagreement. The task force, therefore, returned to Kuala Lumpur. In Jeddah, Tunku Abdul Rahman Putra had an audience with King Faisal, whose constant patronage and steadfast support, coupled with the total dedication of Tunku Abdul Rahman Putra, contributed immeasurably to bringing the idea of the IDB to fruition.

Fund (IMF). The Islamic Dinar, which is a unit of account in the IDB, is equivalent to one SDR of the International Monetary Fund.

The King donated a sum of one hundred thousand US dollars for the setting up of a temporary headquarters for the institution and for the training of staff.

The Secretary of the Committee, accompanied by the legal adviser, Tan Sri Abdul Aziz Zain, and Dr. Rais Saniman, paid a brief visit to the Asian Development Bank and held consultations with the Deputy Director of their legal department, Mr. G. F. Rea. Thus the draft of the working paper, designed to serve as the basis for discussion by the Preparatory Committee, was finalised.

It is noteworthy that the urge for an international development bank for Muslim countries and the quest for a truly Islamic bank more or less coincided and led to the decision to set up an international development bank for Islamic states operating on the basis of Shariah. Though a very significant development in itself, this made the task of establishing the Bank much more complex, requiring much more exploration and original work. As a matter of fact, ideally, there should have been a meeting of the Preparatory Committee for a full-scale discussion of the various issues involved. Only after such a meeting had taken place and some kind of guidelines had emerged should the actual drafting of the Articles have been undertaken. But there were contrary considerations which it was impossible to ignore. The paramount need was for the institution to be set up as soon as possible. Three years had already been lost since the idea of the Bank was first mooted. Moreover, as far as the task of resolving various questions concerning conformity with Shariah was concerned, it could not be accomplished in a few plenary sessions of the Preparatory Committee and had to be pursued by concerted efforts extending over a length of time. Thus, a broad mandate that the Bank must conform to Shariah was incorporated in the Agreement establishing it but the various complex issues were, so to speak, swept under the carpet at the preparatory stage. That this put the management of the Bank on the horns of a dilemma cannot be denied. On the one hand, the management was expected to make the earliest possible start and on the other, before becoming operational a great deal of exploratory work was necessary to ensure conformity with Shariah.

The Preparatory Committee met in Jeddah from 14 to 21 May, 1974. It examined and discussed at length the working paper prepared by the Secretariat. The Saudi Arabian Monetary Agency made all the arrangements for the meeting and having regard to the technical nature of the discussions, after the initial proceedings, the chair was taken by the Governor of the Saudi Arabian Monetary Agency, the Vice Chairman of the Committee.

On the conclusion of the Preparatory Committee meeting, its Chairman was received in audience by His Majesty King Faisal who very graciously made available one of the royal offices, Qasre Niaba, to house the Bank until the construction of a permanent headquarters building.

While approving the draft Articles of Agreement, the Preparatory Committee authorised its Chairman to have the draft Agreement carefully examined from the legal standpoint and also with a view to ensuring that the English and French versions fully conformed to the Arabic text. After the conclusion of the Preparatory Committee meeting, the Secretariat reassembled in Kuala Lumpur in July, 1974, for the purpose of finalising the Articles of Agreement, before they were presented to the meeting of Finance Ministers. It was joined by Mr. George Shuster from the Asian Development Bank who assisted with regard to the legal aspects. Apart from changes of style and those designed to improve presentation, a few changes of substance were also made in the draft agreement. These related to a time limit for ratification by founder members, a uniform period for the payment of subscription by new members, the protection of the Bank's equity investments in a country withdrawing from membership and a time limit for appeal to the Board of Governors against decisions of the Board of Executive Directors.

A Conference of Finance Ministers was held in Jeddah in August, 1974, and adopted the draft Articles of Agreement as broadly approved by the Preparatory Committee.* The principal change made by the Conference related to the subscribed capital of the Bank which was reduced from one billion Islamic Dinars,† as originally proposed, to 750 million Islamic Dinars.‡ A clause was also added to the effect that each member shall declare the initial number of shares it shall subscribe to the capital stock, before the expiry of the date specified in paragraph 1 of Article 66. The last date for signing by founder members was fixed as 15 Shawal 1394H, corresponding to 31 October 1974. In Article 68, it was laid down that the Agreement shall come into force when instruments of ratification or acceptance shall have been deposited by signatories whose subscriptions in the aggregate comprise not less than 500 million Islamic Dinars.

The meeting of Finance Ministers also devoted itself to the task of raising subscriptions towards the capital of the Bank and a three-member committee was appointed for the purpose. The Chairman of the Preparatory Committee had proposed, by way of a tentative basis for subscription, that about 75 per cent to 80 per cent of the total subscribed capital might come from the oil rich countries whereas the remaining 20 to 25 per cent of the subscribed capital might be provided by other members on some basis such as their Fund quotas.

* The Articles had been drafted in English and later translated into Arabic which was made the authentic text. This led to some discrepancies which had to be rectified later by reference to the Board of Executive Directors for interpretation.

† Islamic Dinar is the unit of account of the Islamic Development Bank and is equivalent to one Special Drawing Right (SDR) which is the unit of account of the International Monetary Fund.

‡ The Pakistan delegate, Mr. Ghulam Ishaq Khan, who took a leading part in the discussions of the Preparatory Committee, made a strong plea for the Bank to start with a much larger financial base considering the financial strength of the oil exporting countries and the enormous needs of the least-developed Muslim countries.

The meeting of Finance Ministers felt that a more flexible approach was warranted and on finding that it was difficult to secure pledges for the entire one billion Islamic Dinars of subscribed capital proposed in the Charter, the meeting decided to lower the figure of subscribed capital from one billion to 750 million Islamic Dinars. The committee set up for raising subscriptions was authorised to visit various countries to ensure that the requisite amount of 750 million Islamic Dinars was pledged before the end of October, 1974. However, through the good offices of the Chairman of the Conference, Sheikh Mohammed Abalkhail, the entire amount of 750 million Islamic Dinars was pledged before the expiry of the time limit, without the Committee having to undertake any visits to individual countries.

In regard to interim arrangements, the paper circulated by the Chairman of the Preparatory Committee had proposed that "a person in such capacity as may be determined by the meeting be designated as the head of the organisation and charged with the responsibility and authority to select such staff as is necessary" and that "the person be made responsible for completing the various documents for the meeting of the Board of Governors and other interim arrangements." The Conference of Finance Ministers, however, did not approve of the foregoing proposal and decided that the interim arrangements should be assigned to the Chairman of the Conference, the Minister of State for Finance and National Economy, Government of Saudi Arabia, who was authorised to follow up all the preliminaries necessary for the establishment of the Bank and to convene the first meeting of the Board of Governors when he deemed that conditions thereof had been fulfilled. The Preparatory Committee was thus wound up and the responsibility passed to the Saudi authorities who, in turn, decided to establish a small task force in Jeddah for this purpose led by the Secretary of the Preparatory Committee. Invitations were also sent to the Governments of Egypt and Malaysia to provide one member each for the task force. From this point onwards, Saudi Arabia fully assumed the task of establishing the Bank and the Saudi Arabian Monetary Agency bore almost the entire responsibility for the various organisational steps required for establishing it.

The task force started work in the middle of September, 1974, and prepared a paper spelling out the work which lay ahead. This was subsequently discussed with a two-member team from the World Bank consisting of Dr. El Fishawy and Mr. Hans Pollan.

During the course of consultations, two broad questions were explored: first, the desirability of having a feasibility study undertaken to give the Bank a sound start and secondly, the question of preparing certain basic documents for the Bank which had not been prepared by the Preparatory Committee. The head of the task force prepared a memorandum dealing with these questions. The memorandum observed that the term "feasibility" in the context of what was needed was something of a misnomer. A feasibility study was normally undertaken before starting a project to test its viability. As far as the IDB was concerned, the basic features of the Bank, its functions, capitalisation, and organisational structure had been clearly decided upon in the Articles of Agreement. As such, the time and occasion for a feasibility study of the conventional type had long passed. In other words, what was required was not so much to look at the feasibility of the institution but to endeavour to make the Bank succeed, by addressing the fundamental problems that needed to be tackled. The memorandum emphasised that there were two basic objectives inherent in the IDB: first, to assist in the economic and social development of the Muslim countries and communities, and second to work in strict conformity with the principles of Islamic Shariah. The IDB had been conceived as an institution to operate on truly Islamic principles. This clearly dictated that new techniques and methods should be devised, in order to give the institution a personality of its own. The memorandum argued that, at first sight and at least in the short run, there appeared to be some incompatibility between the objectives of making the Bank operational in the shortest possible time and the devising of working methods conforming to Shariah which, by its very nature, would take time. What seemed necessary was to take a middle course in the beginning, namely to start without undue delay on principles which would conform to the Shariah to the maximum extent possible and as the Bank proceeded on this path, it should constantly strive through "Ijtehad" and experimentation and innovation to evolve new concepts. This task was both complex and difficult and required a highly dedicated and competent team which believed in the viability and practicability of the economic model set out in Shariah and which had the ingenuity and knowledge required for undertaking it. The memorandum suggested that the IDB instead of treating capital as the sole source would do well to augment its resources by other means. The capital could serve as a basis for income generation and for meeting expenses and keeping the Bank going. In due course, however, the IDB should be expected to serve as an investment outlet for the surplus funds of oil rich countries and that the future of the Bank depended largely on its ability to mobilise the surplus capital which was available in these Islamic countries. The memorandum concluded by pointing out that the Bank should try to become operational as early as possible and, in this connection, take to co-financing with other international development banks. There were also considerable opportunities for equity investment in countries where foreign capital was being displaced by national capital.

Next the following documents for the inaugural meeting of the Board of Governors were drafted:

(1) Rules of Procedure for the Board of Governors
(2) Bye-laws of the Bank
(3) Regulations for the election of Executive Directors
(4) Rules of Procedure for the Board of Executive Directors.

These drafts were first examined by a group consisting of Mr. Said Ahmad, Dr. Mohamed A. Wahid Jamjoom, Mr. Yousuf Rahim and Dr. S. A. Meenai and later considered and finalised by the task force consisting of Dr. S. A. Meenai, Deputy Governor, State Bank of Pakistan; Mr. Hanafi Labib Hussein, Chairman, Industrial Development Bank of Egypt; Mr. Yousuf Rahim, Executive Director, Asian Development Bank; Dr. Tawfiq Shawi and Dr. Mohamed A. Wahid Jamjoom of the Saudi Arabian Monetary Agency. In finalising these documents the task force had also the benefit of advice from the two World Bank experts Messrs Fishawy and Pollan.

At the suggestion of the Governor of the Saudi Arabian Monetary Agency, an Action Plan for the consideration of the Chairman of the Finance Ministers Conference, the then Minister of State for Finance and National Economy, Kingdom of Saudi Arabia, was also prepared. The task force then addressed itself to the preparation of the draft notice and the agenda for the inaugural meeting of the Board of Governors and prepared a number of draft resolutions for the purpose. On completion of its work, the task force dispersed in the last week of December, 1974.

To sum up, the establishment of the IDB followed almost a whole year of preparatory work. The task was first undertaken by the Secretariat of the Preparatory Committee and later by a task force. While the preparatory work had been more or less completed by December, 1974, the inaugural meeting of the Bank could not be held before July, 1975.

Chapter 3

Inauguration of the Bank

The intention was to convene the first meeting of the Board of Governors as soon as possible after the Agreement establishing the Islamic Development Bank became effective. However, the receipt of ratification instruments and the first instalment of subscriptions took some time and the legal requirement in this regard could not be fulfilled almost until the middle of Rabial Thani, 1395H, corresponding to the third week of April, 1975. To be precise, the Agreement came into force on 12 Rabial Thani, 1395H, corresponding to 23 April, 1975, with the deposit of the instruments of ratification or acceptance by the signatories, whose subscription in the aggregate comprised not less than 500 million Islamic Dinars. Initially, a meeting in Jamadial Awal, 1395H, corresponding to May, 1975, was contemplated. However, owing to the holding of a Conference of Foreign Ministers in Jeddah and the preoccupation of Finance Ministers with their annual budgets, it was decided to convene the Inaugural Meeting of the Board of Governors in Riyadh, beginning 17 Rajab, 1395H, corresponding to 26 July, 1975.

As soon as the date for the Inaugural Meeting of the Board of Governors had been fixed and invitations had been sent out, the Saudi Arabian Monetary Agency started preparations for the meeting. There was one particular matter which deserved special attention. It pertained to the appointment of a President for the Bank. From the beginning, it was realised by the Preparatory Committee that the success of the Bank would depend to a very large extent on the person appointed as President. At one time, there appeared to be a feeling in certain quarters that the Chairman of the Preparatory Committee, Tunku Abdul Rahman Putra, should be requested to head the Bank for a short period to give it a proper start in terms of political stature. However, at the meeting of Finance Ministers held to approve the Articles of Agreement it became clear that most of the members thought that what was required was a professional person sufficiently young to be able to shoulder the burden which the office would involve. The matter, however, remained open until the Inaugural Meeting of the Board of Governors when, after due deliberation, the Government of Saudi Arabia, the largest subscriber to the Bank's capital, decided to put up its own candidate for the presidency.

The Inaugural Meeting began on Saturday, 17 Rajab, 1395H, corresponding to 26 July, 1975. It was opened by Prince Salman ibn Abdul Aziz, Governor of Riyadh, followed by a speech by Sheikh Mohammed Abalkhail. After the inauguration, the meeting elected Sheikh Mohammed Abalkhail, the Chairman of the Board of Governors, to preside at the Inaugural Meeting and until the end of the First Annual Meeting. The Chairman proposed that thanks be extended to the Preparatory Committee and the Task Force as well as to the member states and organisations who had assisted in the establishment of the Bank. After the passing of the proposed resolutions, countries which had been late with the fulfilment of some of the conditions for membership, namely Libya, Tunisia, Somalia, Guinea and Niger, were admitted as members. The Conference elected Dr. Ali Wardhana, Minister of Finance of Indonesia and N'Faly Sangare, Minister of Banking of Guinea, as Vice Chairmen of the Board of Governors until the end of the First Annual Meeting of the Board of Governors. Dr. Saeed Ahmad Meenai, Secretary of the Preparatory Committee and head of the Task Force, was chosen as the Secretary of the Inaugural Meeting. The Governor of Saudi Arabian Monetary Agency then read out his report on behalf of the Depository. After this, resolutions were adopted in regard to the admission to membership of Yemen, Syria and Afghanistan.

The meeting then proceeded to examine and approve the Rules of Procedure of the Board of Governors. Next the Draft Bye-laws of the Bank were taken up for consideration and certain matters, such as the terms and conditions of service of the President, role of Executive Directors, appointment of Vice President by the Board of Executive Directors, the determination of the financial year for the Bank and mode of selection of the auditors came under discussion. It was decided to maintain the provision that the Vice President be appointed by the Board of Executive Directors. Similarly, the provision in the Articles and Bye-laws about the residence and continuous availability of Executive Directors was maintained. The Hijra Year was adopted as the Bank's financial year and the auditors were to be appointed by the Board of Governors. The meeting then examined and approved the Regulations for the election of Executive Directors and appointed the representative of Kuwait to take charge of the elections. Dr. Ahmad Mohamed Ali, at that time Deputy Minister of Education, Kingdom of Saudi Arabia, was appointed as the first President of the Bank.

On the matter of election of Executive Directors long informal discussions were held in camera and there were also meetings with the Chairman of the Conference. It was decided eventually that of the six elected Executive Directors two should come from Asia, two from non-Arab Africa and two from Arab members of the Bank. The elections were unanimous. The meeting was then addressed by the newly elected President of the Bank. After deciding that the Bank should open formally on 20 October, 1975/15 Shawwal, 1395H, and that the next meeting of the Board of Governors be held in Jeddah during April 1976/Rabial Thani, 1396H, the meeting adjourned on Monday, 28 July, 1975/19 Rajab, 1395H.

At the conclusion of the meeting of the Board of Governors, the newly elected President of the Bank met the Secretary of the Inaugural Meeting, for the purpose of surveying the immediate problems to be tackled and the steps required to be taken for the inauguration of the Bank. They both travelled to Jeddah and inspected Qasre Niaba, which was formerly the office of the late King Faisal and had been assigned to the Bank to serve as its temporary headquarters and made a tentative survey of requirements. The President then embarked upon the task of having the necessary physical arrangements made and to have the building renovated and altered to serve the needs of the Bank.

The first meeting of the Board of Executive Directors was fixed for the third week of August, 1975. Meanwhile, the President had secured some temporary accommodation for the Bank in the SAMA* building. Some part-time help for typing and accounting was also obtained.

The first meeting of the Board of Executive Directors was held in the board room of the SAMA from 23 to 25 August, 1975. The Board reiterated that the Executive Directors be required to reside in Jeddah and work full time. The Board decided to send three separate missions to the Asian Development Bank, the African Development Bank, the World Bank and the Inter-American Development Bank for the purpose of examining their working, organisational structure and policies and for exploring the possibilities of co-operation and assistance. Dr. Meenai, the Executive Director from Pakistan, was requested to act as the Co-ordinator for these missions. The mission to the Asian Development Bank consisted of Dr. Meenai and Mr. Omar Abdullah Sejeini, the Executive Director for Saudi Arabia; the mission to the African Development Bank consisted of Dr. Meenai and Mr. Hamid Algabid, the Executive Director from Niger; whereas the mission to the World Bank and the Inter-American Development Bank consisted of Dr. Meenai and Mr. Hassan Zaki Ahmad, the Executive Director from Egypt.

* Saudi Arabian Monetary Agency.

The mission to the Asian Development Bank visited Manila from 1 September to 10 September, 1975, and held extensive discussions with the President, Vice President and other officials of the ADB. Apart from examining its organisational structure, practices and policies, it explored the possibility of co-financing and also the question of obtaining staff on the basis of secondment. The authorities of the ADB were highly responsive. The mission to the African Development Bank visited Abidjan, where it held similar discussions with the AfDB, which evinced keen interest in the possibility of co-operation with the newly established IDB. The mission to the World Bank visited Washington where detailed discussions were held with the World Bank officials from senior Vice President to the heads of various departments. The World Bank was particularly responsive to the possibility of co-financing. The mission also visited the Inter-American Development Bank and noted some of its special features such as its role in promoting trade in capital goods amongst its members. Through their visits to the various international development banks, the missions arranged with them that they made available to the IDB the various reports prepared by their economic missions and also their sectoral studies related to the member countries. The purpose was to provide an authentic source of data to the IDB before it developed some capacity to undertake its own appraisal of the economies of the member countries. The missions also assembled a good deal of material by way of documents and papers from the institutions on the various aspects of their activities which they thought would be useful for the IDB.

Broadly speaking, the missions to the international development banks had three purposes. In the first place, their objective was to gain acquaintance with the working, organisational structure and policies of the institutions they visited, so as to learn from their experience. Secondly, besides gaining their goodwill, they wanted to explore possibilities of co-operation and assistance from other institutions. Thirdly, it was their desire to use the opportunity for the purpose of developing and firming up certain ideas they had concerning the newly set up Bank.

On their return to Jeddah towards the middle of October 1975, the missions prepared detailed reports on their visits which were submitted to the Board of Executive Directors. Two other basic documents were also prepared. The first document dealt with the organisational structure and the administrative framework for the IDB and the second document discussed the policy approach which the IDB should follow. The missions reported that the situation was particularly favourable for co-operation between the IDB and other international development banks. In the first place, the latter were experiencing a shortage of funds. Secondly, as a result of the improved capacity of the developing countries to prepare projects and, more particularly, owing to the efforts made by the other international financial institutions in respect of project preparation there was a large pipeline of projects available for financing. Another factor which made such co-operation mutually beneficial was that, viewed from the standpoint of the IDB, it would enable it to market some of its resources even before developing too large a staff strength. On the other hand, looking at it from the point of view of the other international development banks, this kind of co-operation would mean that they would be able to engage in some projects which they would not be able to finance entirely on their own. The missions thought there were distinct possibilities for co-financing with other institutions. However, what was necessary was that before undertaking a serious exploration of such possibilities, the IDB develop a capacity to make up its mind quickly without keeping the other institutions waiting too long. Another apprehension which arose in this regard was that such financing might have the effect of reducing the flow of resources from other multilateral institutions to certain recipient countries. It had, therefore, to be borne in mind that the whole purpose of establishing the IDB was to enlarge the flow of financial resources for the development of the member countries and if the co-financing arrangements resulted in other institutions reducing their commitments and assistance to these countries it would not mean much improvement for the member countries of the IDB. The missions had, however, obtained an assurance from the international institutions they had visited that this would not happen and had been informed that assistance by the co-financing institutions had actually increased in the case of countries where joint-financing and parallel financing arrangements had been devised.

The Board of Executive Directors considered the foregoing documents at its second meeting held from 25 to 29 November, 1975, and as proposed in the documents, the Board decided to follow three main directions:

(1) To try to become operational in the shortest possible time through co-financing arrangements;
(2) To develop the Bank as an independent international development financing agency;
(3) To promote the Bank's role as a truly Islamic institution having a distinct personality of its own operating on the principles of Shariah.

On the basis of the paper on Organisational Structure, the Board decided that the Bank should start with a modest organisation having seven departments, namely:

(1) Secretary's Department
(2) Legal Department
(3) Operations and Projects Department
(4) Economic and Policy Planning Department
(5) Finance Department
(6) Administration and Personnel Department
(7) Audit Department.

The Board also agreed that the Bank should take immediate action to assemble a team of professionals already well versed and experienced in development banking from the international and regional development financing institutions on secondment basis. In this connection, two staff members, Messrs M. Zaki Azam and Shamshad Ali Khan, were loaned by the ADB. The World Bank deputed one of their professional staff members, Dr. A. Khafaji and the African Development Bank made available to the Bank one of their senior lawyers, Mr. Saeed Abdalla Mohammed.

Simultaneously, the Bank took steps to complete the various steps required for the establishment of its organisational structure, such as the preparation of job descriptions, specifications of various positions in the Bank and also a set of staff regulations and financial regulations.

The Bank decided to have access to the relevant manpower market by advertising the positions internationally. This step did not, however, prove very productive, insofar as it led to an extremely large number of applications which required a sizeable organisational strength to sort out. An attempt was made to use the computer for the purpose but the results were not altogether satisfactory. There were, in fact, several basic factors which made the problem of recruitment difficult. First, as a new institution, the Bank did not succeed in attracting senior and experienced personnel from other international institutions or from the market. Secondly, the housing and other difficulties in Jeddah, particularly the lack of English medium educational facilities, further complicated the problem. Added to that, was the fact that the Bank required bilingual staff which were very difficult to get.

The difficulties and problems encountered by the Bank in establishing its organisation, coupled with the desire to become operational at the earliest, mainly led the Bank to a rather unorthodox approach. Unlike other international institutions, the IDB decided to prepare a document setting out its procedures and policies and despatch it to the various member countries with a request that they would propose and forward projects and financing proposals to the Bank for its consideration. Soon after this, the President of the Bank, and also some of the Executive Directors, undertook visits to the member countries for the purpose of inviting them to submit projects to the Bank directly without waiting for the Bank to mount any identification missions. At the same time, the international development banks and regional financial institutions were approached to send co-financing proposals to the Bank in the light of the policy document which was made available to them. It was in this manner that the initial difficulties in building up a project pipeline for the Bank were overcome and it was against this background that the IDB commenced its operations.

Chapter 4

Progress Over the Years

Before attempting a critical and comprehensive analysis of the various aspects of the Islamic Development Bank's working, policies and operations, it would be appropriate to present a broad but synoptic view of its progress over the years.

During the Bank's first year, the most urgent task was to establish an office for it and to assemble a skeleton staff. The Qasre Niaba palace, made available to the Bank by the late King Faisal to serve as its temporary headquarters, had been renovated and altered to suit the requirements of the Bank. Next, the organisational structure of the Bank was approved and a number of local staff members were appointed. At the same time, before recruiting a professional staff of its own, the Bank made arrangements to assemble a team of professionals on secondment from some other international and regional development banks for a short period. The staff strength rose to 78 at the end of the first financial year. An emblem was chosen for the Bank on the basis of a competition. The Bank's financial and staff regulations were approved and a structure of salaries and benefits for the staff was established. The Bank received a gift of a plot of land measuring 50,000 square metres for its permanent headquarters from the Kingdom of Saudi Arabia. In order to overcome the housing difficulties for its staff, the Bank undertook the construction of a housing complex. The first administrative budget was prepared and duly approved and a firm of external auditors was appointed.

The Islamic Development Bank

From its inception, the Bank sought to establish close relations with the World Bank group, the African Development Bank, the Asian Development Bank, the Arab Fund for Economic and Social Development, the Arab Bank for Economic Development in Africa, the Kuwait Fund for Arab Economic and Social Development, the Abu Dhabi Fund for Arab Economic Development and the Saudi Fund for Development. These institutions were requested to indicate to the Bank possibilities of co-financing arrangements in respect of member countries. At the same time, the Bank contacted the various specialised agencies of the United Nations such as the UNDP, FAO, UNESCO, and WHO, with a view to promoting co-operation with them. The Bank also sought to establish a close relationship with the national development banks, with a view to using their technical apparatus and expertise for identifying smaller projects in member countries, for equity financing for the IDB. During the first year of operation three new states, namely the Yemen Arab Republic, the Syrian Arab Republic and the Republic of Afghanistan, became members of the Bank.

The problem of placement of funds not immediately needed in operations was thoroughly explored and certain crucial decisions were made on the subject including the establishment of an investment committee to undertake "Ijtehad" in this respect. The initial determination of the basis and magnitude of a service fee was also made.

During the first year, the Bank received as many as 159 projects submitted by 19 member countries. Despite limitations of professional staff, it mounted several missions to review projects in the field and also participated in meetings with potential co-financiers. Thus it was possible for the Bank to commence its financing operations in the very first year. It approved a loan of 6 million Islamic Dinars to the Song Loulou Hydroelectric Project in Cameroon, on the basis of co-financing with the Saudi Development Fund and the Kuwait Fund. It also approved equity participation to the tune of 7 million Islamic Dinars in the Jordan Petroleum Refining Extension project.

While the first year of the Bank was largely devoted to preparation, the second year witnessed a rapid expansion in the Bank's operational activities. As many as 31 projects involving total financing of US$182.3 million were approved. They included operations in the field of agriculture, education, industry, infrastructure and public utilities. During the year the Bank also started its activities in the field of foreign trade financing and similarly a beginning was made with leasing. The organisation of the Bank was strengthened and an Operations and Projects Department was established. A Vice President was appointed for the Bank with the increase in its activities. An office building was constructed during the year to serve as the temporary headquarters of the Bank. The membership of the Bank increased to 32 with the admission of the Republic of Chad, the Republic of Lebanon, the Republic of Senegal, the Republic of Uganda, the People's Democratic Republic of Yemen and the Palestine Liberation Organisation. The Bank organised two meetings during the year, one with Muslim scholars and experts and the other with some "Ulema" which covered a wide-ranging agenda related to the Bank's activities.

During the third year the financing operations of the Bank reached the level of US$270 million, showing an increase of 53 per cent over the preceding year. Of this, foreign trade operations accounted for nearly US$170 million. The membership of the Bank rose further with the acceptance of the Republics of Mali and Upper Volta.* The Bank moved to its new office building in November 1978. One important development relating to the Bank's organisation was that the Board of Executive Directors became non-resident and part-time. A meeting took place with national Islamic banks to explore ways and means of establishing closer co-operation with them. A co-operation agreement was negotiated with IFAD. A detailed organisational chart was prepared for the Bank and the staff strength of the Bank increased from 118 to 173.

The fourth year saw further expansion in the Bank's financing operations and the total financing approved by the Bank amounted to US$490.9 million, showing a 75 per cent increase over the previous year. Of this amount, US$338 million represented foreign trade financing operations. A significant feature was that the proportion of loan financing declined whereas financing on the basis of equity participation and leasing rose. An investment deposit scheme was approved by the Bank, under which the Bank was expected to receive deposits from individual as well as institutional depositors. A comprehensive study was undertaken on resource mobilisation and a special assistance account was established by the Board of Governors with the help of interest proceeds from deposits with foreign banks. The special account was designed for the promotion of training and research in Islamic banking, provision of relief financing in cases of natural disasters and calamities and the promotion and furtherance of Islamic causes. A retirement plan was also approved and the staff strength rose to 226.

During the fifth year, the Bank approved several more operations and the amount of financing approved by the Bank increased. The number of operations increased from 50 to 62, whereas the amount of financing rose from US$490.9 million to US$647 million, representing an increase of 30 per cent. Of this, foreign trade financing accounted for as much as US$476 million. In addition to project financing and foreign trade financing operations, the Bank also sanctioned some special operations, including the provision of financial assistance to the Government of Pakistan in the field of health to reduce the burden following the inflow of Afghan refugees, a health project in Somalia and an educational project in the Arab occupied territories. The membership of the Bank rose to 40 with the admission of the Federal Islamic Republic of Comoros and the Republics of Djibouti, Gambia and Maldives.

* The name of the country has since been changed to Burkina Faso.

A comprehensive scheme for the establishment of the Islamic Research and Training Institute was formulated. Three committees, namely the Administration Committee, the Operations Committee and the Finance Committee of the Board of Executive Directors were established to facilitate the work of the Board of Executive Directors. Meetings were held with representatives of Islamic banks and national development banks to promote co-operation with them. The staff strength rose to 265.

In the sixth year, the Bank approved financing to the tune of US$622.72 million for 63 operations. Of this amount US$138.28 million were for project financing and US$484.44 million were on account of foreign trade operations. A significant development during the year was that the ratio of loan financing decreased significantly whereas the proportion of equity increased from 30 per cent to 40 per cent. Additionally, the Bank approved nine special operations from the special assistance account. During the year the Republic of Gabon became a member of the Bank. Another significant development was that the Board of Governors resolved to raise the subscribed capital of the Bank to the level of the authorised capital and invited member countries to subscribe to it. At the same time the Bank undertook a critical evaluation of its activities, policies and organisation with a view to improving its performance. The statute of the Islamic Research and Training Institute and its first budget were approved by the executive directors. Preparations also began for the designing and construction of a permanent headquarters building for the Bank.

The seventh year witnessed a further expansion in the operations of the Bank both in terms of the number of operations and the volume of financing approved. The number of operations increased from 61 to 69 whereas the volume of financing rose from US$622.72 million to US$661 million representing a rise of 16 per cent. Of this, project financing accounted for US$219.59 million and the rest represented foreign trade financing operations. In addition, the Bank undertook five operations out of the special assistance account.

During the eighth year, the Bank approved 68 operations of the value of US$719.34 million. This total comprised US$221.52 million for project financing and US$497.15 million for foreign trade financing operations. During the same period, seven operations were sanctioned from the special assistance account. A significant change was that the share of loans increased sharply whereas the share of equity participation declined to 7.6 per cent in 1983 from nearly 17 per cent in the previous year. This was because the Bank decided to adopt a cautious approach to equity financing owing to the fact that sound equity projects were difficult to identify and supervise. The organisation of the Bank was further strengthened and, in line with its expanding activities, another Vice President was appointed. The headquarters agreement with the Government of Saudi Arabia was signed. The Bank also installed a computer. The total staff strength increased further with the number of professionals approaching a hundred.

During the ninth year, the amount of financing approved increased by 38 per cent, attaining a level of 920 million Islamic Dinars (US$962 million). At the same time the number of operations approved by the Bank rose to 78, compared with 68 in the preceding year. It may be noted, however, that the increase in total financing approved by the Bank was accounted for by the substantial expansion in foreign trade financing, whereas the level of project financing during the year failed to increase even in money terms. In fact, it amounted to ID205.70 million (US$212.97 million) as against ID206.91 million (US$221.52 million) in the previous year. Perhaps even more significant was the fact that only one equity project was approved during the year. Thus, while the amount of equity financing approved during the year declined sharply, leasing operations expanded significantly, accounting for more than 60 per cent of the total financing approved by the Bank during the year. The technical assistance approved during the year, ID2.9 million, also registered a decline of nearly 50 per cent over the previous year. Viewed from the standpoint of sectoral allocations, there was a welcome increase in the relative share of agriculture. Additionally, the Bank approved the sum of US$50 million for assistance to Sahelian member countries in combating the problems caused by drought. The Bank also made a beginning with the implementation of its programme for technical co-operation amongst the member countries.

During the tenth year, the total financing approved by the Bank increased marginally to ID1,005.22 million. What was, perhaps, more significant was the fact that total project financing during the year rose by 32.8 per cent. At the same time, the amount of foreign trade financing registered a decline of 6.2 per cent. In terms of functional distribution, loans accounted for 36.1 per cent, leasing/line of leasing and instalment sales for 57.9 per cent and technical assistance for 2.4 per cent. Like the preceding year, the amount approved by way of equity financing remained very low. Only one operation, representing 3.6 per cent of the total project financing, was approved during the year. Viewed from the standpoint of sectoral distribution, the share of agriculture increased to 36.3 per cent compared to only 14 per cent in the previous year. The respective shares of utilities and the social sector increased very markedly whereas those of industry, mining, transport and communications fell sharply. As for special assistance operations, they were maintained at the level of the preceding year. There were two other notable developments during the year. Firstly, the Bank undertook a projection of its resource needs and came to the conclusion that taking the average financing of the preceding three years as a base and a planned increase of 10 per cent annually, the Bank would require resources of the order of US$1,650 million and began considering ways and means of getting them. Secondly, the Bank undertook an Evaluation Exercise of its ten years' performance by a panel of outside experts so as to evolve policies and strategies for its future operations.

After undertaking a close examination of the operations, resource position, managerial capacity and the organisation of the Bank, the Review Committee made a comprehensive report to the Bank.* In the main, the Committee emphasised the need for strengthening the financial resource position of the Bank and its managerial capacity and advised it to achieve closer proximity with the private sector. The Committee felt that for effective resource mobilisation the institution must maintain its own financial credibility and high standard as a sound financial institution. The Committee also urged the Bank to expand its catalytic role in the development process of member countries, to become more selective in the identification of projects particularly in equity participation, to retain a certain degree of flexibility in resource generation and conduct of operations and finally to strengthen its relations with other financial institutions. As regards resource mobilisation, the Committee highlighted the need for mobilising additional resources from the financial markets which would require the development of appropriate financial instruments conforming to Shariah and also the development of a secondary market to deal in these instruments. It proposed the establishment of a high-level advisory group to undertake a comprehensive assessment of the resource prospects of the Bank. As for operations, the Review Committee emphasised the need for a core programme for the next few years covering food security, development and promotion of foreign trade, development of technical ability and the promotion of effective co-operation among member countries. The Committee also proposed that the IDB should enlarge its role in assisting the export effort of member countries. In regard to placement, the Committee advised that the Bank should find ways and means of investing its liquidity in conventional markets in ways conforming to Shariah. The Committee felt that the Bank's concessionary financing should be focused on the least-developed member countries while its less concessionary funds should be directed to its relatively more advanced members. In regard to the administrative and organisational set up of the Bank, the Committee emphasised the need for restructuring the organisation of the IDB in order to make it compatible with the task that lay ahead. The Committee also recommended greater decentralisation and flexibility in decision making and improved personnel policies.

In addition to the work of the Review Committee, the Bank also engaged an internationally reputable firm of management consultants to review the organisational and administrative set up of the Bank, which completed its task during the year. Their report contained a number of recommendations relating to the development of a business strategy, organisational changes, development of management capability, accountability, delegation of authority, decision making, human resource management and information systems. The report also highlighted the need for a careful review of the Bank's operational policies. As far as the organisational structure was concerned,

* Eleventh Annual Report 1985–1986 (p. 45).

the report suggested that the Operations and Projects Departments be restructured, a Peoples and Productivity Department be established, and an Information Design Project be set up, whereas the strategic planning support function be assigned to the Economic and Policy Planning Department. Currently, the Bank is studying the reports of the Review Committee and the management consulting firm with a view to taking appropriate action.

The eleventh year of the Bank's operations witnessed a decline in the level of financing compared to the preceding year. Project financing and technical assistance were lower at ID175.73 million (US$192.53 million) against ID269.63 million (US$295.41 million) in the previous year. There was also a decline in the amount of foreign trade financing. The Bank attributed the overall decline in its financing to the recessionary conditions and the scarcity of projects in member countries. These trends persisted during the twelfth year.

Chapter 5

The Legal Framework

The present chapter* is designed to describe briefly the legal framework within which the Islamic Development Bank operates. It is mainly composed of the Articles of Agreement, the Bye-Laws and the various regulations of the Bank. In this connection, mention may be made of the following:

(1) Articles of Agreement establishing the Islamic Development Bank
(2) Bye-Laws of the Islamic Development Bank
(3) Rules of Procedure of the Board of Governors
(4) Regulations for the Election of Executive Directors
(5) Rules of Procedure of the Board of Executive Directors
(6) Financial Regulations
(7) Staff Regulations.

1. Objectives and purpose

The objectives of the Bank are set out in the Articles of Agreement. The Preamble refers to

* The chapter is based on the Articles of Agreement, Bye-Laws, Rules and Regulations of the Bank.

(a) the need for fostering the well-being of the peoples of the Muslim countries and for achieving a harmonious and balanced development of these countries on the basis of Islamic principles and ideals;
(b) the need for mutual financial and economic co-operation among the Muslim states in the economic, social and other fields of activity;
(c) the need for mobilising financial and other resources both from within and outside the member countries and for promoting domestic savings and investments and a greater flow of development funds into member countries.

The charter of the Bank lays down that the international financial institution being established shall be "development, investment and welfare oriented, based on Islamic principles and ideals and a practical expression of the unity and solidarity of the Muslim Ummah." More specifically, the purpose of the Bank, as expressed in Article 1 is "to foster economic development and social progress of member countries and Muslim communities individually as well as jointly in accordance with the principles of Shariah." In this regard, two facts deserve special mention. First, that the mission and task assigned to the Bank embraces the Muslim Ummah as a whole and is not confined to the member countries alone. Secondly, while the Bank is required to operate in accordance with the principles of Shariah, this is a broad and general requirement applying to all the Bank's activities; beyond it, no guidance is provided in specific terms.

2. Functions and powers

The Bank has been assigned the following functions and powers:

(1) To participate in the equity capital of productive projects and enterprises in member countries;
(2) To invest in economic and social infrastructure projects in member countries by way of participation or other financial arrangements;
(3) To make loans to the private and public sectors for the financing of productive projects, enterprises and programmes in member countries;
(4) To establish and operate special funds for specific purposes including a fund for assistance to Muslim communities in non-member countries;
(5) To operate trust funds;
(6) To accept deposits and to raise funds in any other manner;
(7) To assist in the promotion of foreign trade, especially in capital goods, among member countries;
(8) To invest suitably funds not needed in its operations;
(9) To provide technical assistance to member countries;

(10) To extend training facilities for personnel engaged in development activities in member countries;
(11) To undertake research for enabling the economic, financial and banking activities in Muslim countries to conform to Shariah;
(12) To co-operate, in such a manner as the Bank may deem appropriate, with all bodies, institutions and organisations having similar purposes, in pursuance of international economic co-operation;
(13) To undertake any other activities which may advance its purpose.

The foregoing list of functions clearly demonstrates that the Bank has been assigned a very wide-ranging task which in many ways surpasses that assigned to other international development banks.

3. Membership

The necessary condition for membership of the Bank is that the country should be a member of the Organisation of Islamic Conference. This is, however, a condition establishing the eligibility for membership and does not constitute an obligation on the IDB automatically to accept a country as its member simply by virtue of its membership of the OIC. A country has to apply to the IDB for admission to the Bank which in turn lays down the terms and conditions for admission. The present membership is composed of two categories:

(1) The founder members, which were already members of the OIC and which accepted and signed the Agreement establishing the Bank and fulfilled all other conditions of membership within six months of such date.
(2) Other states which applied for admission to the Bank after its establishment and which were consequently admitted as members by the Board of Governors.

The minimum number of shares to be subscribed by a member is 250 with a par value of ID2.5 million.

The question of membership was never keenly debated in the context of the Islamic Development Bank. The Preparatory Committee proposed that the eligibility would consist in prior membership of the Organisation of Islamic Conference. The task of determining whether a country in terms of its political status was considered Islamic or not was avoided at the level of the IDB which confined itself merely to the technical conditions for membership such as the amount of capital subscription. As the institution had been conceived as an Islamic institution, the question of inviting developed industrialised countries in order to boost its resources was never raised. The situation which has evolved over the years is that all the members of OIC, with the exception of Iran and Nigeria, have become members of the IDB. This, however, leaves outside the fold of the Bank many countries with very large Muslim populations. The present membership stands at 44 countries.

4. Financial structure

The Unit of Account of the Bank is known as the Islamic Dinar, the value of which is equivalent to one Special Drawing Right of the International Monetary Fund. At the time of the Bank's inception, the authorised capital stock of the Bank was fixed at two billion Islamic Dinars divided into 200,000 shares having a par value of 10,000 Islamic Dinars each. The subscribed capital of the Bank was initially fixed at 750 million Islamic Dinars. Subsequently, in the year 1980 the subscribed capital of the Bank was raised to the level of its authorised capital and the member countries were invited to participate in the increase. The subscribed capital is paid by the member countries in fixed instalments in freely convertible currencies acceptable to the Bank.

In proposing an initial capital structure for the Bank, the Secretariat of the Preparatory Committee had proposed that it be fixed at a high level considering the financial strength of the prospective members and also the wide ranging functions to be carried out by the Bank. However, at the meeting of the Preparatory Committee in 1974 as a result of the consultations held, it was decided to set the capital base at 750 million Islamic Dinars. There was also a great deal of discussion at the meeting on the basis for the allocation of capital subscription among various prospective members. The Secretariat had its own proposals worked out on the basis of an integrated formula including GDP, per capita income, tax revenues, export income and foreign exchange reserves. After a great deal of discussion, a compromise was reached in regard to the allocations on the basis of various countries voluntarily taking up a certain amount. There was also a long discussion in regard to the minimum membership fee. The relatively poor countries emphasised the need for a token amount and it was eventually agreed to accept 2.5 million Islamic Dinars as the minimum membership fee.

The Articles provide that the authorised capital of the Bank may be increased by the Board of Governors by a vote of two-thirds of the total number of Governors, representing not less than three-quarters of the total voting power of the members. If the Board determines that an increase in the capital stock is warranted, each member shall have a reasonable opportunity to subscribe to it. At the same time, no member is obliged to subscribe in the event of an increase in the capital stock.

5. Use of resources

The Articles provide that the resources of the Bank shall be used exclusively to implement the purpose and carry out the functions of the Bank on the basis of sound economic principles.

6. Operations

In conducting its operations, the Bank has been required to

(1) safeguard its interest in respect of its financing including obtaining guarantees for its loans;
(2) pay due regard to the prospect that the recipient and its guarantor will be in a position to meet their obligations;
(3) take into account the needs of the relatively less developed member countries;
(4) promote complementarity in the economies of the member countries;
(5) foster the well-being of the people in member countries through economic and social development and the enlargement of opportunities for gainful employment;
(6) avoid a disproportionate amount of its resources being used for the benefit of any member;
(7) ensure that the financing made available by it is used strictly for the purpose for which it was provided;
(8) maintain a suitable ratio between its equity investments and loans;
(9) accord priority to projects including joint ventures which promote and strengthen economic co-operation among member countries;
(10) carry out effective inspection and follow-up of projects;
(11) not finance any undertaking in the territory of a member if that member objects to such financing;
(12) provide financing for the foreign exchange component but in suitable cases, especially in the case of less developed member countries, provide financing for the local currency component after assuring itself that the country's domestic resource mobilisation effort justified such action;
(13) operate, as far as sources of procurement are concerned, on the basis of international competitive bidding and also on the basis of a margin of preference for procurement from member countries;
(14) satisfy itself that in respect of programme loans to member countries, the well-being of the people through economic and social development is promoted;
(15) modify at its discretion the terms of amortisation or extend the life of loan or both provided that it is satisfied that such relaxation is

justified in the interest of the particular recipient and the operation of the Bank;

(16) the total amount of equity investment, amount of loans outstanding and other ordinary operations of the Bank must not at any time exceed the total amount of unimpaired Subscribed Capital, reserves, deposits, other funds raised and surpluses including its ordinary capital resources;

(17) the Bank's loans shall be denominated in Islamic Dinars except in special cases where the Bank determines otherwise;

(18) all obligations to the Bank under Loan Agreement shall be discharged in a freely convertible currency acceptable to the Bank.

7. Service fee

The Bank levies a service fee to cover its administrative expenses. The amount of the fee and the manner of levying it are determined by the Bank. In conformity with Shariah, the Bank is not allowed to make any commitment charge.

8. Equity participation

As regards equity participation, the Articles of Agreement make several stipulations:

(1) In participating in equity capital, the Bank must satisfy itself that the project or enterprise is currently or potentially revenue yielding and that it is, and will be, properly managed.

(2) The Bank must not acquire a majority or controlling interest in the share capital of the project or enterprise in which it participates except when it is necessary to protect the Bank's interest or to ensure the success of such project or enterprise.

(3) The Bank must apply such terms and conditions as it deems proper including voting rights to nominate one or more directors to the Governing Board of the project or enterprise.

(4) The Bank must retain the option to sell its equity participation on such terms and conditions as may be considered appropriate. The Bank must not, however, sell any part of its equity participation to any non-national of the member country except with the consent of such member country.

(5) The Bank must not assume responsibility for managing any project or enterprise in which it has invested except when necessary to safeguard its investment.

(6) The Bank must not provide loans to an enterprise in whose equity it has participated except in special cases approved by not less than two-thirds of the total voting power of the members.
(7) The Bank must seek to revolve its resources by selling its investments whenever it can appropriately do so.
(8) The Bank must seek to maintain reasonable diversification in its equity investments.
(9) The member country must not impose any restriction on the remittance of profits and repatriation of capital by the Bank in convertible currency acceptable to the Bank.

This subject came under a great deal of discussion during the various stages. While including equity financing as one of the main functions of the Bank, the Secretariat had taken care to emphasise the risk and difficulties involved in the matter in relation to the provisions concerning other international development banks which had been deliberately prohibited from undertaking such financing in the initial years of their working. However, the founders of the Bank attached a great deal of importance to it even to the extent of incorporating in the Articles of Agreement a provision about maintaining a ratio between equity and loan financing.

9. Board of Governors

Each member is represented on the Board of Governors and appoints one Governor and one Alternate. All the powers of the Bank are vested in the Board of Governors. The Board may delegate to the Board of Executive Directors any or all its powers except the power to:

(1) admit new members and determine the conditions of their admission;
(2) increase or decrease the authorised capital stock of the Bank;
(3) suspend a member;
(4) decide appeals from interpretations or applications of the Agreement given by the Board of Executive Directors;
(5) authorise the conclusion of general agreements for co-operation with other international organisations;
(6) elect the President of the Bank;
(7) elect the Executive Directors of the Bank;
(8) determine the remuneration of the Executive Directors and the salary and other terms of the contract of service of the President;
(9) approve, after reviewing the auditors' report, the general balance sheet and the statement of profit and loss of the Bank;
(10) determine the reserve and the distribution of the net income and surplus of the Bank;

(11) amend the Articles of Agreement of the Bank;
(12) decide to terminate the operations of the Bank and to distribute its assets; and
(13) exercise such other special powers as are expressly assigned to the Board of Governors in the Articles of Agreement establishing the Bank.

At the same time, the Board of Governors has full powers to exercise authority over any matter delegated to the Board of Executive Directors. The Board of Governors must hold an annual meeting and such other meetings, as may be provided for by the Board or called by the Board of Executive Directors according to the Rules of Procedure. The majority of the Governors, according to the Rules of Procedure, constitute a quorum for a meeting of the Board provided that such majority represents not less than two-thirds of the total voting power of the members. Any meeting of the Board at which there is no quorum has to be adjourned for 48 hours. At the end of each annual meeting, the Board elects a Governor to serve as Chairman and two other Governors to serve as Vice Chairmen until the end of the next annual meeting. The Secretary of the Bank serves as the Secretary of the Board of Governors. The Board of Governors may establish at any of its meetings such committees as it may deem necessary or appropriate to facilitate its work. Whenever a formal vote is required, a written text with the proposal has to be distributed to the members. No Governor or Alternate is entitled to vote at any meeting by proxy or by a method other than in person. The Board is also authorised to decide matters without calling a special meeting and by circulating a proposal and requesting for a vote by the Governors within a stipulated period. If the replies received do not include the majority of Governors exercising two-thirds of the total voting power, which is required for a quorum of a Board of Governors, the proposal is considered as lost. The Governors and their Alternates perform their duties without remuneration from the Bank. The Bank may reimburse them for reasonable expenses incurred in attending meetings.

10. Board of Executive Directors

The Board of Executive Directors is composed of ten members,* who must not be members of the Board of Governors. The Executive Directors should be persons of high competence in economic and financial matters and should be elected in accordance with the rules and regulations made by the Board

* The number was increased to eleven in February 1985 with the addition of a permanent executive director from Turkey after it increased its capital subscription. This has raised the number of "appointed executive directors" to five out of eleven.

of Governors. The Bye-Laws provide that of the ten members, four shall be appointed, one each by the four member countries having the largest numbers of shares and six shall be elected by all the Governors other than those representing the four member countries. The Executive Directors hold office for a term of three years and may be re-elected. The Board of Executive Directors is responsible for the direction of the general operations of the Bank and in particular to

(1) prepare the work of the Board of Governors;
(2) take decisions concerning the business of the Bank and its operations in conformity with the general directions of the Board of Governors;
(3) submit the accounts for each financial year for approval of the Board of Governors at each annual meeting;
(4) approve the budget of the Bank.

The Articles of Agreement provide that the Board of Executive Directors shall normally function at the principal office of the Bank which signifies a resident Board. However, there has been a change since 1979 and the Board of Executive Directors has become non-resident. The quorum for a meeting is a majority of the Executive Directors representing not less than two-thirds of the total voting power of the members. At the request of the President or any Executive Director, meetings may be held in Executive Sessions which are attended only by the Executive Directors, the President and Vice Presidents. Any other officer may attend with the approval of the Board granted separately for each session. If an Executive Director shall so request, action by the Board on any matter shall be postponed not more than once for not less than two days. The Executive Directors shall vote in person or in accordance with Section 6 of the Bye-Laws which lay down "that when an Executive Director is unable to attend to the business of the Bank, he may designate a fellow Executive Director to represent him also on the Board in his absence." The Executive Directors are entitled to remuneration at such rates as are established from time to time by the Board of Governors. When the Board of Executive Directors has to consider any matter particularly affecting a member who is not represented by an Executive Director of its own nationality, it shall duly inform the member. Similarly, in case a member submits a request that has to be considered by the Board of Executive Directors, if the Executive Director representing this member is not of its nationality, in both cases it has the right to be represented through a special representative at the meeting. When a vacancy occurs on the Board of Executive Directors at a time other than the regular election, the President informs the member who appointed or elected the former Executive Director of the existence of the vacancy who in turn elects or appoints a new Executive Director.

11. Voting powers

Each member country has 500 basic votes plus one vote for every share subscribed. Except as otherwise expressly provided, all matters before the Board of Governors shall be decided by a majority of the voting power represented at the meeting. As far as the Board of Executive Directors is concerned, each Executive Director is entitled to cast the number of votes that counted towards his election which votes need not be cast as a unit.

12. President

In contrast to some of the other multilateral institutions such as the World Bank and the African Development Bank where the President is appointed by the Board of Executive Directors, the President of the IDB is elected by the Board of Governors. He must be a national of a member country. The President, while holding office, cannot be a Governor or Executive Director. His term of office is five years and he may be re-elected. He is the Chairman of the Board of Executive Directors and the legal representative of the Bank. He is the chief executive of the Bank and conducts under the direction of the Executive Directors the current business of the Bank. The President is responsible for the organisation, appointment and dismissal of the officers and staff in accordance with the rules and regulations adopted by the Bank. In appointing the officers and staff, the President shall, subject to paramount importance of securing the highest standards of efficiency and technical competence, pay due regard to the recruitment of personnel on as wide a geographical basis as possible.

13. Vice President

One or more Vice Presidents are appointed by the Board of Executive Directors on the recommendation of the President. A Vice President must be a national of a member country and holds office for such term, exercises such authority and performs such functions in the administration of the Bank, as may, from time to time, be determined by the Board of Executive Directors. In the absence or incapacity of the President, the Vice President, or, if there be more than one, the ranking Vice President, shall exercise the authority and perform the functions of the President. While holding office as Vice President, he cannot be a Governor or an Executive Director. He may participate in the meetings of the Board of Executive Directors. Unlike other institutions, the IDB's Charter lays down a statutory role and status for the Vice President by requiring that his appointment has to be made by the Board of Executive Directors on the recommendation of the President.

14. International character of the Bank and prohibition of political activity

The Bank must not accept loans or assistance that may in any way prejudice, limit, deflect or otherwise alter its purpose or functions. The Bank, its President, Vice President, Executive Directors, officers and staff must not interfere in the political affairs of any member, nor must they be influenced in their decisions by the political character of the member concerned. Only economic considerations must be relevant to their decisions.

15. Offices of the Bank

The principal office of the Bank is located in Jeddah in the Kingdom of Saudi Arabia. The Bank may establish agencies or branch offices elsewhere. So far the Bank has not established any branch office, though it has had under study a proposal for the establishment of some regional offices.

16. Financial year

The Bank's financial year is the Hijra year. As provided in the Bye-Laws, in determining the Hijra year, the official Saudi Calendar "Ummul Qura" is followed.

17. Channels of communication

Each member must designate an appropriate official authority with which the Bank may communicate in connection with any matter arising under the Agreement establishing the Bank.

18. Reports

The Bank must transmit to its members an annual report containing an audited statement of its accounts and shall publish such report. It must also transmit quarterly to its members a summary statement showing results of its operations.

19. Allocation of net income

The Board of Governors is empowered to determine annually what part of the net income shall be allocated to reserves, depositors, special funds and members provided that no part of the net income or surplus of the Bank shall be distributed to members by way of profit until the general reserve of the Bank shall have attained the level of 25 per cent of the subscribed capital.

20. Withdrawal and suspension of members and termination of operations of the Bank

No member has the right to withdraw from the Bank before the expiry of a period of five years from the date of its membership. If a member fails to fulfil any of its obligations to the Bank, the Board of Governors may suspend such member by a vote representing not less than three-quarters of the total voting power of the members. Before any member is suspended from membership of the Bank, the matter shall be considered by the Board of Executive Directors which shall inform the member sufficiently in advance of the complaint against it and shall give the member a reasonable opportunity to explain its case orally or in writing. The Board of Executive Directors shall recommend to the Board of Governors whatever action it considers appropriate. The member shall be informed of the recommendation and of the date on which the matter has to be considered by the Board of Governors and it shall be given a reasonable time in which to present its case orally or in writing before the Board of Governors. While under suspension, a member shall not be entitled to exercise any rights under the Agreement establishing the Bank, but shall remain subject to all its obligations. A suspended member shall automatically cease to be a member of the Bank one year from the date of suspension unless the Board of Governors decides to restore the member to good standing. In an emergency the Board of Executive Directors may temporarily suspend operations in respect of the new commitments pending an opportunity for further consideration and action by the Board of Governors. The Bank has the right to terminate its operations by a resolution of the Board of Governors approved by voting of two-thirds of the total number of Governors representing not less than three-quarters of the total voting power of the members. In the event of such termination, the liability of all members for the unpaid portion of the subscribed capital of the Bank shall continue until all claims of creditors, including all contingent claims shall have been discharged. No distribution of assets shall be made to members on account of their subscriptions to the capital stock of the Bank until all liabilities to creditors shall have been discharged or provided for.

21. Status, immunities, exemptions and privileges

To enable the Bank effectively to fulfil its purpose and carry out the functions entrusted to it, it has to be accorded certain status, immunities, exemptions and privileges in the territory of each member country. It has the legal status of an independent international institution possessing full juridical personality and enjoys immunity from every legal process except in cases arising from or in connection with the exercise of its powers to raise money or to buy and sell or underwrite the sale of securities. Property and assets of the Bank are immune from all forms of seizure, attachment or execution before the delivery of final judgement against the Bank. The archives of the Bank and in general all documents belonging to it also enjoy immunity wherever located. All Governors, Alternates, Executive Directors, the President, officers and employees of the Bank are immune from legal process with respect to acts performed by them in their official capacity. The Bank may, however, at its discretion waive any of the privileges, immunities and exemptions conferred upon it by its Articles. The Bank, its assets, property, income and its operations and transactions are exempt from all taxation and from all customs duties and no tax is levied in respect of salaries and emoluments paid by the Bank to its employees.

22. Languages

Unlike other multilateral institutions which have only one or two working languages, the IDB has three languages in use. The official language of the Bank is Arabic and the Arabic text is regarded as the authentic text for both interpretation and application. In addition, English and French are used as working languages.

23. Interpretation and amendments

Any question of interpretation or application of the provisions of the Agreement establishing the Bank arising between any member of the Bank or between two or more members of the Bank must be submitted to the Board of Executive Directors for decision. The member concerned has the right within six months of the date of the decision by the Executive Directors to have the matter referred to the Board of Governors. Their decision will be final. In cases pertaining to disagreement between the Bank and a country which has ceased to be a member or between the Bank or any member after adoption of a resolution to terminate the operations of the Bank, such disagreement shall be submitted to arbitration by a tribunal of three arbitrators representing the Bank, the country and the third arbitrator to be appointed by the President of the International Court of Justice or such other authority as may be prescribed by rules and regulations adopted by the Board of Governors. The Articles of Agreement may be amended only by a resolution of the Board of Governors approved by a vote of two-thirds of the total number of Governors representing not less than three-quarters of the total voting power of the members with the exception of the right to withdraw from the Bank, the limitations of liability and the rights pertaining to purchase of capital stock the unanimous agreement of the Board of Governors shall be required. According to the financial rules, the President is required to submit to the Board of Executive Directors for approval before first Zul Qaddah each year, the administrative budget of the Bank for the following year. There is also a provision for submission of a supplementary budget when such need arises. The President is also required each year before first Zul Qaddah to submit a technical assistance budget of the Bank for the following year and also an operational programme of the Bank for the following year showing possible activities in different sectors and countries. The President is authorised to invest funds not immediately needed for the operations of the Bank, subject to the rules and regulations for the purpose. The President is also authorised to undertake temporary borrowing for the current requirement of the Bank provided that at no time the aggregate amount borrowed exceeds 10 million Islamic Dinars. Each year the accounts of the Bank are audited by the external auditors appointed for the purpose by the Board of Governors. Under the Bye-Laws the external auditors have to be of international repute.

Chapter 6

Policies and Procedures

In the case of most international development financing institutions, policy documents are known to have emerged over a period of time through an evolutionary process. Instead of starting with an omnibus policy document covering the entire terrain on which their operations would be spread, international development banks have generally resorted to the preparation of separate memoranda on specific policy issues which in course of time and in the aggregate have assumed the dimensions of a comprehensive single document on policies and procedures. In sharp contrast to this, as observed earlier, the Islamic Development Bank chose to adopt the opposite course of spelling out its policies and procedures in as detailed a manner as possible even going to the length of fixing specific quantitative criteria in respect of the return expected on equity and profit-sharing projects, much before embarking upon the operational course. This departure from convention was largely dictated by its desire to inform the member countries and prospective co-financiers about the policies and procedures which it proposed to follow in turn enabling them to forward projects to the Bank thereby paving the way for the commencement of financing operations. The Bank realised that over the years the policies would have to be modified in the light of experience and the emerging situation and yet it thought that this was the only way to enable it to make the earliest possible start in the direction of rendering service to its member countries. In the preparation of this document,* the IDB had to place reliance in a large measure on the policies and procedures of other similar institutions though an attempt was made to bear in mind the special requirements and character of the Bank stemming from the mandate it had been given to operate in conformity with Shariah.

Ordinary operations

Ordinary operations were divided as follows:

(1) Equity participation in projects/enterprises;
(2) Investment in economic and social infrastructure projects;
(3) Loans for public sector projects, enterprises and programmes;
(4) Loans for private sector projects, enterprises and programmes.

Pre-requisites for financing

It was laid down that the Bank would finance projects/enterprises which were technically sound and economically and financially viable. In this connection, proper feasibility studies were required to be submitted to the Bank. The Bank would then examine the applications subjecting the projects to rigorous appraisal and evaluation. It was made clear that preference will be accorded to (a) projects with a high financial and economic rate of return; (b) sub-regional and regional projects and to those projects which promote complementarity in the economies of the member countries. Priority would also be accorded to projects which demonstrated "clear efforts towards self-assistance and have strong social orientation".

Considerations relevant to financing

In this regard the following stipulations were made:

(1) The Bank will make an analytical appraisal of the financial position of the recipient and the guarantor, the balance of payments and debt servicing position of the member country and other pertinent matters in addition to the financial viability of the projects and enterprises it would seek to finance.
(2) The Bank will pay due regard to the needs of relatively less developed countries and will evolve a suitable strategy for them, taking into

* This chapter is entirely based on and derived from the Bank's document on policies and procedures.

account their GNP and per capita income, stage of economic development, agricultural and industrial situation, technological development, balance of payments, debt servicing position and all other pertinent matters.

(3) The Bank would pay due regard to promoting the well-being of the people in member countries through economic and social development and through enlarging the employment opportunities. For this purpose, efforts would be made to evaluate the social aspects by quantifying the social benefits accruing from a project.

(4) The Bank would avoid a disproportionate allocation of its financial resources to any member and for this purpose it would formulate annual and multiyear operational programmes.

(5) The Bank would seek to ensure that the funds made available by the Bank were exclusively used for the purpose for which they were provided through necessary stipulation in the legal agreements and through review and follow-up missions.

(6) The Bank will accord priority to projects which promote and strengthen economic co-operation among its members and for this purpose would direct attention to multinational projects and joint ventures in the light of availability of raw materials, technology, financial resources, management capability and marketing arrangements.

(7) In order to avoid financing projects in the territory of a member country, which objects to such financing, it was required that the project and the financing application should be submitted through the appropriate government agency or the channel of communication agreed upon between the Bank and the member countries.

(8) While the Bank would primarily finance the foreign exchange component of a project, in suitable cases and particularly in the case of less developed member countries, it may also consider financing a portion of local currency expenditures.

(9) As far as procurement of goods and services was concerned, the Bank stipulated that they will be subject to international competitive bidding with a reasonable margin of preference for procurement from member countries.

(10) Generally speaking, the Bank would consider both new projects or those for expansion and modernisation, satisfying itself in all cases that the financing provided by it would result in the creation of new productive facilities.

Equity participation

The policy document laid down that in line with its objective of participating in the equity of projects which were productive and revenue yielding, the Bank will direct attention to the financial and management aspects. In regard to equity participation, certain other conditions were also stipulated. For instance, it was laid down that the Bank will accord priority to such projects where it was satisfied that its participation would make for a more balanced relationship with foreign capital or induce the flow of foreign capital by promoting confidence and would result in the transfer of technology and expertise. Perhaps the most important stipulation in the policy document was that the Bank will seek equity participation in projects/enterprises having a high financial rate of return in the region of at least 20 per cent. It was also provided that the Bank's equity share will not normally exceed one-third of the total equity and that the Bank would operate on the basis of a lower limit of ID2 million and an upper limit of ID20 million for a new project.

Profit sharing

In addition to loans and equity participation, the policy document clearly envisaged financing of projects on the basis of profit sharing. It was stated that to ensure an adequate income to the Bank, the net income earned by a project would be shared on a pro rata basis taking into account the quantum of investment by the Bank. The amount of profit to be shared by the Bank will be determined "on a declining scale" as the Bank's capital was repaid. For profit sharing, a higher financial rate of return, that is at least 25 per cent, was prescribed.*

Service fee

As regards service fee, it was to be fixed according to the proportions which the administrative expenditures of the Bank bear to its total resources. In determining it the Bank would also take into account the annual administrative cost it would incur in formulating and processing social and infrastructure projects. It was estimated that the service fee, which would become due from the date of commitment, would vary between 2.5 per cent and 3 per cent.

Repayment and grace periods

The amortisation and grace period was to be fixed in a flexible manner taking into account the nature, economic and financial prospects of the project, gestation period and the financial and economic situation of the country. In

* This rate of return could not be achieved in practice.

the case of economic and social infrastructure projects the maximum period of repayment could be forty years with a maximum grade period of ten years.

Procurement

Procurement will be on the basis of international competitive bidding and at the "best market price" available. Preference may be given to procurement from member countries including the recipient country.

Consultants

Consultants may be recruited from member as well as non-member countries with preference given to the former. The Bank will maintain a register containing particulars of consultants to facilitate the selection process.

Co-financing

Having recognised that co-financing arrangements provided the best means of becoming operational quickly, the Bank attempted to spell out its policies in this regard. It was made clear that co-financing was possible by way of equity investment, loans or grants or in any combination of these three forms. As for the objectives of co-financing, it was explained that the Bank looked upon it as a way of providing additional resources to member countries and commencing operations quickly to enlarge its exposure in terms of countries and among the high priority projects and finally to benefit from the expertise and experience of other institutions. Two types of co-financing were envisaged, namely parallel financing under which the Bank and its co-financiers would finance specific and identifiable segments of a project and joint financing where the Bank would provide financing collectively with other institutions. Co-financing could be undertaken with international and regional development financing institutions, national agencies, bilateral donors and private investors. The Bank made it clear that it would prefer that co-financing arrangements should not impair its independent character, priorities and operating principles.

Technical assistance

It was explained that technical assistance operations would be undertaken with a three-fold purpose:

(1) Transfer of technology to member countries;
(2) Preparation of feasibility studies; and
(3) Formulation of bankable projects and to help supervision of projects and enterprises during construction and initial operation.

Priority would be accorded to those projects which have potential for financing from the Bank. Technical assistance could be financed by loan or by grant or by a combination of the two depending upon the nature of the operation and the economic situation of the recipient as also the resource position of the Bank. The Bank could finance technical assistance up to ID80,000 as grant and the balance as loan in appropriate cases. Technical assistance involving pre-investment and feasibility studies would be financed on a loan basis whereas advisory technical assistance would qualify to be financed mainly by grant. The recipient would be required to provide the local currency cost.

Functional targets

The policy document set out the following functional targets:

Investment for profit sharing	40–45%
Equity participation	30–40%
Loans	20–25%

Sectoral priorities

The sectoral targets were as follows:

Agriculture and relative fields	30–40%
Industry and related fields	25–35%
Public utilities	10–15%
Transportation and communication	10–15%
Social sector	10–15%
Others	5–10%

These percentages could be revised from time to time.

While these policies and procedures for financing operations were laid down several years ago and some of the stipulations such as those relating to the rates of return have turned out to be difficult to meet and the sectoral and functional priorities have also not been realised, the policies of the bank have yet to be formally revised and the document prepared originally still holds.

Local cost financing

The document made a distinction between local currency expenditure and expenditure by way of procurement of imported goods available locally. Such expenditures were to be treated as a part of the foreign exchange component. It was felt that priority should be given to the least developed member countries, to projects which have a relatively low foreign exchange component but relatively high economic and social benefits and also to public utility projects having a significant social impact.

Guarantees

As far as the issue of guarantees was concerned, the Articles of Agreement had only stated that in conducting its operations, the Bank shall pay due regard to safeguarding its interests in respect of its financing, including "obtaining guarantees for its loans". The document on Policies and Procedures required that where the recipient of the Bank's finance was not the government of a member country, necessary guarantee might have to be obtained from the government or from an instrumentality acceptable to the Bank, such as the Central Bank or a commercial bank of repute. In the case of regional or national projects and enterprises, the Bank will require the concerned governments, or such instrumentalities acceptable to the Bank, to provide the necessary guarantees for its investments and loans. In November, 1976, the Board of Executive Directors approved a document relating to the general conditions applicable to loans and guarantees. It provided for a guarantee from the government in cases of operations other than equity financing wherever the beneficiary was not a government itself. In the latter case, the beneficiary being government, no other guarantee was envisaged. This was, in fact, in conformity with the practice followed by other international financing institutions, whose general conditions applicable to loan and guarantee agreements clearly laid down that in case the recipient was a member, all references to the terms guarantee and guarantor should be disregarded. There are several advantages accruing from a government guarantee:

(i) It secures the full faith and credit backing of the member government as far as the repayment obligation to the Bank is concerned.
(ii) It confers upon the institution the legal right of prompt collection from the government in the event of a default.
(iii) The guarantee, being provided by government, becomes a contractual obligation under international law.
(iv) Having provided the guarantee, the government acquires a financial stake in the success of the enterprise and becomes obliged not to take

any measures likely to harm the interest of the project.
(v) The guarantee provided by the government is free of charge.

Subsequently, in September 1978 the Board of Executive Directors resolved that the Bank should follow the following procedures in respect of a guarantee for the financing it provides:

(a) When the Government of the Member State is the beneficiary from financing by the Bank or one of its agencies or instrumentality or political subdivision of the Member Country;
(b) Or if the Bank provides financing to an institution/organisation or a company owned by the Government or in which it has a share or is owned by any one of its agencies;
(c) Or for cases where the Bank provides financing to an institution or company operating in one of the Member States which is not owned by the Member State or any of its agencies. In such cases, the Bank in order to safeguard its interests with regard to its financing shall obtain the necessary guarantee from the Central Bank or any other body that performs its functions in the Member State or a reputable commercial bank acceptable to the IDB.

This led to a number of difficulties and protests. It was argued, for instance, that the central bank was no more than the creation of the Government and it was impossible to conceive of it as providing a stronger guarantee than the government itself. Hence, at the annual meeting in Kampala, the Board of Governors adopted a resolution stating that the original position relating to the requirement for guarantee which existed prior to the date of the amendment be restored and in recognising the need for timely repayment and having regard to the fact the device of charging penal interest is not available to the Bank, the Board of Executive Directors may undertake studies taking into account the various views expressed at the Third Annual Meeting. The matter was thus studied by the Board and a compromise was struck. It was decided that while the Bank may continue to follow the traditional path in regard to obtaining of guarantees, the central bank of the country concerned should be assigned a more direct and active role in ensuring that payments due to the IDB are actually made on time. It was, therefore, required that in every case where either the government is borrower or where a loan was guaranteed by the government, a letter be obtained from the Finance Ministry or any other authorised ministry of the beneficiary state instructing the central bank of the concerned country in categorical terms that the payment on account of loans be effected on the dates on which they fall due. Furthermore, a copy of this letter of authority should be provided to the IDB together with an acknowledgement from the central bank indicating that the directive had been received and noted. These two letters are treated as basic documents enabling the country concerned to contract the loan. This arrangement has a two-fold advantage. In the first place it serves as the requisite authority for the central bank to act on behalf of the government in making payment immediately it becomes due. In the second place it assigns the central bank a definite role and responsibility for ensuring that payments to the Bank are regular and punctual. This decision of the Board of Executive Directors was ratified at the Fourth Annual Meeting of the Board of Governors in March 1980 and continues to be followed.

In summing up, it may be observed that if the IDB were to become operational as early as it did, it was natural that instead of developing tailormade procedures and systems, it adopted those followed by other international development financing institutions. As far as loan financing and technical assistance operations were concerned, except for the service fee, not many procedural innovations were warranted. It was in respect of other modes of financing such as equity, leasing, profit sharing and foreign trade financing operations that special procedures and systems were needed. At any rate, it would be highly beneficial now for the Bank to undertake a comprehensive review of its document on policies and procedures with a view to making such modifications as are necessary in the light of the experience gained during the past years and also with the specific object of evolving policies, procedures and systems best suited to its distinctive operations and special character.

Chapter 7

Financing Operations

1. Overall level of financing

As observed earlier, the primary concern of the Islamic Development Bank on its establishment was to commence its financing operations* as soon as possible. To achieve this a two-fold method was adopted. First, instead of following the conventional path of project identification by mounting missions to member countries, the Bank decided to put together a document setting out its policies and procedures and invited member governments to send projects and proposals for the Bank's financing. Secondly, early contact was established with international and regional institutions with a view to co-financing.

The IDB was thus able to make the quick start which it desired. However, in this regard, two points deserve attention. In the first place, the lack of long and comprehensive preparations quite naturally affected the efficiency and quality of its operations. Secondly, there was not enough opportunity for exploring and considering Shariah aspects and problems. Having embarked upon the operational course, the Bank had little time to look back and concentrated on increasing the number of its operations so as to help as many

* The Bank has three main types of financing operations, namely, project financing, foreign trade financing and special assistance account operations.

of its member countries as possible. The average level of financing per operation had to be small for several reasons. Firstly, considerations of safety dictated that the amounts committed per project should be small. Secondly, in this way a much wider field could be covered in terms of recipients as well as the number of operations. Thirdly, by undertaking a large number of operations, the Bank gained much-needed experience and was able to establish a working relationship with several co-financing institutions.

While this effort was underway, it was soon realised that if the Bank was to make an adequate and sizeable transfer of resources to its member countries, it had to diversify its modes of financing. The Articles of Agreement had only mentioned loans, equity investment, profit sharing, technical assistance and foreign trade financing. To these were added, in course of time, two more modes of financing, namely, leasing and instalment sales. Subsequently, three other financing techniques were devised, namely, the line of equity, the line of leasing and line of instalment sales.

The first operation approved by the Bank was a loan to the Song Loulou Hydroelectric Project in the Cameroon on the basis of co-financing with the Saudi Fund for Development and the Kuwait Fund for Arab Economic and Social Development. During the twelve-year period from 1396H (1976) to 1407H (1987), the total financing approved by the Bank has amounted to ID5,927.48 million. Of this, ID1,572.45 million represented project financing, and ID4,355.03 million foreign trade financing. In addition to this, the Bank approved ID179.37 million by way of special operations. A breakdown of the project financing approved by the Bank on an annual basis is provided in the following table:

Year	*No. of project financing operations*	*Amount (ID million)*
1396H (1976)	2	13.45
1397H (1977)	23	99.70
1398H (1978)	15	69.91
1399H (1979)	21	91.14
1400H (1980)	27	131.57
1401H (1981)	28	114.78
1402H (1982)	31	136.18
1403H (1983)	33	157.50
1404H (1984)	31	200.89
1405H (1985)	45	243.45
1406H (1986)	35	179.71
1407H (1987)	48	134.17
TOTAL:	339	1572.45

In judging the Bank's performance in terms of growth of its operational effort, it would be fair to mention some of the main constraints. As far as resource availability was concerned, though the Bank was in a comfortable position, as a young and inexperienced institution, it had to chart its course with a great degree of caution. True, the magnitude of resources and assistance required by the member countries was enormous. However, the Bank's ability to step up its operations was governed largely by the size and quality of its project pipeline. In planning the tempo of growth, it had to take account of the fact that unlike other institutions, in its case, resource mobilisation presented a much greater challenge in that traditional methods of mobilising resources from the market were ruled out and in the ultimate analysis resource mobilisation depended on the Bank's success in devising resource mobilisation techniques in conformity with Shariah. This was a highly complex and time-taking task and therefore the Bank was left only with one single avenue for replenishing its resources, namely, to seek an increase in its subscribed capital. In this background, it would have been clearly unwise for the Bank to adopt a carefree attitude in regard to resource availability in determining the rate at which its operational programme was to grow. Leaving aside the resource problem, by far the most important determinant of the operational effort of the Bank was its organisational and professional strength. The Bank had serious difficulty in building up an adequate organisation rapidly for a number of reasons such as the shortage of personnel having the requisite qualifications and experience, language requirements, geographical considerations and the recruitment approach adopted by the Bank. Even when the organisational strength grew with the passage of time, the work load grew faster if for no other reason than the following up of projects after their approval.

Besides these, there were some other factors having a bearing on the level of the Bank's activities. For example, co-financing which made it possible for the Bank to commence operations quickly, had certain implications for the size of its operational programme. The Bank had to take care that what it provided by way of resources was not so large as to displace what the original would-be financiers might have provided. It was vital to optimise the balance of funds of the financing participants. Moreover, if the Bank was to develop as an international development financing agency, it could no longer remain solely dependant on co-financing with other institutions and had to undertake operations on its own on an increasing scale. This obviously, so to speak, made a demand on the Bank's overall organisational capability. Furthermore, it was quite understandable that governments were generally reluctant to forward projects, which were in the most advanced stage of preparation and for which financing was needed urgently, to an institution deemed to be still in a stage of infancy.

There were at least two other factors which had a restraining effect on the overall size of the Bank's operational effort. Firstly, the emphasis on equity built into the Bank's policies and the statutory requirement that a balance be maintained between its loans and equity operations, owing to the complexities and shortage of sound equity proposals, had indirectly a restrictive effect on the overall size of its operational effort and more particularly on the tempo of its growth. A second factor interfering with a faster increase in its operational effort was that some of the prospective recipients whose projects had reached an advanced stage of processing became ineligible for financing by virtue of a payments default. This resulted not only in a waste of the effort put in on the projects concerned but also in a shortfall in the Bank's overall annual performance.

Having discussed and analysed the various factors responsible for the rather slow growth of the Bank's operational programme, it has to be clearly recognised that, as far as the future is concerned, there is a strong and undeniable case for a substantial expansion in the financing activities and operational efforts of the Bank. Notwithstanding the various constraints and difficulties involved, and considering that it has a membership of 44 countries, some of which are the poorest in the world, and embraces a population of nearly 800 million people, it is only through an adequate enlargement and improvement of its operational effort that the Bank can satisfy the aspirations associated with its establishment. This is a task which calls for scientific planning, imaginative policies and hard work to surmount the obstacles and difficulties which lie in the path. With an experience extending over a decade, however, this can hardly be regarded as an impossible task. At the same time, it would require the working out of a proper strategy for the purpose. It will have to be composed of several elements. As far as resource availability is concerned, a vigorous effort will be called for, devising and developing new modes of mobilisation designed to attract resources from the market so as to be able to reduce dependence upon capital increase as the sole means of replenishing the Bank's resources. In fact, resource mobilisation will have to be related to the various types of operation which the Bank undertakes and a strategy formulated with due regard to the requirements and special features of each type of operation. The fact that some international institutions have succeeded in recent years in mobilising massive resources from some IDB members such as Saudi Arabia, is both a challenge for the IDB and also a measure of the scope which seems to exist in this direction. Simultaneously, an effort will have to be launched to mop up the plethora of liquidity existing in some of the member countries in the private sector. This will, on the one hand, make possible an expansion of the project financing by the Bank by releasing some of the long-term capital resources of the Bank presently locked up in short-term operations like foreign trade financing and on the other, assuming that such mobilisation will yield large funds, the Bank will be enabled to make a larger resource transfer to its member countries through its foreign trade financing. Apart from more active resource mobilisation, a number of other steps will be required. The Bank's administrative and professional strength will have to be augmented substantially. At the same time, the average level per operation will have to be raised sufficiently. What is more, the Bank will have to make much more frequent use of a combination of the different modes of financing, particularly equity with leasing. In a word, as far as the size of the annual operational programme is concerned, the Bank will be well advised to adopt a much bolder and more ambitious approach in the sure knowledge that after almost a decade of working it would be unrealistic for it to hope for the degree of interest and support, so vital for its future development, without a clear demonstration of soundness and efficiency combined with adequate courage and enterprise.

2. Functional distribution of financing

The document on policies and procedures issued in 1975 before the commencement of operations had established quantitative functional targets for the Bank to follow and it would be interesting to see how far they had been adhered to in terms of the Bank's financing operations ended 1404H (1984). In this connection, it may be pointed out that the functional targets laid down in the document only related to three types of operation, namely, profit sharing, equity participation and loans. No targets were prescribed for leasing, foreign trade financing and technical assistance. The reason for this was that at the time the policy document was prepared, leasing and instalment sales as distinctive types of operation had yet to be devised. As for technical assistance, by its very nature, it could hardly absorb a very substantial proportion of the Bank's resources and therefore it was thought unnecessary to establish a target for it in percentage terms. Hence too rigid an application of the targets prescribed in the policy document for profit sharing (40–45 per cent), equity (30–40 per cent) and loans (20–25 per cent) would hardly be meaningful. And yet it would be both useful and interesting to look at the situation as it has actually emerged during the ten years of the Bank's operations to 1405H (1985). This is set out in the following table:

(Amount in ID million)

Year	*Loans*	*Equity*	*Leasing*	*Profit sharing*	*Technical assistance*	*Foreign trade financing*
1396H	6.00	7.45	—	—	—	—
1397H	55.41	33.23	5.22	—	0.84	43.61
1398H	25.46	24.36	10.00	4.27	0.82	127.44
1399H	33.74	37.79	16.25	—	1.37	262.43
1400H	52.68	35.04	36.47	—	3.38	358.75

1401H	31.28	45.98	30.69	—	6.83	367.89
1402H	45.03	28.70	56.91	—	4.45	377.55
1403H	73.45	10.61	86.43	3.06	5.99	460.46
1404H	71.46	6.00	125.27	—	2.96	671.61
1405H	98.62	8.73	92.10	—	6.63	667.27
1406H	28.27	—	—	—	2.43	572.84
1407H	34.70	0.75	—	—	6.00	453.15

Several conclusions seem to emerge from the foregoing table. In the first place, foreign trade financing accounts for by far the bulk of the total resources provided by the Bank to its members. Being a short-term placement operation, this does not have the same impact and significance from the developmental standpoint as the other types of financing provided by the IDB. However, two points may be made in this respect. First, though basically a short-term operation, it is conducted with such regularity and frequency that it acquires the character of a rolled over or standing credit facility. Secondly, it affords much needed balance of payments support to the recipients. What is perhaps even more crucial is that this being an operation financed out of the surplus funds of the Bank, so far it has not restricted the size of the Bank's project financing. Secondly, the preceding table shows that, as far as the ratio between loans and equity is concerned, after moving markedly in favour of equity, it has taken a sharply reverse course in recent years. This is for the reason that while loan financing has risen substantially, equity financing has been on the decline on account of the unhappy experience the Bank has had with some of its equity investments.

Here, perhaps, a word is necessary about the rationale as also the effect of the requirement contained in the Articles regarding the maintenance of a balance between loans and equity operations of the Bank. It has to be realised that underlying this provision, there was no inherent bias against loan financing but mainly a desire to spur the Bank to make concerted efforts to expand its equity operations. The provision seems certainly to have exercised a pressure on the Bank to enlarge its equity operations. At the same time, however, it had a restraining effect on the loan operations of the Bank as long as a corresponding increase in equity financing was not feasible. Eventually, the balance had to be upset and the target of loan financing exceeded in the interest of raising the overall level of the operational programme.

Finally, there are two other features relating to the Bank's experience with different types of financing, which deserve to be highlighted. First, leasing and instalment sales which were not even mentioned in the Articles of Agreement or the policy document of the Bank have come to occupy the highest importance among the various operations undertaken by the Bank and hold promise of becoming even more important in the future. The second feature relates to the fact that, contrary to the high target laid down in the policy document, profit sharing operations undertaken so far by the Bank are extremely meagre.

There was not much mention of profit sharing as a mode of operation in the Articles of the Bank, though the policy document prepared after the establishment of IDB referred to it specifically. The Bank became aware of it in those cases where equity financing was not feasible.

The importance attached to profit sharing as a mode of operation in the functional targets set by the IDB in its policy document stemmed partly from its manifest Islamic character and partly from the expectation that it would prove to be the principal source of income to the Bank as loan financing was concessionary in nature.

It would be highly rewarding for the Bank to sponsor a comprehensive study on the subject of profit sharing in relation to its operations with a view to formulating guidelines on the subject, having sufficient conceptual and operational clarity. So far, the Bank has undertaken only three profit sharing operations of the total project value of ID17.63 million representing about 1 per cent of the total financing approved by the Bank. The first was undertaken in 1978 in the Badr Housing Complex in the UAE, the second in 1983 in an Auqaf project in Morocco and the third, in 1988, was the King Abdul Aziz Mosque Project in Jeddah, Saudi Arabia. Possibilities of entering into such arrangements in conjunction with Islamic banks seem to merit special attention if for no other reason than the fact that profit sharing has been given the pride of place in the Islamic system of financing.

More recently, the IDB has introduced a new mode of financing known as al-baya-li-ajal or instalment sale. The mode, which is considered to conform to Shariah, has been designed for those cases which cannot be covered by lease financing. Under this arrangement, the ownership of the asset sold is immediately transferred to the beneficiary whereas the price of the asset is recovered in instalments. The Bank buys an asset and immediately resells it to the recipient at a higher price to be paid in instalments over a period of time. The timely payment of the instalments is guaranteed by the Government or by a first class commercial bank. This mode of financing is expected to enlarge the scope for the financing of productive assets, particularly those which cannot be covered by leasing either because they are not separately identifiable or because their life span is not sufficiently long. Otherwise, as far as the period of financing and the return on it are concerned, it will be more or less the same as in the case of lease financing. The Bank has so far undertaken 23 operations totalling ID193.40 million by way of instalment sales. One of the main advantages of the instalment sale arrangement is that since the ownership of the asset is transferred immediately to the beneficiary, the required commercial bank guarantee can be provided by mortgaging the assets to the guaranteeing bank. This may prove to be significant for expanding operations with the private sector in member countries.

3. Sectoral distribution of financing

In terms of the distribution of financing among various sectors, it is noteworthy that 17.3 per cent of project financing approved during 1396H (1976) to 1407H (1987) went to the agriculture and agro-industry sector, 35.6 per cent to the industry and mining sector, 21.4 per cent to the transport and communications sector, 13.2 per cent to the public utility sector, 10.3 per cent to the social sector and 2.2 per cent to other sectors. The following table provides a breakdown of financing according to sectors:

(Amount in ID million)

Year	*Agriculture & agro-industry*	*Industry & mining*	*Transport & communication*	*Public utilities*	*Social sectors*	*Others*	*Total*
1396H	—	7.45	—	6.00	—	—	13.45
1397H	11.12	38.93	44.27	—	5.39	—	99.71
1398H	13.00	32.96	6.50	19.68	—	4.27	76.41
1399H	1.70	47.75	24.18	9.41	5.04	3.05	91.13
1400H	14.67	59.98	21.83	22.17	12.91	—	131.56
1401H	27.10	60.07	23.22	5.12	—	4.23	119.74
1402H	5.50	59.29	33.63	34.26	5.00	0.09	137.77
1403H	6.16	45.20	75.35	8.27	39.34	10.21	184.53
1404H	28.79	74.62	34.43	21.20	41.37	0.49	200.90
1405H	116.48	60.76	7.28	45.43	35.48	3.32	268.75
1406H	30.27	72.02	40.56	12.84	12.13	—	167.82
1407H	25.77	19.51	36.06	30.91	11.22	10.75	134.22
Total:	280.56	578.54	347.31	215.29	167.88	36.41	1625.99

The above table shows that broadly speaking, in terms of sectors, industry and mining has occupied the first place, transport and communications the second, agriculture the third, public utilities the fourth and social services the last place. In a way, it was understandable that in a situation which was characterised by almost total dependence upon recipient governments and co-financing institutions as far as the building of the project pipeline was concerned, coupled with the Bank's concern for stepping up its operations and serving as many countries as possible, the Bank could not achieve an ideal sectoral distribution of its financing. Even so, one hopes that the Bank in future years will be able to direct a much larger part of its financing to agriculture than it has done so far. Even in the case of the World Bank, the financing activities picked up slowly in the agricultural sector largely as a result of a shortage of well-prepared projects. Indeed, the need for expanding the role of the IDB in financing agriculture can hardly be over-emphasised. This is for several reasons. In most of its member countries which are experiencing a rapid population growth, there is an acute need to step up the production of food. Agriculture in most countries is the source of livelihood for the bulk of the country's population. As a sector, agriculture seems to provide a much greater promise as a source of employment compared to many other sectors. It is also responsible for providing the largest portion of the foreign exchange earnings of most of the low income member countries. Even viewed from the standpoint of income distribution, agriculture deserves special attention as the source of income and welfare of the major part of the country's population.

What seems to be required in the IDB's case is a broad approach to the problem. While stepping up its direct lending for agricultural projects, it must also look for projects in the field of livestock, agricultural estates, seed production and forestry. There is also a need for identifying possibilities by way of projects designed to produce fruits and vegetables. Attention has also to be directed to the field of fisheries. Another sub-sector needing attention is the financing of dairy products, like eggs, milk, butter and poultry. The demand for such products is known to be increasing in many countries with the growth of money incomes. By covering the broad areas set out above and at the same time emphasising the need for improved project preparation in the agricultural sector and, if necessary, providing technical assistance for it, the IDB will not only be able to expand its role in the overall agricultural sector but also achieve greater success in the direction of assisting the least-developed member countries and in developing opportunities for financing the agricultural sector on the basis of equity.

The other requirement is to undertake sector studies which should consider not only priorities within the sector but also draw attention to constraints to agricultural development and suggest modifications to institutions or agricultural policies which are needed to facilitate investment and development and are essential pre-conditions to the financing of specific projects. It would also be worthwhile to seek projects in the following fields:

(1) Water resource development including irrigation, both surface and ground water, land reclamation and drainage, sanitation and flood control.
(2) Medium-term and long-term agricultural credit programmes for agricultural development and livestock.
(3) Agricultural industries and commercial development of farms and fishing areas, storing, packaging, processing and marketing of agricultural projects and industries.

So far as the overall problem is concerned, the Bank should consider the possibility of sponsoring a comprehensive rural survey for its member countries along the lines of that undertaken by the Asian Development Bank soon after its establishment. There are some IDB member countries whose agricultural sector has not been surveyed and whose priorities have not been decided. The IDB can take care of this area with a view to helping the member countries.

In financing industry, the IDB has to bear in mind that within its membership it has two categories of country:

(1) Those which have already attained some degree of industrialisation though mostly it has been achieved through excessive protection and by employing the import substitution strategy rather than by establishing industries which have the competitiveness and potential for exports.
(2) Those countries which are only just embarking on the task of establishing industries and are faced with handicaps such as the shortage of skilled labour, management and entrepreneurship and also suffer from a shortage of capital resources and inadequate domestic markets.

The Bank would serve its own objectives as also the interest of the member countries if it adopted a different approach in the case of the foregoing two categories of country. In the case of those countries where the infrastructure base has already been developed and external economies are available, the Bank should readily involve itself in financing the industrial sector. However, in the case of those countries which suffer from a critical shortage of skills and entrepreneurship and where the domestic markets are much smaller, the IDB must concentrate on the provision of technical assistance in the field of project identification and promotion. Generally speaking, more attention has to be directed to the pre-investment work. The aim should be to promote the efficiency of industrial production through more vigorous and comprehensive project appraisal. It may also be worthwhile to get involved in projects involving more than one country in order to overcome the handicaps of a limited market. Similarly, greater attention has to be directed to the promotion of small-scale industries and improving technology.

The financing of transportation and communications has been an important field of operation for the IDB since its inception. In fact, this covers a wide field including aviation, waterways, shipping, ports, railways and road services. In undertaking future operations, it may be useful if a project by project assessment is supplemented by a comprehensive analysis of the transport sector as a whole. This is particularly required in the case of some of the least-developed member countries where the urge for improving and expanding the transport facilities is strong. What the IDB must try to ensure is that the countries achieve an appropriate mix of transport and other investments.

The need for developing a core programme for producing a meaningful impact on the economies of member countries is undeniable. However, the main constraint in this regard appears to be the modest size of the Bank's annual programme which needs to be remedied through a multiyear programme and country programming.

4. Geographical distribution and breakdown by country

It has been the IDB's endeavour from its inception to provide financing to as many of its member countries as possible and also to diversify its operations in each of them. The position, as it has emerged during the ten years since the establishment of the Bank, shows that as far as project financing is concerned, the leading beneficiaries have been Turkey, Jordan and Pakistan, whereas taking the foreign trade financing operations into account also, Turkey, Algeria, Pakistan, Bangladesh, Morocco and Jordan have been the principal recipients of resources.

As far as financing to individual countries is concerned it is necessary to make two significant points. First, that it is essential to establish clear-cut criteria regarding the eligibility of the various member countries for assistance from the Islamic Development Bank. It is well known that in the case of other international development banks, the relatively developed countries are not eligible to receive financial assistance. It is not suggested that the IDB adopt a principle identical with any other institution. What is required is that it should address itself to this question so as to evolve appropriate criteria. For example, financing by the IDB may focus exclusively on the capital deficit members whereas the Bank should seek to assist its capital rich members in other ways, taking into account their needs and economic circumstances. As a matter of fact, in future, this should constitute a major challenge for the Bank which is expected to help all its member countries with due regard to their special requirements. Apart from the general criteria, it may also be useful to establish general rules of eligibility for various types of operation, such as loan financing, equity, leasing, instalment sale and technical assistance. As a general rule, concessionary financing, that is loans and technical assistance, should be exclusively used for the benefit of the least-developed member countries, whereas other modes of financing such as leasing, equity, profit sharing and foreign trade financing must be concentrated on the relatively more advanced countries. The second point relates to the need for establishing country programmes. It was understandable that the Bank could not embark on this exercise until it had, so to speak, come of age. However, with almost a decade of experience, it is time that it made a proper beginning with country programming. For it is only through this technique that the Bank would be able to systematise and regulate its financing to its members.

It is significant that so far the IDB has not succeeded in enlarging its relationship with the private sector and its financing has concentrated almost solely on public sector projects and enterprises. This does not accord with the Articles of Agreement of the Bank which require the Bank to assist both the public and private sectors. The principal reason for the present situation is that the main channel through which projects have come to the IDB are the governments of member countries. It is possible that governments have been reluctant to forward many private sector projects to the IDB on the ground that it would reduce their own share of financing. With the experience and knowledge gained by the Bank in its member countries, it should try to become more active in financing private sector projects. While in most member countries the private sector is underdeveloped, considerable scope seems to exist in this direction in the capital surplus countries and member countries having large private sectors. The national development banks in the member countries should be able to render useful assistance in this regard. At the same time, this effort would require several adjustments in policy and approach such as greater flexibility in regard to guarantees and also the relaxation of the requirement that private sector projects must come to the Bank through government channels. Moreover, it would also be in harmony with the spirit of Islamic banking if instead of asking for strong commercial bank guarantees, much greater reliance was placed on rigorous appraisal of projects and clients with a view to safeguarding the Bank's investment.

Chapter 8

Loan Financing

It is well known that in the case of international development banks, loans are the sole means of resource transfer. In the case of the Islamic Development Bank, however, as far as its Articles of Agreement and Policy Document are concerned, this particular mode of financing was not given pride of place. The reason for this was obvious. Loans inherently involve interest. The IDB's mandate was to operate on the basis of Islamic principles which prohibit interest. At the same time, by virtue of its charter, the Bank was required to undertake loan financing with the explicit proviso that it should maintain a balance or ratio between its loan operations and equity financing. There could not be any question of charging interest on the loans but the Articles laid down that the Bank would levy a service fee to cover its administrative expenses. In terms of policy, loan financing is intended for infrastructural projects in the agricultural, transport and utilities sectors as well as social sector projects in the field of education and health. The Bank is also required to accord priority to the least-developed member countries in respect of loan financing operations. It is noteworthy that unlike other multilateral institutions, the IDB does not undertake the guaranteeing of loans for member countries.

The loan financing approved by the Bank from 1396H (1976) to the end of 1470H (1987) is set out in the following table:

Year	No.	Amount (ID million)	Percentage of total project financing
1396H	1	6.00	44.6
1397H	11	55.41	55.6
1398H	5	25.46	36.4
1399H	6	33.74	37.0
1400H	9	52.68	40.0
1401H	7	31.12	27.1
1402H	8	45.03	32.7
1403H	11	73.45	39.8
1404H	12	71.46	34.7
1405H	15	98.62	36.1
1406H	7	28.27	16.8
1407H	11	36.08	26.9
Total:	103	557.48	34.7

The foregoing table shows that loan financing has occupied a dominant position in the Bank's operations and has clearly tended to outstrip the importance it was assigned in the Articles of Agreement. The explanation for this is two-fold. In the first place, since loan financing is the traditional mode of financing practised by international development banks, most of the projects and proposals it received from member governments and co-financiers had a loan bias. Secondly it is by no means easy to generate projects suitable for other types of financing. The sectoral breakdown of IDB loans is provided in the following table:

Sector	No. of loans	Amount (ID million)	Percentage
1. Agriculture	23	145.01	29.4
2. Public utility	20	109.37	22.2
3. Social services	20	111.66	22.6
4. Transportation and communications	18	104.35	21.2
5. Industry and mining	2	11.44	2.3
6. Others	2	11.13	2.3

In the agricultural sector, loans were mainly for irrigation and drainage projects, in the transportation and communications sector for roads and ports development, in the public utilities sector for power generation and water and sewerage facilities and in the social sector for educational projects.

The above table reflects the Bank's policy of focusing its loan financing on infrastructural and social projects.

As regards geographical distribution, it may be noted that taking the ten-year period since the inception of the Bank, the principal recipients of loans have been Tunisia, Bangladesh, Mauritania, Algeria, Malaysia, Mali, Yemen AR, Niger, Senegal and Iraq. In terms of per capita income, 31.43 per cent of the loan financing went to 11 countries having a per capita income of less than US$375, 34.91 per cent to countries with per capita income of between US$375 and US$1,000 and 33.66 per cent to countries with per capita income of more than US$1,000.

It is high time that the IDB critically examines its policy guidelines in respect of loan financing in the light of its experience over the years. In this connection, a number of suggestions may be made. The present policy that infrastructural projects have to be financed on the basis of a loan should be made more flexible. This is for the reason that some infrastructural projects, like the Suez Canal and the Bosphorus Bridge, can be highly remunerative and as such can bear a much higher cost of financing than the service fee charged by the Bank to cover its administrative expenses. It would be beneficial both for the Bank and the recipients that such projects instead of being necessarily financed by means of loans, are assisted by other means of financing such as leasing. Thus the Bank will be enabled to obtain a reasonable return on its financing and what is more, the project would be able to mobilise adequate financing from the Bank as the latter would not be inhibited by the fact that loans made on the basis of a service fee involve a financial sacrifice. In other words, the Bank would be prevented from providing resources to high-yielding projects at an unduly low price whereas it would become possible for remunerative projects to obtain a large chunk of resources from the Bank without necessitating an undue financial sacrifice from it by way of concessional financing.

As far as the policy directive about the maintenance of a suitable ratio between loans and equity investments is concerned, it has to be understood that the real purpose of this statutory requirement was to encourage and boost equity financing by the Bank. There is no doubt that it has exerted some pressure on the Bank to make greater efforts to expand its equity financing activities as a necessary condition for increasing its loan operations, thereby attaining a respectable level of financing in overall terms. However, what is equally evident is that this provision has tended to squeeze loan financing by the Bank if it has not been possible for it to achieve a matching or corresponding increase in its equity business. Moreover, as a result of its anxiety to maintain a ratio, the IDB may have been led into accepting equity projects which it might not have approved otherwise. If the foregoing analysis is correct, it follows that a clear-cut change is called for in the Bank's policy. What is required is to seek to expand the equity financing activity by laying it down as an independent objective to be pursued on its own, rather than as a pre-condition for increasing loan financing. This will, on the one hand, serve as a safeguard against the risk of the Bank being forced into unsound equity investments and on the other, by separating the loan operations of the Bank from its equity business, it would prevent the loan operations being squeezed as a result of a lack of suitable opportunities and other problems and difficulties in the field of equity financing. The loan financing by the Bank, instead of being determined by the size of equity financing, must be governed by the resources available for it and the needs of the least-developed member countries.

As a matter of fact, having regard to the developmental role of loans as a mode of financing, their concessional nature, the importance of financing agriculture and last but not least the paramount need for helping the least-developed member countries, the Bank must do everything possible to maximise its loan activities consistent with resource availability. Any apprehension that such an approach poses the risk of the loan financing becoming unduly large is groundless and unjustified by virtue of the fact that there are at least two major factors which would seriously limit the dimensions of loan financing by the Bank, namely, the restricted availability of free or costless resources and the low return on loans by way of the service fee. True, thanks to the abundant resources in the form of its subscribed capital for which it has not had to incur any cost, the Bank has so far not become sufficiently aware of this constraint. However, as time passes by and as, in the aftermath of lower oil prices, capital raising from its member countries becomes much more difficult, the full impact of this factor is bound to be felt.

This leads to two further suggestions: first, that the Bank would do well to address itself to the task of mobilising resources for loan financing by methods such as the establishment of a Special Fund as also through a diversion of capital resources from its other activities which, being more remunerative, are easier to finance by attracting resources from the market. Secondly, recognising the serious difficulties in mobilising adequate resources for loan operations, it would be advisable for the Bank to become much more selective in this respect by confining the access to such resources solely to its least-developed member countries. In other words, the Bank would be well advised to give up its present policy of mixing the loans with other types of financing for all member countries, regardless of their economic status and per capita income levels and of merely ensuring that there is a reasonable interval between two loans to the same country irrespective of the total loan financing already provided to it.

Once the list of countries eligible to receive loan financing from the IDB has been established, an attempt could be made to devise a formula for allocating the loan funds amongst them. Broadly speaking, the allocation could be made on the basis of their respective per capita GNP levels and size of population, coupled with an awareness of their external payments position reflected in their debt situation and debt service burden. At the same time, the relatively poor absorptive capacity of the least-developed member countries, in so far as this is a reflection of weak institutional structure, lack of skilled manpower and other characteristics of under-development, should not be held against it in determining its loan financing allocation. As far as sectors are concerned, having regard to the heavy dependence of the least-developed member countries on agriculture, together with the fact that loans are specially suited for financing agricultural projects, the IDB should treat agriculture, particularly food production, as its top priority as far as its loan financing is concerned.

It is also worth consideration that in the case of other institutions, the benefit of concessional financing or the low cost of credit is passed to the recipient country which in turn makes the financing available to the borrowing entity at an ordinary or market rate. Contrary to this, on grounds of Shariah, the IDB seems to insist that the loan should be passed on to the ultimate beneficiary on exactly the same terms as it had been originally made by the Bank. This aspect deserves to be studied with a view to devising some method whereby the Government of the member country gets the full benefit of concessional financing and not necessarily the borrowing entity. Finally, it would also be desirable for the IDB to allow more liberal terms to the recipients in terms of the periods of grace and repayment* in its future loan operations compared to the loans granted by it in the past.

This leads us to issues connected with the service fee charged by the Bank. As observed earlier, the Articles of Agreement only stated that the Bank shall levy a service fee on the loans it makes to cover its administrative expenses, the amount of the fee and the manner of levying it to be determined by the Bank. In this regard, it would be appropriate to refer to the background in which this provision was made. The draft prepared by the Secretariat of the Preparatory Committee had stated that the Bank would be making interest free loans but when the draft was discussed with the Vice Chairman in Jeddah, the term interest free was dropped. The argument was that use of the term would be superfluous as the Bank was required to operate on the basis of Shariah anyway. When this particular clause was discussed by the Preparatory Committee, it was felt that there should be some charge attached to loans: otherwise, this would give rise to unlimited demand for loan financing. It was thus decided to insert a clause about a service fee to be charged on the loans. When the policy document was prepared, an effort was made to elaborate this rather bald statement by spelling out that the administrative expenses sought to be covered by the service fee were not the overall or total expenses but those which related to its loan operations only. In the light of these directions, before embarking upon its operations, the Bank undertook a comprehensive exercise to determine the quantum of the

* Article 2.13 of the Policies and Procedures document envisaged a maximum repayment period of 40 years and a maximum grace period of 10 years. This has not been applied so far, and over the years the repayment period has actually shrunk from 30 to 25 years.

service fee, by estimating its administrative expenses and it was decided to charge a service fee ranging between 2.5 and 3 per cent annually. This rate has remained unchanged since it was first fixed. In order to distinguish it from interest in the loan agreement it is set out as a sum of money or amount rather than in percentage terms. It becomes due from the date of commitment which is defined as 90 days after the signing of the agreement or the date of fulfilment of the conditions of effectiveness, whichever is earlier.

It is essential to underline the fact that, while the term service fee has been derived from other international development banks which have set up separate institutions such as the IDA, the Asian Development Fund and the African Development Fund, the service fee charged by the former represents basically a concessional price for the resources which they provide. In sharp contrast to this, the service fee charged by the IDB on its loans has the character of a charge solely to cover the precise expenses incurred by it in the process of making the loan as also those which it will incur during the life of the loan. In other words, any strict comparison between the service fee charged on the Special Fund or concessional lending by other international development banks and the quantum of the service fee levied by the IDB is not justified. Broadly speaking, the service charge on IDA loans and other Special Fund lending is a concessional price or low rate of interest determined in relation to the prevalent interest rate structure and is not based, as is the case with the IDB, on a meticulous calculation of administrative costs connected with the process of making loans.

In actual practice, the task of estimating the administrative expenses on the basis of which the service fee is to be determined would have been much easier had there been a totally separate organisation for loan financing, as distinct from the other operations and functions performed by the Bank. Moreover, it is relatively easy to estimate the direct costs related to project identification, appraisal and follow-up. What is much more difficult is the estimation of the indirect costs through a re-allocation of the overheads. The task becomes highly complex owing to the time factor in that it involves the estimation of costs over the entire life span of the loan, say 30 to 40 years. The process is further complicated by the fact that costs have to be allocated to both new as well as on-going projects. Apart from the difficulties in calculation, there are a number of other factors to be taken into account. Loans are supposed to be the most concessional among the various operations undertaken by the IDB. Having regard to the fact that it has proportionately the largest membership of the least-developed countries combined with its declared policy of assisting its poorest members by according them special treatment, and also bearing in mind its Islamic character demanding the utmost compassion for the weakest of its member countries, it would not be unreasonable to expect that its assistance to its least-developed members would be substantially more concessional than that provided by other institutions.

In summing up, a number of suggestions can be made for the consideration of the Bank. Above all, confronted with formidable difficulties inherent in an accurate and exact estimation of administrative costs as a basis for fixing the service fee, the Bank would do well to try to solve the problem by devising a policy approach rather than through a mathematical formula. The policy situation is to be based on three elements, namely, first, the paramount need for the most concessional assistance to the least-developed member countries, second, the vital need for conforming to Shariah in respect of service fee and, third, the formidable problems involved in the calculation of administrative costs to serve as a basis for fixing the service fee. This seems to open up a whole series of possibilities and options. First, considering that the resources it uses for financing loans are free and costless, and following a dual approach to mobilising resources for loan financing through the device of a special fund and keeping the overall loan financing within reasonable bounds by confining it to its least-developed member countries and restricting it solely to infrastructural and social projects, after its overall income position improves sufficiently, the Bank may abandon its practice of levying a service fee on its loans. Levying a service fee may be permitted by Shariah but surely it is by no means compulsory and there could be no objection if it were dispensed with in the interest of its poorest member countries. The second option for the Bank could be to let the indirect costs of loan financing be absorbed by the other operations of the Bank and to base the service fee on direct costs only, which can be calculated with much greater ease and precision. It may also be worthwhile to separate the loan financing entirely from the other operations of the Bank. This would facilitate the mobilisation of resources for loans through the establishment of a Special Fund and permit resort to the market for resources required for its other activities.

Chapter 9

Equity Financing

It may be observed at the outset that equity financing operations being highly complex and risky by nature, international development banks were as a rule required to concentrate primarily on loan financing. In fact, in the case of certain institutions, there was a prohibition on equity financing in the initial years. Even at present, the situation has not basically changed. True, an affiliate of the World Bank, the International Finance Corporation, undertakes equity financing. However, in this connection two points deserve attention. First, by far the bulk of its financing has taken the form of loans. Secondly, it has mostly undertaken equity financing in combination with a loan operation, thereby establishing a position as the lender whereby its interests as an equity holder in the project are also partly safeguarded. Lately, the Inter-American Development Bank has made a very modest beginning in the area of equity financing with the help of the Venezuelan oil facility. Similarly, as recently as 1983, the Asian Development Bank has introduced an equity financing facility on a very limited scale by establishing a small fund for it, so that its overall financial situation is not endangered by operations which are known to carry much greater risk.

In sharp contrast to the foregoing situation, equity financing was made one of the principal functions of the Islamic Development Bank. This was for three reasons. First, it was felt that the equity gap in its member countries represented a formidable obstacle to development. Secondly, equity financing was deemed to be a source for the Bank to earn sufficient dividend income to offset the fact that its loan operations were to be conducted only on the basis of a service fee, which could do no more than help the Bank meet part of its administrative costs. Thirdly, equity financing was deemed to be a highly desirable operation viewed from the standpoint of Shariah, insofar as it avoided the interest problem. The result was that not only was equity financing accorded a prominent place in the Bank's Articles of Agreement, but also a specific provision was incorporated, establishing the need for maintaining a ratio between equity financing and loan financing.

These aspects were further emphasised and enlarged on in the Policy Document prepared by the Bank. An attempt was made in the Document to lay down the basic policy approach and guidelines which the Bank would be following in respect of equity financing, including matters such as equity to be confined to productive and currently or potentially revenue yielding projects with due attention to the quality of management, the Bank not to acquire a majority or controlling interest in the share capital of an enterprise, the Bank's right to be represented on the board of directors, the option to sell its equity participation, avoidance of management responsibility, ban on combining equity with loan, the need for revolving its resources by selling its investments at the appropriate time, the need for diversification of equity projects, giving priority to such projects where the IDB's participation will have a catalytic effect and finally the decision to seek equity participation in projects and enterprises which promise a high financial rate of return that is in the region of at least 20 per cent.

During the twelve-year period since its inception, the IDB has undertaken 63 equity financing operations of the order of ID267.66 million. This represents 16.7 per cent of the total project financing approved by the Bank. The annual breakdown is given in the following table:

Year	*Number of operations*	*Amount (ID million)*	*Percentage of total project financing*
1396H	1	7.45	55.4
1397H	8	35.73	38.3
1398H	5	26.86	42.0
1399H	8	39.79	43.7
1400H	10	37.04	29.7
1401H	10	45.98	41.2
1402H	8	28.70	18.6
1403H	5	15.61	8.5
1404H	1	6.00	2.9
1405H	3	8.73	2.6
1406H	2	10.00	5.6

1407H	2	5.75	4.3
Total (over 12-year period)	63	267.66	16.7

The table clearly shows that the Bank started its equity financing operations enthusiastically and gradually built up this activity to its highest level in the year 1401H. However, since then, the operations have dropped sharply in view of the Bank's unhappy experience with several of its equity investments, so much so that during 1404H only one equity financing operation was approved, for ID6 million, which represents the lowest figure for a single year since the establishment of the Bank. At the same time it may be noted that its total portfolio of equity investment is almost as large as that of the IFC built up over a much longer period. In terms of sectoral distribution, the investments covered various sectors such as mining, banking, utilities, and agriculture though the primary focus was on industry. As far as the geographical distribution was concerned, the leading beneficiaries were Morocco, Jordan, Pakistan, Tunisia, Indonesia, Senegal, UAE and Cameroon. Generally, the disbursement rate has been much quicker in equity projects compared to other types of project financing. Being free of cost, equity capital is called by the project sponsors in the very early stages. Out of 60 projects approved by the Bank up to the end of 1405H, 43 projects were fully disbursed, 6 partly disbursed and 21 undisbursed. Fully disbursed projects included 24 direct equity projects and 19 projects through line of equity. As regards their implementation, 19 of the direct equity projects are in operation.

It appears that many of the projects financed by the Bank are facing difficulties of one type or another related to project implementation, production, marketing and other operational or financial aspects. In many cases, when the projects have been delayed, the problem of cost overrun has occurred. Sometimes the delay in implementation has been caused by problems with the suppliers of machinery and technical know-how. A number of enterprises have faced marketing difficulties due to domestic factors and international recession. Some companies cannot compete in the market due to their high cost of production. Another major factor has been the devaluation of currencies which has increased the interest burden as also the foreign debt liability impairing profitability and creating serious liquidity problems. The IDB's equity investments have not only suffered a loss in value estimated at ID60 million, but have yielded a very low return. The return from equity has even been lower than the service fee charged on loans. Only five companies have distributed some dividend income so far. This has necessitated a provision for meeting losses in the balance sheet of the Bank of the order of ID35 million.

There are a number of factors responsible for the difficult situation which the IDB faces in regard to its equity investments. As observed earlier, owing to its anxiety to become operational as early as possible, coupled with the fact that building up of organisational strength takes time, the Bank had to depend heavily on recipient governments and international and regional financial institutions to propose projects for its financing. While in the case of other modes of financing, this did not do as much harm, it turned out to be very costly in relation to equity investments. They were mostly public sector projects, where profitability and financial soundness are by no means paramount considerations. Again, the gestation period in cases of equity projects is generally long, whereas the funds are called in at a very early stage of project implementation. The IDB not having much experience of its own, the main emphasis was placed on the Internal Rate of Return (IRR) which was calculated in relation to the life of the project. Other profitability indicators, more relevant for equity investment, such as yield, price earning ratio, etc. were not adequately used. Sometimes equity was taken in projects having a large infrastructural element without ensuring that the infrastructural component must be financed from concessional sources. Investments were made in projects in some of the least-developed member countries out of a desire to assist them without regard to the fact that their basic economic structure was inadequate and needed to be developed before equity financing from the IDB could be justified. The Bank had to operate on the very limited project pipeline consisting mainly of first time project proposals starting from scratch. Furthermore, the Bank was over-anxious to expand the network of equity financing to cover as many of its member countries as possible. In the cases of certain countries, equity investment was hard to obtain due to their suspicion of foreign investment and in the face of their national laws. It may be observed by way of example that while Turkey and Indonesia have made special provisions in their investment laws allowing the IDB to participate in equity, there are still some countries, such as Algeria and Syria, where restrictions still exist.

There are also broader factors, such as the lack of a capital market, ineffective macro-economic policies and the poor quality of economic management in the case of IDB member countries, which have had a bearing on the IDB's equity investments. There is a general reluctance in IDB member countries to offer equity to foreign organisations. The member countries are oriented towards loan financing. The financing structure of the companies in IDB member countries is characterised by a high loan component and a small equity base. The entrepreneurs do not like to lose control over the project by offering equity to others. One of the major reasons for the poor performance is that the Bank has tended to depend heavily on governments and co-financiers for identifying, evaluating, appraising and the following up equity projects. It has failed to see that most of these institutions are oriented in favour of loans and are quite indifferent to factors which are important from the point of view of equity holders. The Bank has also not been sufficiently attentive to the motivation of other shareholders as far as dividends are concerned. Many of the shareholders have other interests in the project such as technical fees, supplies of machinery, and a management function, which enable them to give less importance to the dividends. Even when the Bank undertook independent appraisal, because of lack of expertise, it did not apply the proper criteria for equity. It has also not tried to undertake equity in combination with other modes of financing thereby establishing a greater hold on the project. Equity requires an active role, unlike loans where financing institutions can remain largely passive. Equity investments in IDB member countries are difficult to unload because of the narrowness of the capital market so that any effort to sell the stocks may disturb the market and bring about a drastic fall in share values.

Owing to lack of professional strength, the Bank could not be active in the field of identifying sound equity projects. At the same time, having regard to the mandate contained in its charter regarding equity financing, particularly the need for maintaining a ratio between loans and equity investments, it felt obliged to step up equity operations. In the absence of a cadre of specialists in this type of activity and unable to draw on the experience of other international development banks for the simple reason that in this particular field they themselves lacked it, the IDB could not undertake an adequate appraisal of projects either. Factors such as dividend expectations, degree of competition, quality of management, overall economic environment, macro-economic policies affecting the project, the need for a technical partner, the prospects for revolving the investment and the risk of exchange depreciation did not receive the attention they deserved. While the policy document had laid down the minimum expected return from an equity project at 20 per cent, this was never rigorously applied and in processing proposals for equity participation, the Bank appears to have been primarily influenced by developmental considerations. The IDB's concern for development was quite understandable. What was not understandable was that once the project was approved, the Bank seems to have become fairly oblivious of the fact that it had been accepted for developmental reasons and, therefore, instead of confining itself to the role of a conventional equity investor, it was incumbent upon it to assume a highly effective role in its implementation and management. In other words, while the initial investment decision was based on developmental considerations, the subsequent contact and relationship with the project were modelled and patterned on ordinary commercial equity participation. While approaching equity projects with a certain degree of over-enthusiasm at least partly based on the belief that equity investments were highly remunerative whereas loan financing was a concessional operation and without understanding fully the implications of such investment and without acquiring the necessary know-how and experience, the IDB sought to secure its interests by insisting that it would be invariably represented on the board of directors. However, looking back, it is fairly evident that such an approach did more harm than good. This was for two reasons. In the first place, the Bank could not evolve an effective system of representation on the boards of companies. Secondly, the knowledge that it was watching the affairs of the company at the level of the board, distracted attention from the vital need for effective and active follow-up of its equity projects. All this led to a situation where the IDB could not pursue the task of vigorous follow-up of its equity investments. Furthermore, for lack of leverage the Bank has been unable to mobilise much-needed support for projects which were highly commended by the member countries and which now need to be rescued by appropriate action at the level of Governments.

Turning to the measures required to correct the situation, it is possible to list several steps. One of the basic requirements seems to be that the Bank should participate in the equity of only those enterprises which have a clear prospect of earning a profit and payment of dividend. While the Bank should satisfy itself that the project has a developmental significance, this should only be treated as making the project eligible for consideration. The project actually chosen must have the definite promise of providing the Bank with a reasonable level of dividend income within a specific time frame. Apart from the financial viability, attention should be directed to determine whether the enterprise would be properly and efficiently managed. Attention should also be directed to the external conditions relating to the project. It is important that decisions on equity proposals are speedy and timely. Equity has to be obtained in the very initial stage of a project and in case of delay in decision making either at management or board level, not only does a cost overrun problem arise, but good opportunities are lost. It is essential for the Bank before deciding upon an equity investment to determine if by participating in the project it would be playing a catalytic role by attracting and inducing other foreign investors. This should be a deliberate consideration each time. The Bank should bear in mind that the proportion of equity in the financing plan is adequate particularly to accommodate cost escalation in the countries where inflationary pressures are severe. It should also ensure that there is an adequate provision for contingencies. Applying the basic criteria of soundness and profitability, it is fairly evident that it will be impossible for the Bank to avoid a concentration of equity financing only in a few member countries which satisfy the conditions. Hence, the Bank should not seek to attain a balance between loans and equity in terms of individual member countries and should aim at an aggregate balance. Member countries which do not meet the criteria may be compensated by a large share in the other types of financing. In selecting the projects, special attention should be directed to factors such as the debt equity ratio, risk exposure, existence or lack of developed capital markets, which will have implications for the IDB's disinvestments of shares. It is very necessary for the future that each time an equity investment is undertaken, it should be done with a clear appreciation and evaluation of the disinvestment possibilities. In cases where there is an infrastructural component in an equity project, it should be financed through concessional sources before the main project is accepted for equity financing. Again, if similar projects are approved for a certain industry in member countries in close geographical proximity with each other, the regional aspects should be carefully considered, including plans for development of the industry in other countries of the region which will ultimately generate intense competition and marketing difficulties. Much more attention needs to be directed to the analysis of the project cost, particularly when there is a marked variation in investment costs in the same region. Conscious attention should be directed to the risk of exchange rate depreciation and inflation.

In countries suffering from hyper inflation and continuous depreciation of their currencies, the Bank should, as far as possible, avoid equity investments. In this respect, perhaps, it needs to be pointed out that the impact of devaluation differs from enterprise to enterprise in that devaluation causes more harm to enterprises that have mobilised large chunks of financing from outside and are saddled with large debt-servicing liabilities while producing for the domestic market. As against this, for enterprises which have been financed largely from domestic sources but are export-oriented, exchange depreciation may turn out to be helpful. However, in some countries the authorities allow for formalised indexing of security instruments or denomination of the capital base of companies in foreign exchange. This possibility may be explored by the IDB also. Similarly, wherever possible efforts may be made to safeguard against the risk of devaluation by either designating the value of the Bank's investment in terms of foreign exchange or by entering into some buy-back arrangement at values designated in terms of foreign exchange. So far, quite naturally, the IDB has focused attention on possibilities of equity investments. What is now required, after several years of experience, is also to consider ways and means of subsequent disinvestment and the problems it is likely to pose. It might be useful for the IDB to consider the possibility of taking part in equity participation funds set up at national level in member countries. There are many such institutions in the member countries which are responsible for filling the equity gap in enterprises which are located in the relatively less-developed areas of the country.

Much greater attention needs to be directed to the identification of equity projects. There is a clear-cut need for establishing relations with other institutions and regional organisations which are more active in the field of equity, such as national development banks and chambers of commerce and industries. Attention may also be directed to institutions in charge of licensing and of approving equity investment, such as investment promotion bureaux. Generally speaking, by virtue of the fact that most of the equity proposals come from the private sector, they are not so well prepared. This requires some effort on the part of the Bank to offer some technical assistance for the preparation of good equity projects. The Bank would also improve its performance in the field of equity by focusing more on expansion projects rather than new projects. Similarly, before deciding to invest it should direct attention to the need for a technical partner in the project. It should also take into account as to who the other shareholders will be, and whether their interest in the enterprise would be a dividend income or other considerations such as technical fees, supply of machinery and raw materials or technical services. Broadly speaking, the Bank should accord preference to investment in projects where there exists no threat of price control or where there is already a guarantee available regarding realistic pricing, thereby yielding a minimum return for the shareholder. It is also necessary to undertake a comprehensive examination to see what kind of legal guarantee and assurances can be obtained from countries and enterprises in which the Bank takes equity. The investment agreements have to be much more strict and also incorporate such specific matters as a pricing formula and should also incorporate all the necessary guarantees in a rigorous manner with a view to protecting the Bank's interests and investments. There should be necessary safeguards by way of follow-up and reporting requirements. It is significant that many of the equity investors combine equity with a loan to the enterprise. This definitely strengthens the position vis-à-vis the project. As lenders, they can include many of the covenants including the right to monitor the project which safeguards their interest as an equity holder also. In this connection there seem to be two possibilities. One is to combine equity with leasing and the other is to confine the participation to equity, but by virtue of the leverage that the IDB may have, persuade the enterprise to accept certain covenants. There is a strong case for combining equity with leasing. This would have the advantage of securing the Bank's position and would give an assured return from the project. Another advantage would be that the Bank would thus be able to raise its average level of financing and involvement in each project. With a view to providing an incentive to member governments to offer sound opportunities for equity investment, the Bank may consider adopting a practice whereby the investments made in a member country would initially be counted as assistance. However, once the investments start yielding a certain annual return, the equity investment may be excluded from the assistance provided to the recipient country and be classified as investment. Efforts should also be made to link the disbursement of equity funds with the implementation of the project. While this is dependent largely upon the legal structure and practices in various countries, the board representatives should ensure that the call up of capital be in accordance with the project implementation under the agreement. True, the Bank would remain bound like other shareholders by all actions taken by the company in conformity with its memorandum and articles of association. However, recognising that in most cases there is pressure, particularly from the indigenous shareholders, to call for the entire subscription in one go before resorting to other modes of financing, the IDB should resist this pressure. It can even try to negotiate and incorporate specific conditions regulating disbursement at the time when the subscription agreement is signed. In this way, the disbursement would be staggered over a period of time.

There is also urgent need for strengthening and intensifying the follow-up and reporting requirements relating to the equity investments of the Bank. For this purpose, in addition to strengthening its own professional staff by recruiting professionals with expertise in corporate finance, market analysis and business management as well as in macro-economic and financial analysis, outside help may also be mobilised by way of a panel of experts. In the case of loan financing, the need for follow-up extends only until the project has been implemented. But in the case of equity financing, the follow-up is required all the way till the time that the Bank pulls out of the equity. In order to ensure an effective follow-up, the practice of sending missions from headquarters is likely to be more useful than to have a local presence. This, of course, does not rule out the possibility of appointing some representatives on the board from the member countries concerned. Such persons can be selected on the basis of their experience, qualifications and expertise avoiding any conflict of interest and can be invited for consultation and briefing at the headquarters from time to time.

As regards representation on the boards of companies, the Bank should evolve a more effective system of representation. Instead of seeking representation in each and every company where it holds equity, it may be desirable to be selective. Representation has to be by qualified and experienced people. There has also to be continuity of representation. The representatives should be properly briefed in regard to the issues discussed at the meetings and should be required to make a comprehensive report to the Bank as to what transpired at the meeting together with periodic progress reports about the enterprise. It is also necessary to build up an adequate organisation within the Bank composed of financial analysts, economists and others with sufficient experience in the field of equity which should deal with the equity investments of the Bank. In the case of projects which are not well prepared, the Bank, instead of rejecting them outright, should help the sponsors to improve them, if possible, through technical assistance with the provision that funds provided as technical assistance loan may be converted into equity in appropriate cases.

Finally, there is a great need for developing comprehensive guidelines for the appraisal of equity projects. It is essential to aim at a more active involvement by the Bank's lawyers in equity projects. This would involve a study of the investment laws of the country, company laws, taxation laws, charter of the company, and bye-laws. Use should also be made of local lawyers in appraising a project in relation to taxation laws and company legislation. The Bank must also direct much more attention to the macro-economic factors and policies in that they have a direct impact on the variance and performance of equity projects. While critically reviewing the project itself, much greater attention needs to be directed to the external factors and to try to project them in relation to their effect on the project itself and its success. This requires a comprehensive study of the economic situation and the policy parameters. Attention should also be directed to the cash needs of a project and the whole sequence in which equity and loans have to be mobilised. One critical area requiring special attention in equity projects relates to marketing, which has to be evaluated very critically. Many a time while judgements on technical matters may be fairly accurate, assessments about marketing may turn out to be erroneous. When an appraisal team sets out, it should not go with an understanding that it has to undertake an appraisal which would justify placing it before the board and having it approved. An appraisal should be totally objective and only designed to help the Bank decide whether to support the project or reject it. In order to make sure that all the important aspects of the project have been considered including technical viability, managerial, financial and economic aspects, an attempt should be made to standardise the appraisal report. Each appraisal report should have a brief summary of the main findings related to the description of the project and its purpose, technical, managerial and marketing aspects of the project, breakdown of investment costs and the proposed financing plan. It should contain information about sponsoring and executing agencies, project implementation schedule as well as a statement of conditions to be included in the subscription agreement and recommendations for justification for special arrangements before the signing of the agreement or the commencement of disbursements. There should also be an analysis of a sector and industry to which the project belongs. The appraisal report should pay special attention to the marketing aspect, both the demand and supply position. Sometimes countries in the same region undertake the development of similar industries, which results in an over-expansion and over-supply. There should also be an attempt to assemble as much information as possible in regard to the history of the project and the various stages of its development and also of the project sponsors. As far as the operational and financial record is concerned, factors such as management and organisation, labour relations and technical aspects have to be carefully studied.

Before concluding, it is necessary briefly to turn to what has been designated as a line of equity. This facility was devised as early as 1977 and was the product of the IDB's desire to enlarge the scope for equity financing and to serve the needs of small projects. Strictly speaking, a line of equity is an invitation to a national development bank to identify and appraise equity projects within a specified amount and forward them to the IDB for its consideration. The banks are supposed to have a financial stake in the project also and receive a percentage share in the dividend income which accrues to the IDB on such investments. The maximum and minimum limits for such financing are ID100,000 and ID2 million respectively. For this purpose, national development banks are appraised with particular attention to their technical expertise and experience, together with their ability to identify and evaluate equity projects. Their role is principally to identify such projects and to forward them for consideration to the IDB with an evaluation report. The first line of equity was approved for the Malaysian Development Bank in 1977. Since then the Bank has approved sixteen lines of equity amounting to nearly a hundred million US dollars to fifteen banks in fourteen member countries. In some member countries, two lines of equity have been approved for two different institutions. Perhaps a stage has been reached where the Bank should seriously review the line of equity arrangements. Experience has shown that the criteria laid down for granting lines of equity have not been properly followed and national development banks approved for the purpose neither have the technical expertise nor adequate number of equity projects. In most cases, the utilisation of the facility has been unduly slow. There is evident need to limit such involvement, considering the large number of investments already made and the difficulty in managing and supervising such projects. Due attention should also be directed to the actual equity financing record of institutions to which lines of equity are granted. The Bank should ensure that such institutions did not use the Bank's lines of equity for the purpose of providing rehabilitation finance to sick companies or for the purpose of making their loans more secure. As a matter of fact, the lines of equity should be confined only to such institutions as have the necessary technical and professional expertise for appraising such projects and which have available a sufficient number of viable projects in the field of equity. Those national development banks which lack technical and professional expertise should be considered for the grant of technical assistance for training their staff before qualifying for the grant of a line of equity. At any rate, with the possibility of the grant of a line of leasing, the Bank has an alternative mode available to it for co-operating with national development banks which is also a much safer mode. As far as the present policy relating to the line of equity is concerned, apart from the technical ability of the concerned national development institution, the Bank should take into account the actual record and experience of these institutions as far as equity investments are concerned, as also the overall situation in the country and its policies in relation to equity. The development finance companies should be asked to have an involvement in the project in the form of equity rather than a loan. So far it seems to have been the Bank's policy that it is not prepared to place much reliance on the judgement of the national development finance company and makes up its mind through an independent process. This is not a healthy situation because on the one hand judgement has to be made only in terms of the appraisal report from the national development banks and on the other it spares them from any moral responsibility. If they were made to feel that the IDB was placing reliance on them, it is likely that they would be more responsible and recommend projects which are safe and sound. Similarly, it would be advisable to base the decision to grant a second line of equity to any national development bank on the actual performance of projects it had identified and recommended under the first line of equity granted to it. It might also be helpful to enhance the remuneration of equity projects recommended by them and to explore possibilities of negotiating buy-back arrangements with national development banks. This would not only facilitate disinvestment of shares but would have the effect of heightening the interest of development finance companies in the investments made by the IDB in projects recommended by them.

As for those projects in which the IDB holds equity and which are facing difficulties, an effort should be mounted to examine comprehensively each of them with a view to identifying the factors responsible for their lack of success and the possibilities of rehabilitating them. In fact, each of the projects must be kept under close and constant surveillance in terms of their long-term outlook so as to try to apply corrective measures before they are actually overtaken by difficulties.

In conclusion, it would be appropriate to express the hope that instead of shying away from equity operations, having regard to its mandate and the interests of member countries, the IDB will use its experience in the field, bought at a high price, to improve its capacity for financing equity operations on a sound basis. By doing so, it will also, so to speak, blaze the trail for other institutions that are cautiously setting foot in this complex field of development financing.

Chapter 10

Lease Financing

It is important to note that in the Articles of Agreement establishing the Islamic Development Bank there was no mention of lease financing among the functions of the Bank. Presumably this was for two reasons. Firstly, in framing the charter of the Bank the focus was on the other international development banks, none of which undertook lease financing. As a matter of fact, there was hardly any need for it in their case as they were free to use interest bearing loans as their principal mode of financing. Secondly, lease financing did not readily suggest itself when the IDB's articles were being formulated, as it was well known that leasing by way of hire purchase operations was directly built on traditional lending based on interest. Leasing of this kind merely meant the extension of credit to the purchaser by the supplier with the help of finance obtained from banks and the leasing fee and terms were a direct function of the prevailing rate of interest. As far as the other type of leasing was concerned, namely, the renting out of assets, machinery and capital equipment for a period and under which the leased items eventually returned to the lessor, it was clearly not feasible for an international development bank to undertake such operations. However, soon after starting on its operational course, the IDB realised that apart from loan financing on the basis of a service fee, designed exclusively for infrastructural and social projects, and equity financing, which had the character of risk capital, another vehicle for resource transfer was badly needed which did not involve as much risk as equity financing and which could serve projects which were sufficiently remunerative and as such did not qualify for concessional loans. It was in this context that the IDB was led to lease financing.

The IDB first undertook lease financing in 1977 and from then until the year 1987, the Bank undertook 59 such operations, amounting to ID518.73 million and representing 32.5 per cent of the total financing approved by the Bank. The annual breakdown is provided in the following table:

Year	*Number of operations*	*Amount (ID millions)*
1397H	2	7.22
1398H	2	12.50
1399H	2	16.25
1400H	6	38.47
1401H	3	30.69
1402H	7	57.99
1403H	8	75.00
1404H	11	120.47
1405H	9	92.10*
1406H	8	62.54
1407H	1	5.00

The table clearly shows that lease financing by the Bank has picked up rapidly in the past four years. The items covered by leasing have generally concerned hardware, including shipping vessels of different types, locomotives, railway wagons, generator sets, port handling equipment, tractor assembly plant, cement plants, oil rigs and various types of capital equipment. As far as the geographical distribution was concerned the principal beneficiaries of IDB's lease financing were Turkey, Pakistan and Jordan. Moreover, lease financing has gone almost wholly to public sector projects and enterprises.

Judging by the rising tempo of lease financing by the Bank in recent years, it appears that having regard to the profitable and safe nature of leasing as also due to the unhappy experience it has had in respect of its equity investments, the IDB is increasingly drawn to lease financing operations in preference to both loans and equity financing.

It is worth noting that in order to ensure that the leasing operations undertaken by the IDB fully conformed to the Islamic principle of profit sharing, in the place of the prevailing interest rate, projected profit or the

* This has to be viewed together with the fact that the Bank approved ID210.83 million of instalment sales and ID10 million as line of leasing during the year.

expected rate of return was made the basic parameter for the fixing of the leasing fee. As for the period of repayment, it was determined on the basis of the estimated cash flow. In other words, leasing in the case of the IDB emerged as a profit sharing operation for an intermediate term of not longer than ten years. Under the leasing arrangement, the IDB authorises the lessee as its agent to contract for the purchase of the leased item. The lessee is assigned the responsibility for negotiating all matters pertaining to the sale and delivery of the asset and is required to ensure that the item is fully insured during transit and until delivery. The delivery is made directly to the lessee by the supplier, and the former has to make sure that the equipment matches the specifications in all respects. For the choice of the leased item, as also during installation and after delivery, the risk and responsibility rests with the lessee and the lessor is not liable to any claim relating to loss or damage to the equipment. The lessee is expected at all times to keep the leased item in good repair and working order and to carry out any repairs which become necessary. The lessee has also to indemnify and protect the lessor from any claims arising out of the use of the equipment during the entire period of agreement. The equipment has to be kept fully insured by the lessee at its own expense. Until the ownership passes to the lessee, the equipment remains the sole property of the lessor, which fact is acknowledged by fixing a plate on the equipment to this effect and the lessor is guaranteed full access to the leased asset for purposes of inspection. This served as a major factor favouring the use of leasing as the IDB assets being exempted from import duties, taxes and levies of all kinds under its Articles of Agreement, it conferred a substantial benefit on the project in terms of reduction in investment cost for the reason that the ownership of assets remained with the Bank which was the lessor. In the case of leasing arrangements, apart from the usual guarantees, the items leased by the Bank are also insured. The guarantee is against non-payment whereas the insurance is against damage or loss of assets. Repayment schedules are based on implementation profiles, the first payment becoming due six months after the leased facility goes into production.

Practical experience has shown that one of the major problems in drawing up the schedule for the payment of the leasing fee as also the price of the asset is the uncertainty attached to the actual time when the leased item would be delivered and switched into use. In some cases there have been unexpected delays in the supply of the item and as leasing fee is linked directly to use, this upsets the repayment schedule and necessitates refixing both the period and the leasing fee. In certain cases, in order to make the item an integral whole, some amount of local cost financing is also involved. This does not, however, seem to present much of a problem for though a part of the leased asset involves local cost financing paid for by the IDB in terms of foreign exchange, a kind of substitution takes place and the foreign exchange released by local cost financing partly meets the foreign exchange needs of the project by making it possible to utilise the balance for meeting some of the other foreign exchange costs. Similarly, one of the essential conditions to be satisfied for making leasing accord with the Islamic principles is that the item or asset leased should be an integral whole and capable of being used by itself. This indeed is a rather difficult condition to meet and sometimes in segregating one item for lease financing from the project as a whole, there is a risk of excessive flexibility in applying this criterion. It may be mentioned that in a good many cases, particularly in the developed countries, the attractiveness attached to leasing is based largely on the tax advantage that it enjoys. As far as the tax burden is concerned, it is less in the case of income derived from leasing compared to that accruing from interest. This enables the lessor institutions to offer attractive rates of leasing fee. This does not, however, hold in the case of the IDB which is in any case exempted from all taxation.

Of late, there has been significant development in that the Bank has embarked upon leasing certain items in projects which are not by themselves income yielding. This is in contrast to the earlier practice of applying leasing to projects having the ability to meet the rental charges from self-generated cash flows. This has been justified on the ground that the leasing fee is only a payment for the use of the asset to the lessor and it makes no difference whether the lessee makes a profit or not.

As far as the concept is concerned, especially in relation to the repayment arrangement, it is possible to distinguish three different cases or forms. In the first case, a physical asset may be leased to a party which enters into a firm purchase commitment and undertakes to repay both the rental for the use of the asset and also the price of the asset and repayment is completed during the period of the lease so that at the end of the lease the ownership is transferred to the party. This mode of leasing is perhaps the closest to the hire-purchase concept. The second form is one where there is a firm contract to purchase but the party does not pay for the price of the physical asset during the period of the lease but only makes the rental payment. When the lease period is about to run out, the party acquires ownership of the physical asset which was leased to it by paying its price. This form of leasing is rather removed from the usual concept of hire-purchase. The third form of leasing can be one which is traditional and in which there is no firm commitment to purchase and the party merely pays the rental for a certain number of years on certain conditions. This does not mean that it could not acquire the physical asset by negotiating appropriate conditions after the expiry of the lease period. This concept is the one furthest removed from the concept of hire-purchase.

It is evident that leasing represents a highly promising area of operation for the IDB. This is for a number of reasons. In the first place, the risk element is minimal in that the investment is fully covered by the government and also commercially insured. Secondly, the return is highly satisfactory and is received at fixed intervals instead of being subject to uncertainty, as is the case with the dividends on equity. Thirdly, the investment is not for a very long period and the funds invested return to the Bank on a pre-determined date.

What seems to be required is a two-fold effort. On the one hand, the Bank should develop tangible guidelines for leasing with reference to its experience in this field and also take advantage of the information which it can receive from other relevant leasing organisations. It is vitally important to adopt such methods and procedures as remove its leasing activities from a hire-purchase system and bring them closer to the principles of Shariah. In particular, matters such as the determination of the rent linked to the profitability of the project and the determination of the final sale price as also whether the sale price should be received in instalments over a period of time or calculated at the end of the contract when the leased assets become the property of the lessee should be carefully examined. Generally speaking, the Islamic character can be fully protected through a dual approach based first on the need for ensuring that the item leased is an integral whole capable of independent use and then by fixing the rental on the basis of the going rate of leasing fee obtaining in the market for similar items unrelated to the prevailing rate of interest and taking into account the depreciation factor in fixing the price to be realised for the asset. The main difficulty will be that for many of the items a standard rate of leasing fee may not be readily available from the market and the IDB will have to develop a schedule of leasing fees of its own for various types of item through a process of derivation and by exercising its own judgement. Secondly, while the Bank must try to enlarge these operations with a view to applying them and extending them to various sectors and types of operation, it should be fairly selective and avoid the temptation of getting involved with leasing activities for which it has no technical expertise. For example, as far as the leasing of ships is concerned, it may be worthwhile for the IDB to consider what priority to attach to it. This is for two reasons. Lease financing for ships and aircraft is, relatively speaking, not so scarce or difficult to obtain as for items involved in industrial production and agriculture. Secondly, leasing of ships requires highly specialised knowledge and experience which is difficult to command for an international bank. Anyhow, if as a matter of policy, the IDB decides to continue its ship leasing activities, it should avoid sole dependence on consultants and create some professional strength of its own in this field.

As under the Articles of Agreement, it is not possible to combine equity financing with loan financing, increasing use should be made of a combination between equity and leasing partly to buttress the equity and partly to enlarge the Bank's participation in the project without running too much risk. This would enable the Bank to raise the average level of its financing per project to more respectable levels.

Another direction in which it should move is the possibility of mobilising funds from outside which are directly linked to its leasing activities. Such deposits will be safe as the leasing investments will be fully guaranteed and commercially insured. Also, the return will be higher than those on the foreign trade financing which is a short-term investment. Furthermore, now that the Bank has discovered that there are serious constraints on the total amount of foreign trade financing which it can undertake without exposing itself to undue risk, it would be desirable to turn its thoughts to directing some of its funds and outside deposits to leasing activities. As a matter of fact, one straight possibility is to mobilise resources for it under the Investment Deposit Scheme. The main difference will be that deposits would have to be for the medium term and yield a higher return compared to the present Investment Deposit Scheme under which deposits are accepted for foreign trade financing.

Before concluding, brief mention may be made of what has been designated as the line of leasing facility which is, in fact, a counterpart of the line of equity arrangement. Its object is also to reach the small enterprises in the member countries through the medium of national development banks and to offer them financing. The real difference between the two types of arrangement is that in one case the financing offered is in the form of equity and in the other case by way of leasing. In terms of this facility, national development banks are appraised and those found suitable are granted a "line" that is a block amount of funds up to which they can identify and appraise projects and recommend them to the IDB for lease financing. The limits for investment under this arrangement are a minimum of ID0.25 million and a maximum of ID2 million. The national development banks are only expected to identify and appraise suitable projects and to send the evaluation report to the IDB for consideration and the latter is completely free to make a decision after taking into account all the relevant factors. In the case of such financing the guarantee is provided by the concerned national development bank as a primary obligor duly backed by a guarantee from the concerned government in respect of repatriation of rentals and sale proceeds of assets leased by the Bank. The concerned national development bank is also required to perform a supervisory function on behalf of the IDB, to hold share certificates and to collect and remit rentals to the Bank. In lieu of these services, the national development bank is entitled to a remuneration at the rate of 3 per cent of the return received by the IDB on such financing. The Bank has so far approved five line of leasing arrangements totalling ID40.8 million. Experience has shown that the facility would become much more popular if the national development banks' appraisal of projects is accorded greater trust and reliance and their remuneration for the effort they make is reasonably raised. The condition of a counter guarantee by the national development bank as also the requirement of participation by them in the project may also be suitably amended to encourage the utilisation of this mode of financing.

Chapter 11

Technical Assistance

Like other international development banks, the Islamic Development Bank has been assigned the task of providing technical assistance to its member countries. In the IDB's case, the technical assistance function is more vital because of the preponderance of the least-developed countries in its membership. Technical assistance has great importance in connection with pre-investment work and for project generation. It can enable the IDB to develop a proper pipeline of projects and also assist the least-developed members by enlarging their absorptive capacity. It is evident that most of the least-developed countries cannot accept and process development finance efficiently without technical assistance. By providing technical assistance, the IDB can serve as a catalyst for overall development and investment in the least-developed member countries. On the one hand, technical assistance activities for project preparation can help build up a pipeline of good projects and on the other, such project preparation can stimulate outside investment interest and funds from other international or bilateral sources. Technical assistance for project preparation can take several forms including technical, economic and financial feasibility studies of the project or the carrying out of the detailed engineering design. Again, there is a possibility of advisory technical assistance which may help to establish or strengthen an institution carrying out studies on sectoral policies or for formulating national development plans. The case for an active effort in the field of technical assistance is based on several factors. Firstly, technical assistance constitutes a vital need of the least-developed member countries. Secondly, technical assistance plays a major role in project generation and improving the project pipeline. In the case of some institutions, such as the Asian Development Bank, as many as one-third of the projects come through technical assistance. Thirdly, through technical assistance the process of integration among member countries can be accelerated through technology transfers. Technical assistance broadly has the effect of improving the absorptive capacity of the least-developed member countries.

The Articles of Agreement establishing the IDB contain two specific references to technical assistance. Article 2(ix) relates to the provision of technical assistance to member countries whereas Article 22 states that a special fund may be established by the Bank for providing technical assistance. In addition to providing financial assistance for project financing, the Bank provides technical assistance either in the form of a loan or a grant not exceeding ID150,000, or combination of both, primarily for feasibility studies, preliminary and detailed designs and consultancy services during the execution phase of projects. These operations are a part of the Bank's efforts to identify suitable projects for financing in the future. The total amount approved by the Bank for technical assistance since its inception has now reached ID41.22 million, which covers 102 operations in 27 member countries. A major proportion (89.5 per cent) of this technical assistance has been approved for the least-developed member countries, for whom the Bank approved 98 technical assistance operations up to the end of year 1407H (1987), of which 7 were later cancelled. Of the remaining 91 operations, 13 studies/designs have been completed and documented. Two projects have been picked up by the Bank for financing. One project financed under the technical assistance programme did not come to fruition. Of the 10 other projects thought to be bankable, one project has been taken up by other financing institutions so far. There are 65 projects at various stages of implementation.

The annual breakdown is provided in the following table:

Year	*Number of operations*	*Amount (ID millions)*
1396H	—	—
1397H	3	0.84
1398H	3	0.82
1399H	5	1.37
1400H	3	3.38
1401H	10	6.83
1402H	8	4.44
1403H	12	5.99
1404H	7	2.96

1405H	14	6.18
1406H	13	2.41
1407H	24	6.00
TOTAL:	102	41.22

As far as geographical distribution is concerned, the principal beneficiaries of technical assistance have been Turkey, Niger, Yemen Arab Republic and Senegal.

Member countries are sometimes reluctant to resort to a loan for financing a technical assistance project which may or may not yield a bankable project. Having regard to the role of technical assistance in the context of the least-developed member countries and in building the project pipeline and more particularly to make the terms more concessional, the IDB decided to establish a "Special Account" for technical assistance in the year 1983. At the same time, the limit for technical assistance grants was raised to ID150,000 from ID100,000. Judging in the light of its past experience and lack of success in boosting its technical assistance operations, there is a strong case for the IDB to liberalise the terms on which it is offered. Even though in most cases the technical assistance offered by industrialised countries is tied to and motivated by the expectation of export promotion, the fact that it may be accepted in preference to the possibility of obtaining technical assistance which is not tied to or influenced by selfish motives, underlines the need for making the terms for technical assistance from the IDB more attractive. More assistance may be offered on a grant basis rather than as a loan. The existing limits for grants may be raised further. Technical assistance offers need not be confined to projects with a distinct promise of yielding an opportunity for financing by the Bank. The IDB should equally readily accept any good proposal which would help a member country to obtain financing from another source. Sometimes there is a tendency to curtail the length of technical assistance loans on the ground that the amounts involved are not burdensome. This is not quite right as the concessionality of the loan is linked to the period. What is more, while the IDB has recently lowered the service fee on technical assistance loans to 1.5 per cent, there is a clear-cut need for treating the technical assistance loans as separate from loans in general and to lower the service fee on them further as the cost of administering them is much lower. Considering that many offers of technical assistance remain unutilised owing to local currency shortage, particularly in the case of the least-developed member countries, the bank may be prepared also to share in the local cost of technical assistance projects in specially deserving cases. Instead of confining technical assistance to project identification and generation, the Bank may in selected cases agree to meet the needs of projects on the ground also. Special attention should be directed to the provision of technical assistance to projects received from the private sector, especially those involving equity financing from the Bank. In such cases, the Bank may secure the option of converting the loan into equity in the enterprise. More effort has to be made to establish closer liaison with agencies such as the UNDP and governments of developed countries which offer technical assistance on a tied or untied basis. Technical assistance should be especially directed to the need for developing a pipeline of projects for those countries which have very poor absorptive capacity. Technical assistance for pre-investment and sector studies may be provided on a grant basis whereas technical studies for feasibility studies may be extended on a grant basis or as a loan or as a combination of the two taking into account the nature of the project and the economic circumstances of the member country. After developing its own strategy for financing technical assistance instead of waiting for projects to come, the Bank should formulate a comprehensive programme by selecting areas to which it attaches high priority. The Bank should be constantly on the look out for appropriate opportunities of extending technical assistance. It should screen all projects which it receives from this standpoint and if it finds that a project needs improvement, instead of financing it, it should come up with an offer of technical assistance. Likewise, in the case of projects which can be made acceptable by further technical work, instead of rejecting them outright, it should consider the possibility of providing technical assistance. Considering the needs of some of the least-developed member countries, and the desirability of improving the quality of economic management, it may be worthwhile to enlarge the scope of the Bank's technical assistance programme by establishing a facility under which technical personnel and experts would be available to member countries requesting such assistance for short periods until they can develop their own capacity. Simultaneously, greater attention should be directed to the holding of training workshops locally in preference to deputing personnel abroad, as this would not only be cheaper but also enable a larger number to benefit. It is also necessary to simplify the process for the approval of technical assistance through a delegation of authority to the President of the Bank up to a higher amount than the present limit of ID50,000.

In the year 1983, the IDB launched a programme for technical co-operation among its member countries. The programme is related partly to the Bank's efforts to provide technical assistance and partly to its role of promoting co-operation among the Islamic Ummah. Under this arrangement, short-term assistance is made available on a grant basis with a maximum of US$25,000 for one country and US$60,000 in the case of training programmes and seminars in which three or more countries participate. For a start, a sum of US$300,000 was earmarked for this purpose to be replenished from time to time. During 1984, five different schemes of technical co-operation relating to training, the holding of workshops and the provision of the services of experts were sanctioned, involving a total expenditure of over US$290,000. This represented only a beginning and in order to help this effort member countries have been requested to nominate one of their national development banks or another appropriate agency to serve as a point of contact and to co-ordinate activities under this programme. As for the executive mechanism, applications for assistance are received by the head office of the Bank which in turn makes contact with other member countries and specialised regional entities in order to determine if the assistance sought could be provided by them. In case the response is favourable, the next step is to negotiate the broad terms of the arrangement for technical co-operation and to fix the respective share of cost for each of the three parties. After the completion of this stage, the implementation time-table is worked out.

The Programme for Technical Co-operation is broadly designed to utilise the capacity for technical assistance existing within the membership of the IDB for the benefit of the other members in need of such assistance. By providing the least-developed member countries with access to the experience and expertise of the technologically relatively advanced member countries, it brings the member countries together and paves the way for closer economic co-operation. The coverage of the programme is fairly large and includes consultancy and advisory services in the field of industry, agriculture and other activities, technical advice for managerial problems, advisory assistance for institution building, particularly technical and training assistance to national development banks, the organising of seminars, workshops and short-term training courses, arranging of educational tours and familiarisation tours and promoting all types of efforts for training, exchange of experience and sharing of information and know-how. That the Programme for Technical Co-operation needs to be strongly supported and pursued by the Bank as also by the co-operating parties needs no emphasis. In fact the benefit is mutual. The providers of technical help open up possibilities of export as also of greater involvement in the economies of the recipients whereas the latter get technical advice which is closer and more relevant to their own conditions and which is more sympathetic and, in any case, free of political considerations.

In conclusion, attention may be invited to a matter which by virtue of its importance for the economic development of its member countries seems to deserve maximum attention from the IDB. This relates to the paramount need for the transfer and, even more, for the development of technology appropriate for its member countries. Experience has shown that the transposition of models developed in countries with a well developed industrial and technological base is largely irrelevant in countries at much lower levels of technological development and facing different types of economic and social problems. Industrial history shows that financial institutions have played a critical role in the process of technological development of industrial countries. In the case of developing countries, international development banks have generally concentrated on the financing function. Science and technology are a critically important element in the process of development. It is fairly evident that the financial resource transfers which can be made to the developing countries for development are highly inadequate for bringing about a striking change and improvement in their living standards. As a matter of fact, if international institutions and the international community were to concentrate only on financial resource flows, the least-developed member countries would be subject to the same suffering and hardships for centuries as is the case now. This seems to call for action in two main directions. In the first place, the developing countries themselves have to undertake technology planning as an integral part of their national development plans. What is necessary is not only to have a plan but to have the necessary institutional structure by way of national centres and an adequate effort both in the private and in the public sector to achieve these goals. General co-operation has to develop among the developing countries and also there has to be an effort directed to improving the access of developing countries to the existing world stock of technologies.

The other direction, which is important, is that the IDB should assist in promoting the development of technology for the special conditions which characterise the situation in its member countries. This may well be illustrated with reference to the utilisation of solar energy. A great deal of work is being undertaken on the utilisation of solar energy in the international context, but enough attention is not being given to its utilisation in relation to the specific needs of the least-developed member countries. The main impetus and incentive for such work comes from the commercial viability of such projects. The Bank can promote and strengthen such efforts by directing financial resources to them and also by organising support from the recipient countries which would make certain projects viable and feasible in relation to the size of the market. Moreover, technology consists of a combination of knowledge and equipment. In this context, the capacity to produce capital goods is crucial and the IDB will do well to direct special attention to this field. The interaction and linking of technological research and development with industry is a vital condition for concrete results. It is also necessary to expand industrial training facilities and to try to improve the contractual agreements for the acquisition of technology. What is required is that the IDB should seek to bridge the gulf which generally divides the financing institutions from institutions promoting technology, such as national science councils and agricultural research centres. This may be of help so that the output of scientific research by way of new technologies could be utilised in projects initiated by the IDB. Instead of favouring imported technology, a concerted effort should be made to promote indigenously designed technology. While trying to evolve labour intensive technology, as against capital intensive techniques, an effort should be made to help finance a substantial research and scientific programme to create new types of technology. At the same time, the tendency to duplicate projects has to be resisted and an attempt should be made to evaluate the technological alternatives in the initial stage of the project cycle. In order to perform this role, the Bank may consider establishing a technological assessment and evaluation unit within its organisation.

What is required is not only a transfer of technology but also an effort to ensure that it is assimilated properly and the technology transfer takes place efficiently. Therefore the effort must be to build up domestic capability in the developing member countries to assimilate and adopt imported technology to suit their own requirements and the IDB may try to assist the member countries in creating and devoting adequate resources to research and development in selected areas.

While focusing its technical assistance operations on its least-developed member countries, the IDB must adopt an active, in fact aggressive, policy in this respect. Instead of waiting for the initiative to come from the prospective recipients, it should identify appropriate opportunities for offering it. The objective should be to utilise technical assistance for institution building and generating sound projects in high priority areas, thus making it possible to enlarge its own financing to its poorest members but also assisting them in mobilising larger financial resources from other external sources and institutions by presenting sound and well conceived projects.

Chapter 12

Foreign Trade Financing

Perhaps the most distinguishing feature of the Islamic Development Bank, apart from the fact that it is required to operate in conformity with Shariah, is that it undertakes foreign trade financing on a large scale. The resources which it provides to its member countries under its foreign trade financing scheme every year are twice, in fact sometimes thrice, as large as the project financing undertaken by it annually. This, together with the fact that other international development banks do not finance foreign trade,* has in certain quarters led to the wrong impression that the IDB is primarily a foreign trade financing institution rather than an international development bank.

It may be observed at the outset that though the IDB under its charter was assigned the function of assisting in the promotion of foreign trade, especially in capital goods among member countries, this was not the motivating force for the structuring of the foreign trade financing facility by the IDB. As a matter of fact, the origin of the scheme lay in the problem the Bank faced in respect of the placement of surplus funds not immediately

* Though the expansion of external trade of member countries is specifically mentioned in the preamble of some of the multilateral institutions, many of them do not have a large and specific programme of foreign trade financing for the purpose. The Inter-American Development Bank has a modest scheme in operation based primarily on discounting the trade paper arising out of foreign trade transactions among member countries.

needed in its ordinary operations. Like any other international development bank, the IDB on its establishment found itself confronted with a situation where it had at its disposal large funds received by way of capital subscriptions from the member countries. At the same time, it is well known that there is always an interval between the establishment of an institution and the commencement of its operations. Conventionally, international development banks invest funds not needed in operations in government securities or government guaranteed securities or in time deposits and certificates of deposits with banks. In the case of the IDB, the conventional forms of placement were clearly ruled out by the cardinal requirement of conforming to Shariah as all the above mentioned modes of placement clearly involved interest. As far as the Articles of Agreement were concerned, the only guidance which they provided was contained in Article 2(xiii) which empowered the IDB "to invest *suitably* funds not needed in its operations". As a matter of fact, it was this flexibility which constituted the main challenge of finding new ways of placing the Bank's surplus funds. It was also realised that the problem of placement of funds not immediately needed in operations would not simply solve itself when the Bank commenced operations. In fact, however active the IDB may become in the field of operations, there will always be some liquid funds and the Bank, therefore, needed to devise a permanent mechanism for placing its surplus funds in a manner which conforms to its basic principles.

Against this background, the IDB set out to explore the entire problem of placement in its various aspects and in a comprehensive manner. The study identified the basic issues and considerations involved in the problem and examined the entire position in regard to the placement of the funds of the IDB. It surveyed the various conventional forms of placement of funds practised by other international development banks and laid down the criteria and conditions for the investment of the IDB's surplus funds. After reaching the conclusion that the conventional forms of placement were ruled out by virtue of the requirement dictating conformity with Shariah, in as much as they involved interest, a comprehensive study was undertaken of the other possible modes of placement, such as investment in stock markets and investment trusts, real estate markets and commodity markets and the risks and difficulties involved in adopting them. The broad conclusion which emerged from the study was that the Bank had no option but to explore its own methods of placement of surplus funds through experimentation and with the co-operation of the member governments. Having concluded that the most serious and promising possibility related to the placement of funds at the national level, the Bank came to the conclusion that the most appropriate beginning could be made in the field of foreign trade financing. This was by virtue of the fact that this was deemed to be a field which provided a possibility of relatively short-term investments, thereby meeting the basic requirements of safety, liquidity and a return. It was felt that, on the one hand, the member countries with serious foreign exchange shortage would be assisted through the availability of much needed development imports and, on the other, the Bank would be enabled to place its funds suitably and obtain a return on them on the ground that it was performing a trading role. It was with this background that the present foreign trade financing scheme of the IDB was conceived.

The foreign trade financing undertaken by the IDB is based on the Islamic principle of "Baya-Murabeha" or advance sale. Under this arrangement the Bank agrees to finance the purchase of a commodity in a certain amount and to resell it to the beneficiary against a guarantee. The beneficiary negotiates the purchase of the goods from a supplier on behalf of the Bank not exceeding the amount approved by the Bank. If there is a balance, it has to be paid for by the beneficiary. The imports have to be made from a member country unless the IDB allows procurement from a non-member on the ground that either the goods are not available from a member country or the terms are not competitive. The beneficiary must submit the contract with the supplier for the IDB's approval and must sign it only after approval has been given. The number of shipments, as also the period between them, has also to be fixed. The price payable to the IDB by the beneficiary is the price payable by the Bank to the supplier plus a mark-up expressed in percentage terms. This resale price has to be repaid by the beneficiary on the expiry of a fixed period after the payment of the purchase price is made to the supplier by the IDB in a freely convertible currency. Each resale price is denominated in Islamic Dinars with reference to the prevailing rate of SDR. The goods are delivered direct or to the order of the beneficiary which is responsible for checking all specifications relating to the imported goods. The Bank is in no way responsible for any breach of contract by the supplier. The beneficiary is also required to have the goods fully insured by insurers acceptable to the IDB. The guarantor, which is in most cases the government of the country, undertakes to pay, on demand, the resale price when it becomes due. The commodities eligible for financing must be of a developmental nature. As the operation is in the nature of a placement, it is vitally important that repayments are on time and also that the funds approved by the Bank for the purpose are promptly and fully utilised.

The first foreign trade financing operation was approved in February 1977. Since then, there has been a rapid growth in these operations as seen in the following table:

Year	*Number of operations*	*Amount (ID millions)*
1397H	5	43.60
1398H	14	127.45
1399H	25	262.46

1400H	32	350.75
1401H	31	367.89
1402H	28	377.55
1403H	27	460.46
1404H	42	671.61
1405H	30	667.27
1406H	66	572.84
1407H	53	453.15
TOTAL:	353	4355.03

It would thus be seen that, in the twelve years since its inception, the IDB has made available to its member countries a total amount of US$5 billion by way of foreign trade financing operations. As regards commodities for which financing was made available, the principal items were crude oil (48.2 per cent), intermediate industrial goods (19.39 per cent), refined petroleum products (9.42 per cent), vegetable oil (7.61 per cent), cement and construction material (3.24 per cent), jute and jute products (3.03 per cent), fertilizers (2.93 per cent) and cotton (2.19 per cent). In terms of the geographical distribution, the principal beneficiaries were Algeria, Pakistan, Turkey, Bangladesh, Morocco, Jordan, Tunisia, Sudan, Iraq, Yemen AR and Yemen PDR.

In the year 1984, the IDB introduced a variant of the foreign trade operation under the name of the line of foreign trade financing. This was primarily for the purpose of undertaking foreign trade financing as a placement operation in countries with a strong balance of payments position. As in these countries it would be unrealistic to expect that requests for foreign trade financing would come from the government, an arrangement is struck with banking institutions whereby a fixed amount is made available to them and they undertake foreign trade financing with it. The main feature of the scheme is that the local bank – in its capacity as executing agent – purchases the commodity from abroad on behalf of the IDB and then resells it on a deferred payment basis to a beneficiary institution in the country. The local bank is also required on behalf of the IDB to insure the commodities concerned against various hazards and to check the quantity, quality and specifications of these commodities. So far, the IDB has approved a foreign trade financing line to one institution, namely, the National Development Bank of Libya.

The foreign trade financing operations of the IDB have proved beneficial in several ways. In the first place, they have provided a mechanism for the placement of the surplus funds of the Bank, avoiding interest and yielding a legitimate income for meeting the expenditure of the Bank. Secondly, by requiring that to the maximum extent possible, the financing provided should be used for importation from member countries, it has sought to increase trade within the membership. In some cases, the financing made available by the IDB has also been instrumental in forging new trading relationships between member countries. Thirdly, the foreign trade financing, in so far as it is confined to developmental goods and inputs, has had a favourable developmental impact. While the financing is of a short-term nature, it has a developmental significance in that there is a certain regularity in these operations which enables the recipients to release their own external resources for development. The scheme has been used for importing crude oil, petroleum products, industrial intermediate goods and fertilizers. Fourthly, though it is not a function of the Bank, it has provided a degree of balance of payments support to the recipients, many of whom suffer from an acute shortage of foreign exchange. Some of the countries have maintained a certain level of indebtedness to the Bank by utilising one operation after the other. This has given the member countries a temporary relief in their payments difficulties. Fifthly, the surplus funds invested in foreign trade financing have remained within the membership and to this extent have not gone to the international market. Finally, through its foreign trade financing, the IDB has been able to make a resource transfer to the member countries expeditiously without taxing its professional and organisational strength unduly.

At the same time it would be unrealistic to exaggerate the success which the scheme has achieved or to gloss over and underestimate the problems and difficulties which have arisen. It has to be recognised that the arrangement has not proved to be the ideal mechanism for the placement of surplus funds and falls short of the safety and liquidity criteria and elements which characterise traditional modes of placement. The defaults which have taken place have, in fact, inflicted a heavy cost on the Bank. This is also for the reason that the IDB cannot take recourse to charging interest as a penalty as this is prohibited under the Shariah.

The Bank would do well to recognise that though its foreign trade financing operations had originated as placement operations, they have ceased to be such with the passage of time. This is for the reason that they have now acquired the status of the Bank's normal financing and are thus much sought after, so that it would be well nigh impossible to take resources from this type of financing without substituting other funds. In other words, foreign trade financing now conspicuously lacks the essential, and perhaps the most integral, feature of a placement operation, namely that funds can be withdrawn whenever required. The funds employed in the foreign trade financing of the Bank can hardly be regarded as surplus or liquid funds available for project financing.

As far as the trade promotion effect is concerned, it has not been sizeable. The foreign trade financing has been utilised mostly for the import of crude oil and refined petroleum products and has not resulted in a great deal of additionality. As far as the trade promotion effect* is concerned, it could be

* In order to determine the impact of the foreign trade financing operations in promoting trade among member countries, it needs to be asked as to how many new

enhanced by not only requiring the beneficiaries to import from a member country, but by laying down that the foreign trade finance mode available from the IDB be utilised for financing an import item or commodity not hitherto traded between the concerned member countries. This would, of course, tend to restrict the scope of foreign trade financing by the Bank. There is another difficulty in the scheme. While financing has to focus on more advanced member countries with a strong balance of payments position, their import needs being more sophisticated cannot always be met from within the membership. As far as the developmental impact is concerned, it has been inhibited partly by the short-term nature of the facility and partly by the cost element. As for the balance of payments support, it may be noted that it would be unrealistic for the IDB to play a role in this respect partly because of resource constraints and partly owing to the absence of adequate ability to influence the fiscal and monetary policies of member countries. What is more, in cases of default, the Bank is now prevented from even providing project financing to the concerned countries. In the light of its experience in respect of its foreign trade financing operations, the IDB should invariably carry out a rigorous examination of the credit-worthiness of each recipient and its external position in relation to the prospects for timely repayment of the amount of foreign trade financing made available by the IDB. There is a recognised and obvious need for making credit-worthiness analysis an integral and essential part of the Bank's overall country economic work. In this connection, it may be relevant to invite attention to Article 16 dealing with Considerations Relevant to Financing. Article 16(1)(ii) clearly lays down that in conducting its operations the Bank shall pay due regard to the prospect that the recipient and its guarantor, if any, will be in a position to meet their obligations under the contract. It has to be realised that credit-worthiness analysis forms an integral part of country economic and sector work. As a matter of fact, all aspects of this work have implications for debt servicing capacity. Therefore, the ideal way of approaching this task is to establish arrangements for country economic and sector work. As far as the work on credit-worthiness itself is concerned, success will depend partly on evolving a comprehensive framework for the purpose and partly on ensuring the data used for the purpose is of the requisite quality.

Among the various factors to be taken into account in examining credit-worthiness, special attention has to be directed to the following:

(1) A critical evaluation of the quality of economic management in the country.
(2) An assessment of the outlook for the country's main exports.
(3) A projection of its import requirements.

---

items have been traded between member countries as a result of the Bank's financing and how much of a trade diversion has taken place in favour of member countries.

(4) An analysis of the price trends of exports and imports.
(5) Likely availability of external capital both commercial and concessional.
(6) The current and future debt service liability.
(7) The liquidity position in terms of reserves and potential borrowing capacity.
(8) An assessment of the country's ability to make adjustments to unexpected adverse changes in economic performance.
(9) The position in regard to the exchange rate and over-valued exchange rate as a major factor causing debt servicing problems.

As far as data is concerned, the IDB must make a concerted effort to obtain the most reliable information both from country sources and also from the IMF and other institutions.

The objective should be the utilisation of the extra resources of the Bank according to Shariah. At the same time, there is a need to devise some system in line with Shariah whereby the Bank could recoup the loss caused due to default in payments. For developmental purposes, a separate scheme may be introduced in the form of an independent export-oriented financing facility designed to promote foreign trade in capital goods, and non-traditional items, with a longer repayment period. The objective should be to provide incentives for development of new trade relationships among member countries. The Bank may also consider the possibility of devising a balance of payments support scheme which could be financed from the Special Assistance Account by earmarking a certain amount of funds for this purpose. The scheme should have the specific objective of assisting the poorest member countries in dire need and should have a more flexible approach towards repayment. The facility should be made available only to the least-developed member countries of the Bank. The Bank should also intensify the efforts to expand its trading role. The background against which foreign trade financing operations were introduced and the way the whole situation has developed need to be examined from the Shariah angle. Necessary efforts in this context should be mounted.

As mentioned earlier, Article 2(vii) of the IDB's charter which pertains to the promotion of foreign trade makes specific mention of capital goods. However, so far, it has not been possible to cover capital goods under the Bank's foreign trade financing which has developed primarily as a by-product of the Bank's need for the placement of its short-term funds. However, after five years of experience a stage has been reached when attention needs to be directed to the problem of promoting foreign trade in capital goods among member countries. This would involve two things. First, the financing would have to be for a considerably longer period than the one allowed under the existing Foreign Trade Financing Scheme. Secondly, the mark-up would have to be considerably lower in order to provide sufficient incentive for the trade to develop. Bearing in mind the fact that the existing capacity of member countries to produce capital goods is rather limited, it is unlikely that such financing would be on such a substantial scale that it would constitute a serious strain on the Bank's resources. In this connection it may be useful for the IDB to finance a comprehensive survey to determine the existing capacity and supply situation in respect of capital goods as also the potential demand which exists for their export and sale within the membership with the help of financing from the Bank. The IDB should in the light of these facts introduce a special facility for financing trade in capital goods. In order to conform to Shariah, though the facility will help both the exporting as well as the importing country, financing would be made available by the IDB to the importing country, thereby matching the offer of credit from the suppliers of machinery from outside sources. Under the scheme, finance could be provided to cover the production and pre-shipment stage also. In other words, IDB could have capital goods produced in member countries with the requisite capacity which it could purchase and resell to other member countries requiring them. As far as the mark-up is concerned it will have to be fixed with reference to the terms governing supplier's credit from other sources. The period of repayment should also be determined by applying a similar approach. In fixing the mark-up, the IDB may consider applying a lower rate in the case of (1) imports from member countries and (2) non-traditional and new items previously not traded between the member countries concerned. It may be worthwhile to introduce a new element by offering to finance import items which have hitherto been obtained from non-member countries and which the beneficiaries agree to import from a member country. At the same time it would be desirable for the IDB to strengthen its trading role. In this regard it may be appropriate to recall that at the time of introducing the scheme, the Bank had even initiated discussions for the establishment of a trading subsidiary in which the work of foreign trade promotion and financing could be concentrated. The whole basis on which the present facility was introduced was that the Bank would be assuming the function and role of a trader. However, owing partly to a lack of organisational capability in the Bank to undertake the trading role effectively and partly to the fact that the beneficiaries have their own institutional framework and relationships in the trading field, the role of the Bank as a trader has not been prominent. The final and ultimate goal should be the establishment and development of a fully-fledged trading organisation for the purpose of promoting foreign trade among Muslim countries.

In conclusion it may be noted that hitherto the emphasis in the IDB, as far as export is concerned, has not embraced the overall problem of promoting the export effort of member countries. The Bank seems to have concentrated on the problem of promoting inter-country trade rather than exports as such. In contrast to this the re-financing facility being operated by the Inter-American Development Bank is designed to assist the exports of member countries generally, and not necessarily to member countries. In this connection the foreign trade operations, which in the main are placement operations for the Bank's surplus funds, have not contributed very greatly to additional trade among member countries. Sometimes, the commodity financed is the item traditionally traded between the countries concerned and many a time the Bank allows importation from outside the membership also. The terms and conditions of the foreign trade operations are not well suited to the promotion of exports, particularly in respect of capital goods and engineering items. What is required is a much greater effort at identifying possibilities, potential markets, sources of supply, and to provide necessary information, as also financing for longer terms and at cheaper cost so as to provide an incentive for the trade to increase. As a matter of fact, as far as the capital goods are concerned, the terms have to be so concessional as to have an edge on those provided through supplier's credit. Another important need is to recognise that in some of these member countries, balance of payments problems, that is, the shortage of foreign exchange, stands in the way of full utilisation of the productive capacity of industrial units which need imported inputs for production. The limited production of these units is absorbed by the more profitable domestic market. The increased availability of foreign exchange to such manufacturing units could result in a fuller utilisation of capacity with concomitant effect on costs. The Bank should consider the possibility of establishing a fund for the exploitation of the export potential of its member countries currently not fully exploited due to a foreign exchange shortage. The multiplier effect of a revolving foreign exchange fund could be considerable.

Basically, the IDB should adopt a strategy whereby it can establish a link between trade and development. This requires that it should first finance projects which augment the export potential of the country and later provide financing to enable the countries to export the emerging products with the help of the credit backing made available by the Bank.

The IDB is now contemplating the introduction of a longer-term financing scheme designed to promote exports among the participating member countries.* This, so to speak, complements the foreign trade financing scheme which has been in operation in the IDB for the last several years and provides financing for imports of raw materials and other inputs generally for a period of less than 18 months. The new scheme is expected to provide financing for a period ranging between 18 and 60 months for intra-regional export trade. Any country wishing to participate will have to make a contribution of ID1.5 million. Besides the contribution from the members, the IDB proposes to make a contribution of ID150 million to the scheme. The Bank expects to offer a reasonable return to the providers of funds for the scheme. The scheme will be confined to the financing of non-traditional exports which have been defined as commodities representing not more than 20 per cent of

* The scheme is now in operation and four operations have already been conducted under it.

the FOB value of the country's total exports during the preceding three-year period. Each participating country will be required to select a national agency which will be given the authority to process all applications from the country concerned. One condition would be that the commodities should have been entirely produced or manufactured from basically produced raw materials or parts. Several member countries have evinced interest in participating in the scheme and the scheme is expected to be launched shortly. The Islamic banks are also expected to participate in the scheme.

In this context, certain points deserve consideration. The first question relates to the scale of priorities which the IDB must follow. In other words, the question to be asked is whether absorbing so much of its resources at a time of a general resource squeeze would be justified for the purpose in preference to other demands on the Bank. This is particularly so when it is realised that the first task is to build up the productive capacity of the member countries which has to precede the possibility of export. Furthermore, the scheme, as presently conceived, is somewhat tilted in favour of the relatively developed member countries with the necessary export potential. As far as the least developed member countries are concerned, their most urgent need is to build up their productive capacity in order to expand their export potential. Secondly, the cardinal principle on which the scheme is based, namely, that each participating country will benefit from the scheme in proportion to its own financial contribution to the scheme and those made by institutions in its territory is also questionable. In rationing the funds it would be proper to remember that those who benefit from them would in any case be paying a price for the use of the resources. Judged in terms of the Islamic principle of assisting the needy, as also the entire philosophy governing development, what is required is that the institution should be built on the principle that capital subscriptions and contributions should be made in terms of the financial capacity of the member countries, whereas the excess or benefit from the scheme should be in proportion to the need for such assistance. This is particularly so as many of the providers of funds, such as Saudi Arabia, would hardly be in need of assistance from it, whereas some of the other countries experiencing a difficult foreign exchange situation would be in much greater need of assistance than they would be entitled to on the basis of their financial contribution. As a matter of fact, the IDB itself is built upon this principle in that capital contribution governs the voting power of individual members but not the size of assistance to be made available to them. As far as assistance is concerned, it would be desirable to establish suitable criteria by way of need and other factors. For instance one of the factors to be taken into account would be the extent of competition which the exporting countries face by way of credit backing from their rivals in other countries which are able to provide greater credit backing on account of their relatively more comfortable foreign exchange position. The Bank would also do well to bear sufficiently in mind the risk of overdues and must adopt methods whereby payment default is avoided. In this regard, perhaps, it would be wise to rely on national agencies in the beneficiary countries which should be responsible for prompt repayments. As for contributions, the main incentive should be the return which would be offered by the scheme.

The IDB is also engaged in examining the possibility of establishing a regional export credit guarantee scheme. One of the basic problems to be resolved in this connection is to ensure that the scheme would conform to Islamic Shariah.

Chapter 13

The Project Cycle

Apart from expanding and stepping up the operations of the Islamic Development Bank the importance of and need for achieving a qualitative improvement in its operational activity can hardly be over-emphasised. It vitally concerns the interests of the institution as also those of the recipients. It is obvious that any improvement in the quality of the Bank's operations will help to strengthen its financial soundness and the effectiveness of its role vis-à-vis the member countries. What needs to be realised is that resources being limited and scarce, any sub-standard or poor quality operation is directly and equally detrimental to the interests of the recipients. The recipients should in fact be assisted to utilise their scarce resources in the most efficient manner. Hence the need for improving the quality of the Bank's operations. With the completion of almost ten years of its operations and the substantial increase in its capital resources, it is time that the situation was evaluated critically with a view to determining what steps can be taken to improve the quality and efficiency of the IDB's financing operations. In other words, alongside the policy review to determine what adjustments are necessary, it is equally important to make comprehensive and critical evaluation of the various procedures governing the operational activities of the IDB so as to cover the entire project cycle and to identify areas for improvement and various steps that need to be taken in this field. It was understandable that in its anxiety to become operational and maximise its operational activities and also owing to lack of staff strength and inexperience, the Bank has not been able to introduce and develop comprehensive operational procedures. In view of this, it is vitally important to evaluate critically the situation with a view to introducing and adhering to various procedures for conducting efficient operations by the Bank.

It is noteworthy that in other international financial institutions the bulk of financing results from preparatory technical assistance operations or feasibility studies financed by the institutions. In contrast to this, the IDB has so far received its projects mostly through the mail.

It is time that the IDB should strengthen its own efforts at project generation and at identifying and developing projects through technical assistance and financing feasibility studies. Attention should also be directed to project identification during the appraisal and other missions which the IDB sends to member countries. It will be beneficial to establish contact with a project in the pre-feasibility stage and then provide technical assistance for the undertaking of feasibility studies. In view of the fact that its organisational strength is limited until such time as it is augmented, the Bank could also utilise some of the agencies in the field such as the WHO, UNIDO and UNESCO, charging them with the specific task of identification, even if this involved the IDB bearing the cost of such work. The work of project identification should be based on the sector studies carried out by other institutions as also on the technical assistance provided by the IDB. One project should be made to become a source for generating another project. In order to move in this direction, a mission will have to be mounted for collecting relevant information on the various possibilities with a view to preparing the terms of reference for the feasibility studies. A technical assistance report has then to be prepared and the necessary technical assistance granted by the Bank. The Consultant Selection Committee (CSC) should meet and shortlist some consulting firms and also establish the policy criteria for the consultants' proposals. Invitation letters should then be issued to the selected consultant firms who should be provided with an outline of the technical assistance proposal and the terms of reference. Consultants should be invited to submit proposals without indicating any fee for the services to be performed. The CSC should then meet to evaluate the consultants' proposals and to rank individual proposals based on the merits of each. The first ranked firm should then be invited for negotiations and others in the same order until a technical assistance agreement is executed with the country. Consultants should then be sent into the field. The entire foreign exchange cost should be financed by the Bank and the local currency expenditure may be borne by the government. Consultants should be required to submit an interim report after a month or two of commencement of field-work and their work may be reviewed by the Bank. After a draft final report is prepared by the consultant, it may be discussed between the consultants, the Bank and the government and thus would emerge the final feasibility study which would form the basis for the Bank's appraisal. A project brief should be prepared for each project, describing its objectives, identifying principal issues and establishing a timetable for its further processing. Project identification and generation may be undertaken as a conscious and deliberate function. An identification mission may be sent to those countries where the project pipeline is particularly deficient. An outside consultant or technician should be associated with some of the missions with the conscious object of identification. In the case of projects in fields like equity and leasing a liaison should be established with institutions which are more concerned with these activities, including the private sector. A collaboration meeting with other international financial institutions should be organised annually. A local presence may be established for facilitating the identification and project generation work. In the final choice of projects sufficient weight should be given to the relative economic and social benefits of projects, instead of being guided too much by the fact that the project would fit into a certain mode of financing or would help in meeting the quantitative targets fixed by the Bank.

It would suffice if, instead of trying to prepare independent reports, the IDB were to prepare a comprehensive memorandum on the economy of each member country with the help of country reports prepared by other institutions and to update this information from time to time taking advantage of the occasions when its missions visit the various countries. The Bank may consider the possibility of sending some of its own economists to the member countries for data collection and discussion. In the interim period this need can be met through the operational missions which visit these countries and can be utilised for updating information. It is time that it developed a systematic approach by choosing a sector with the help of the studies available from other organisations. An effort should be made to make as much use as possible of the sector work undertaken by other international institutions which can be made available to the IDB. What seems necessary now is also to prepare a broad multiyear operational plan for the Bank by taking into account:

— the requirements of member countries for capital resources and the expected resource availabilities;
— the resource picture of the IDB;
— the organisational strength and capacity of the institution;
— the availability of suitable projects in member countries.

The long-term plan should establish not only the overall size and volume of operations over the next five years but also establish targets in respect of various sectors and modes of financing. This long-term operational programme, based on resources which will be available and which are likely to be mobilised, should then be split up into the annual operational programme.

The IDB should move actively in the direction of developing a country centred approach, of establishing country programmes and financing targets for its member countries. The next step should be to devise suitable criteria for the allocation of the Bank's resources among various member countries so as to avoid disproportionate amounts of its resources being used for the benefit of any single member country. Country allocations should be based primarily on per capita income levels and size of population. Having regard to the fact that the IDB operations are modest in size, too much emphasis need not be placed on absorptive capacity. After a notional allocation of resources has been made, an attempt should be made to select such projects as fit into their development programme. The usual way of preparing the country programme is through sending programming missions to hold discussions with the authorities. A tentative programme, say for a five-year period, is framed treating the first year as firm and allowing the later years to be treated as provisional or tentative. The effort should be to have an element of over-programming, as all the projects expected to be financed may not turn out to meet the Bank's standard. Country programmes must be discussed and reviewed with the recipient governments annually to make such revision as becomes necessary and with a view to firming up a programme for the ensuing year. Account should also be taken of the credit-worthiness of various countries. The IDB should also try to evolve a budget process as an integral part of its management system. Together with this, an effort should be made to appraise the operational programme in terms of the workload and staff requirements. What is required is not only to develop criteria but also to take into account the performance of various countries.

The Bank has to break new ground and undertake an original effort at devising guidelines and a framework for appraising projects to be financed on the basis of equity, leasing and profit sharing. There appears to be a need for recasting the organisational structure of the Operations and the Projects Departments in order to make them more efficient and effective. As far as the Report and Recommendations of the President are concerned, greater attention should be devoted to major problem areas, especially future policy issues and similar matters which might be of particular interest to the Board. Gradually the Bank's effort should be to make more independent appraisals and to reduce dependence on other sources. It seems necessary to enhance the role of the Legal Department in project appraisal work. They should be enabled to become involved in the work at a fairly early stage. Sometimes they may even be asked to go into the field. It may be useful to publish information about the projects approved for financing so as to evoke greater interest in them, particularly from the consultants. It is necessary to prepare a comprehensive code of conduct for the staff members proceeding on missions and provide guidance to them in regard to preparation for their work, discussions and contact with the country officials and also personal behaviour. Greater resort in specific areas should be had to employing and engaging consultants and to associate them with the Bank's missions so that its staff members learn from them. In fact, the Bank should aim at gaining a constant working experience through joint work with all co-financing institutions instead of remaining confined to providing resources. The appraisal report should devote special attention to the unfavourable points, risks and pitfalls. In fact, there should be a special section in each appraisal report for adverse and negative factors. Each time a mission is proposed, it should be determined whether it requires the assistance of an outside consultant. In undertaking work on various projects it is vitally important to ensure continuity as far as possible. The effort should be to make the appraisal critical and analytical. The mission should not leave with the object of preparing an appraisal for the purpose of seeking an approval by the Board but should invariably look at the weak and strong points and make a judgement after balancing the various considerations. It is time that the IDB also devoted more attention to improving the quality and presentation of appraisal reports by subjecting the drafts to careful examination and editing.

It may be worthwhile to consider whether it would not be desirable to hold detailed negotiations with the recipients before the submission of the projects to the Board of Executive Directors. In case the present practice of negotiating the loan after approval is continued for some time until a stage has been reached for holding negotiations before submitting the appraisal to the Board, it is necessary to hold an initial dialogue with the recipients about the important matters for negotiation and towards this end greater involvement of the Legal Department would be required.

The Bank's interest in each project, instead of dwindling after approval, has to be heightened. The follow-up and supervision requirements have to be clearly defined at the time of appraisal and, after negotiations, clearly set out in the legal documents. The beneficiaries should be required to submit periodical reports and, at the same time, the Bank should send its own staff to the project to see how it is coming on and to check the information provided through progress reports and to have on-the-spot discussion of the difficulties and problems which the project might be experiencing. This could be done through mounting project inception missions, review missions and also special missions in order to deal with any specific problems. Supervision should not only embrace physical work but also factors such as improvements in management and organisation and training. The Bank should use various performance indicators for different types of project in judging the operational results. The major objective should be to use the experience of supervision for gathering such accumulated knowledge as may help in future projects. The ideal approach for the IDB would be to follow a *via media* by requiring the beneficiaries to submit periodic reports, while at the same time sending its own staff to the project to see how it is coming on and to check the information provided through the progress reports and to discuss any difficulties and problems that may have arisen. What is required is to undertake proper planning for supervision so that problems can be detected and tackled before they arise through further engineering studies or by employing consultants to strengthen management and organisation. The IDB should organise missions from time to time with a view to discharging this role. In this connection, the first type of mission should be what may be described as a Project Inception Mission (PIM) which should be mounted soon after the signing of the agreement. In cases where the executing agency is working with the Bank for the first time or is relatively inexperienced in dealing with the execution of projects financed by international banks, the mission should try to establish a working relationship with the agency; advise the recipient on the preparation of legal documents necessary to make the financing effective; explain the procedures and requirements for recruitment of consultants, procurements and disbursements; and explain the reporting requirements of the Bank for the project.

In the long run, the IDB will also have to develop a capacity for a proper audit or post-evaluation of the projects which it finances. This will involve a comprehensive review of all the results so as to make a comparison between the actual and the expected results in regard to the rates of return, costs and benefits. The object will be to learn from experience so as not to repeat past mistakes and to develop new policies and procedures. This work may well be assigned to an independent unit, separate from the operating staff of the Bank and reporting directly to the management and the Board through an independent officer. The audit should be based on a desk review of all materials pertaining to the project and whenever necessary the audit staff should be encouraged to undertake a field review.

Chapter 14

Operational Policies

As the reader may have observed, in discussing the various types of operation undertaken by the Islamic Development Bank, certain specific policy aspects relating to them were also covered. The present chapter is designed to identify and examine some of the general issues deserving attention in the policy area.

1. Developmental orientation and Islamic approach

The IDB has been set up to foster economic and social progress of member countries and Muslim communities in non-member countries. It is essential, therefore, to consider how far it should allow this realisation to condition its attitude and position on various issues such as expected rates of return, volume of loan financing, readiness to finance real estate and commercial construction, urge to raise the service fee and other costs of financing in step with rising interest rates in international money markets and reluctance to provide technical assistance on grant basis rather than as loans. In other words, the question which warrants careful consideration is how far the Bank, consistent with safeguarding its interest, should assist its members by means of expanded loan financing, assuming greater risk, accepting a lower rate of return, charging a low service fee and allowing longer periods of grace and repayment.

Perhaps the paramount factor which should fashion its basic approach is that the Bank is required to operate in accordance with Islamic principles. As a matter of fact, the cardinal condition envisaged in the Articles of Agreement in regard to conformity with Shariah should not remain confined to the avoidance of interest alone. It should condition the Bank's entire approach. It is well known that Islam enjoins upon the institution to extend most help to the weakest. In other words, following the Islamic principles, instead of treating all countries alike and meting out uniform treatment to them, the institution has to show a special concern for those who are the most needy. The Bank's attention has to be directed to various member countries in accordance with the stage of their development. In other words, the least developed have a prior claim on the Bank's resources and efforts compared to the relatively more developed member countries. Of course, as far as the actual flow of resources is concerned, the main constraint is the lack of absorptive capacity. However, what is being suggested is that instead of taking this as a fact of life, the Bank has to do all that it can to enhance the absorptive capacity of the countries which are the poorest by removing the various bottlenecks. Far from shying away from or getting scared by the difficulties and handicaps, it must try to overcome them and help the member countries to surmount them. The second basic requirement following from the Islamic ideal and the development character of the institution is that the Bank adopt a basic needs approach allowing member countries to attain a basic living standard for their people. In other words, in selecting a project due attention has to be directed to these particular aspects. The Bank should avoid getting involved in prestigious projects and instead give high priority to projects designed to improve the lot of the masses.

As far as specific issues are concerned, in conformity with its developmental character several adjustments are required. In the first place, it has to expand its loan financing and at least ensure that that being the most concessional type of financing, loans go to the poorest countries. As regards foreign trade financing operations, they must be accorded a lower priority than the ordinary operations constituting project financing by virtue of the latter having a larger developmental impact. Moreover, the Bank must adopt a more flexible attitude by offering assistance on easier terms and more extended periods to countries deserving such assistance by virtue of their difficult and desperate economic situation. The Bank should also avoid purely commercial operations such as real estate financing. As a rule, the Bank must also direct attention to the social returns of a project. It may be noted that a built-in emphasis on the size of the return does not help the Bank's image in that it leads to the conclusion that it basically looks at projects in terms of their high financial profitability. The developmental character of the institution also dictates much greater attention to the technical assistance effort by the Bank. The IDB should use its powers of persuasion to mobilise the largest amount of concessional resources on the easiest terms as it is on this basis that it can offer liberal and concessional assistance to countries which badly need such help. The IDB has not had to mobilise resources from the capital market in the same way as other international financial institutions. The resource providers should be made to feel that the IDB deserves their liberal help not by virtue of employing their resources at the highest profit but on the ground of the excellent use which it makes of them as far as the broad mission of promoting the well-being of the Muslim Ummah is concerned. It is noteworthy that in the case of many international development banks the largest amount of resources goes to the relatively more developed members. This is largely because of the lower absorptive capacity of the poorer countries. However, what is expected of the Bank is to try to change the situation by attacking the factors which stand in the way of transferring larger resources to the poorer countries so that the IDB emerges as an institution which makes a larger absolute contribution to its poorer members compared to the relatively more developed countries. Perhaps one way of resolving this problem would be to classify the various operations of the Bank as concessional and non-concessional. For example, loan financing and technical assistance could be treated as concessional operations whereas equity financing, leasing and foreign trade financing may be regarded as non-concessional. At the same time this plea for benevolence should not in any way be mistaken as a diluting or lowering of standards in regard to efficiency, soundness and productivity. As far as individual projects are concerned, they must be conceived and appraised by applying the most rigorous criteria. After all the IDB can assist the poorer countries by ensuring that the resources which it makes available to the member countries are used in the most productive manner and their developmental impact is the largest. For this purpose, it should also exercise maximum supervision and follow-up.

2. Co-financing

It may be emphasised at the outset that co-financing was conceived by the IDB as a means of becoming operational at the earliest opportunity. It was, so to speak, a vehicle which carried it to the operational stage rapidly insofar as the Bank was assisted by the technical work undertaken by the co-financiers. This provided a contrast to other international development banks whose motivation is not so much to use co-financing as a means of marketing their own resources but as a device for bridging the resource gap. From the beginning of its operations to the close of 1404H (1984), the Bank participated in co-financing arrangement in 40 projects in 20 of its member countries. The IDB co-financed with co-financiers from both multinational and national institutions. Prominent multinational institutions include the World Bank, Asian Development Bank, African Development Bank, Arab Fund for Economic and Social Development, International Finance Corporation,

OPEC Fund, Arab Fund, Arab Investment Company and the Arab Mining Company. Important national institutions designed for financing regional or least-developed countries were the Kuwait Fund, Saudi Fund, Abu Dhabi Fund, Arab Petroleum Investment Company. The list also includes some important international banking and finance institutions like DEG, ACB, BIAO, CIIS, EXIM Bank and EDF. The co-financing arrangements did not only present a project but enabled the Bank to keep its involvement to the minimum by seeking to fill the gap, not having to make an independent judgement about the project and merely safeguarding its own interest through legal means. All this has enabled it to have a large number of operations to its credit and has also made it possible to serve the largest number of member countries. At the same time, this appears to have exacted a price from the Bank by not forcing it to be sufficiently active as far as project development, generation and identification are concerned. Taking a small portion of the total financing cost in a huge project has denied it any effective role or recognition. It has made it over-dependent on the judgement of the co-financiers, making the appraisal work second hand. At the same time, as the number of projects is too large, it has been beyond the capacity of the IDB to carry out effective follow-up and supervision.

It would be useful for the Bank to critically review its policy in regard to co-financing with a view to determining in the light of experience developments which have taken place since its inception and in relation to its future goals as to what changes are warranted in the Bank's approach to co-financing. Now that the Bank is endeavouring to build its own strength for project appraisal and is keen to become more active in the field of project identification and generation, two new strands may be introduced in its policy relating to co-financing. First, it should confine the co-financing arrangements mainly to large projects. Secondly, it should in appropriate cases assume the initiative in inviting and involving other co-financiers in projects which it proposes to promote. So far the IDB has been invited by other co-financiers. It is time that it should make a beginning in the direction of reciprocating by inviting other co-financiers. In fact, the original inclination to use the co-financing as a means of marketing its own resources should be transformed into a desire to supplement resources and to fill up the financing gap. At the same time, in the case of small projects co-financing may be avoided in order to get a larger recognition and meaningful participation. Simultaneously, an effort may be made in terms of mobilising resources from institutions which are deficient in respect of ability to undertake independent identification and appraisal. Such a willingness to play a leading role by providing assistance in project evaluation and project administration will be able to mobilise resources from institutions which lack technical capacity. The IDB should participate in reasonably sized projects and take a substantial portion of financing instead of taking a small fraction in a giant project. This will enable it to market larger resources without making a massive demand on its technical and organisational resources and would enable it to get more satisfaction, experience and make it more effective in the follow-up, implementation and evaluation of projects.

That co-financing will continue to be undertaken on a large scale by the IDB is obvious. In the first place, the cost of projects is so high, particularly in the infrastructural category, that they can be financed only on the basis of co-financing. Moreover, this will help the IDB to overcome the shortage of projects which it can finance independently, particularly in the least-developed countries. What seems necessary is to establish a focal point to co-ordinate the co-financing activities and liaison with the various potential co-financiers. In this connection the Bank should look at the possibility of involving local private commercial banks with excessive liquidity. The possibilities of co-financing with private sources are particularly relevant for middle-income developing countries. The participation of an international financing institution like the IDB in the same project would give much needed confidence to co-financiers less experienced in the task of project appraisal and administration.

The Bank would also do well to actively use co-financing operations with more experienced institutions for the purpose of training its own staff. This can be achieved mainly through an early involvement and by mounting joint appraisal missions. At any rate it is only through building up its professional strength and expertise that the IDB can aspire to become self-sufficient in the processing of projects embracing the entire cycle comprising identification, appraisal, negotiation, supervision, follow-up and post-evaluation.

3. Average level of financing

Before discussing the various implications and determining what adjustments in policy are warranted, it may be useful to present the basic facts bearing on the problem. It may be observed at the onset that though there have been some fluctuations, the average level of financing has remained unduly low. Taking the present financing operations of the Bank for the past five years, the average level works out to less than US$6 million per operation. It is only after adding the foreign trade financing operations that the average level of financing per operation rises to US$9 million. As regards the various modes of financing, it may be noted that the average size of equity participation stands at US$6.39 million; the average size of lease financing has been at US$9.26 million; the average approval for a loan project has been US$6.71 million; and the average size of a technical assistance operation amounts to US$0.51 million. In the case of foreign trade financing operations, the average was US$12.67 million. What is noteworthy is that if allowance was made for inflation even at the rate of 8 to 10 per cent annually, the average in real terms would be correspondingly lower. It is understood that the average size of World Bank loans including IDA credits in 1980 was US$48.4 million and the comparative figure for the ADB was US$24.3 million.

There were several factors accounting for the relatively low average level of financing in the case of the IDB. The Bank adopted a cautious approach in the initial years owing to inexperience and lack of organisational strength. It has operated on the basis of notional ceilings for various types of operation which are deemed to be low. The Bank was anxious to cover as many countries as possible which necessarily led to a large number of operations involving small amounts. One important factor which affected the average level was the urge to undertake a large number of operations so that the IDB could get involved in more sectors and sub-sectors and also in various forms of financing. The Bank has been keen to help the relatively least-developed members where the size of the operations is obviously smaller. There has been a definite emphasis in favour of equity operations. As the equity base in the member countries is rather small, it has tended to keep the Bank's average level of financing also low. The Bank undertook most operations on a co-financing basis. Without co-financing for a particular project, the level of financing could have been larger. The Bank avoided combining different modes of financing which also kept the Bank's financing level low. The Bank avoided local cost financing and programme lending which has also affected the size of financing. One of the reasons accounting for the low average level is the line of equity arrangements with DFCs and technical assistance operations where the volume of financing per project is generally very low.

There will be several advantages to be expected from an increase in the average level of the IDB's financing operations. In the first place, it will enable the Bank to effect a larger transfer of resources to the member countries. Secondly, by controlling the number of operations, it will keep the strain on the Bank's staff at a reasonable level, making it possible to carry out the needed operations without having to increase the staff strength inordinately. Thirdly, it will contribute to economy and cost effectiveness in the Bank's financing operations. Fourthly, it will help to reduce the burden on the member countries generally and particularly on the least-developed member countries in servicing the mission. Fifthly, by controlling the number of projects, the Bank can be more selective in its operations. Finally, by virtue of larger financial participation, the Bank will have a more effective presence and role in the implementation and supervision of projects and will also receive greater recognition.

The aim should be to expand the total volume of financing while allowing a much slower increase in the number of operations so that the average level would rise over the years. In other words, the effort of the IDB should be to ensure that the number of operations rises slowly whereas the amount of financing expands rapidly. This is a very important consideration. With the recent increase in the Bank's subscribed capital the resource constraints has been largely overcome and, having regard to the increasing requirements of member countries, the IDB has to make a concerted effort at expanding its development financing operations proper as distinct from the foreign trade facility. However, the two major constraints in the way of a larger operational effort are the lack of organisational strength to handle more than a certain number of new operations along with the increasing burden of follow-up of operations approved by the Bank in the past years and the lack of well-conceived and sound projects which can fit into the Bank's scheme of policies and priorities. It follows, therefore, that while concerted efforts are made to expand the Bank's organisational strength and to develop a larger pipeline of suitable projects through the provision of technical assistance and project identification, the Bank should seek to step up the transfer of its resources to member countries by increasing its average participation in individual projects deemed fit for the Bank's financing.

Turning to the methods of achieving an increase in the average level of financing operations several suggestions may be made. The notional ceilings in respect of various types of operations applied by the Bank in respect of its participation should be raised. The Bank may in appropriate cases resort to a combination of the modes of financing in the same operation with a view to enlarging its participation. Hitherto the policy of the Bank has been to confine its participation as far as possible to a single type of financing. However, in future, it may resort to combining equity financing and leasing. One way of increasing the average level is to become involved in regional projects which can absorb larger financing per operation. If the idea is to raise the average level of financing the IDB may have to adopt a more liberal attitude towards local cost financing and in the long run even consider the advisability of undertaking some degree of programme and sector lending. The enlargement of the Bank's participation in individual projects also presupposes a strengthening of the Bank's organisational and operational procedures. While the IDB's approach and inclination to undertake operations on a co-financing basis is quite understandable, it is necessary that it should in the long run develop a capacity to undertake independent operations which will enable it to increase its financial participation in individual projects and generally raise the average level of financing. There is also need for more economic work by the IDB with a view to gaining sufficient knowledge about the economy of member countries in which it undertakes financing, their development prospects and constraints, strategies and policies, their resource availability, absorptive capacity and external assistance needs. Simultaneously, the Bank should gradually move in the direction of country programming. It was understandable that in its anxiety to become operational the IDB has moved in an ad hoc fashion picking up what is available. However, now that its resources have been augmented and with a view to enlarging its financial participation, it has to establish some tentative country programmes and financial targets for various member countries so as to harmonise its operations with the development programmes of the member countries. The Bank's financial participation in individual projects can also be enlarged if it seeks to look beyond an annual programme and to develop a multiyear plan of operations. It is obvious that larger participation in individual projects would also call for improved follow-up and supervision.

To sum up, apart from inflation, the average level of financing has to be raised in order to assist in reducing administrative cost, to contain the burden on the Bank's professional strength and in order to process an increased financing volume. Additionally, the Bank will get more recognition and have a more effective say in administering and implementing the projects if its average level of financing is sufficiently high. Now that the initial stage has been passed, there does not seem to be much justification for making a fractional contribution to huge projects. However, it should be clearly understood that the effort in regard to increasing the average level of financing by the IDB should be made in a flexible manner. It should in no case mean that in the future the IDB will favour only large operations. In fact, it should continue to undertake small operations when justified and particularly when it has to play a catalytic role.

4. Local cost financing

It seems that a stage has been reached when it may be useful for the IDB to review its approach to the problem of local cost financing. Article 16(8) of the Agreement establishing the IDB lays down that the Bank may provide financing for the foreign exchange component of total cost and in suitable cases, especially in the case of less-developed member countries, it may also provide financing for the local currency component after assuring itself that the country's domestic resource mobilisation effort justifies such action. In effect, however, the Bank instead of providing local currency financing, has hitherto sought to meet the situation by taking a rather liberal view of foreign exchange costs by making allowance for costs associated with the imported component of locally produced goods and services. It may be observed at the outset that the World Bank and the International Development Association have been providing foreign exchange loans for financing local expenditures after satisfying themselves that the borrowing country has a suitable development programme, is making an adequate development effort and that this programme requires funds in excess of the resources that can be mobilised locally. It appears that such financing by the International Bank for Reconstruction and Development (IBRD i.e. World Bank) and IDA has remained confined to about 10 per cent of their total lending. As for the Asian Development Bank, it decided in 1974 to provide foreign exchange financing for a portion of the local currency expenditures to be incurred on projects financed by the Bank. However, in order to ensure a slow and cautious beginning, the Bank limited the local cost financing to 5 per cent of its annual lending from ordinary capital resources and 10 per cent of its annual lending from the Asian Development Fund. Until the end of 1977, the Bank had approved 30 loans in which a provision for local cost financing had been incorporated totalling nearly US$90 million. Ten of these loans were from ordinary capital resources and twenty from the Asian Development Fund. Thus, the level of local currency financing remained much below the ceiling of 5 and 10 per cent mentioned above. The situation changed markedly in 1978 when local cost financing was stepped up both from the ordinary resources and from the Fund. In 1978, local currency financing by the Asian Development Bank totalled US$60.6 million in twelve loans to five countries – US$26.7 million from ordinary capital resources and US$33.9 million from the Asian Development Fund. These accounted for 3.4 per cent and 8.9 per cent respectively of the total loans approved from these resources in 1978. The bulk of the financing has gone to the least-developed members.

Apart from the need to keep abreast with other institutions and not lag behind in respect of the range of financing facilities which the IDB provides, there are several other factors to be taken into account. In this connection, it may be observed that developing countries have reached the stage where, quite apart from foreign exchange and external resources, they experience an acute shortage of local currency resources. The potential for domestic saving being low, the Governments of these countries have to take recourse to deficit financing and money creation for implementing their development programmes which through serious inflationary consequences tend to undermine the development effort itself. Alternatively, if, in the interest of safeguarding monetary stability, countries avoid excessive credit creation domestically, then they have sometimes to forgo the utilisation of foreign exchange which is available from outside sources in the absence of the local currency counterpart. Thus there may be a case for local cost financing in the case of member countries who have despite their best efforts suffered from a serious shortage of domestic savings. Another factor deserving attention is that, in the framework of current thinking and emphasis on the eradication of mass poverty and meeting the basic needs of the population, quite a few of the developing countries are moving in the direction of giving priority to agriculture and the socially oriented sectors. All such projects involve a very large component of local cost financing and a relatively smaller foreign exchange component. In other words, if the Bank's financing was confined to foreign exchange alone, it may be tantamount to excluding projects of large socio-economic importance which have a limited foreign exchange element but large local financing requirements. Local cost financing will also be consistent with the IDB's desire to take up a higher proportion of the total cost. It also needs to be appreciated that insistence on foreign cost financing and reluctance to finance local currency cost indirectly encourage capital intensive techniques against labour intensive projects with implications for the employment situation of the member countries. It is noteworthy that the IDB's Articles of Agreement lay great emphasis on the creation of employment opportunities. In fact, Article 16 requires that in conducting its operations, the Bank shall pay due regard to the promotion of the well-being of people in member countries through economic and social development and the enlargement of opportunities for gainful employment. So far the Bank's involvement in the agricultural sector has been limited, but through accepting the possibility of local cost financing the Bank may be able to expand its involvement in agricultural projects which have a relatively high local cost element and in turn avoid concentration in terms of commercial and industrial projects.

Another factor dictating a favourable attitude towards the possibility of local cost financing is related to the IDB's anxiety to accord special treatment to the least-developed member countries. In other words, there is a strong case for some flexibility in regard to the local cost financing in the case of the least-developed countries with their low level of per capita income which serves as a constraint on their capacity to generate domestic savings needed for development. At the same time, these countries are also faced with a serious shortage of foreign exchange and this means that provision of foreign exchange for meeting the local currency cost could also help in easing the pressure on their balance of payments. Local cost financing would thus enable the countries to import other essential developmental requirements. In the case of the least-developed members apart from their low per capita income, the task of mobilisation of additional savings is rendered difficult by their weak institutional framework. The result is that these countries either have to resort to deficit financing or must reduce their development spending. There is thus a case for local cost financing in order to fill their domestic resources gap. Moreover, the shortage of local currency resources in their case also reduces their ability to absorb foreign exchange financing. Local currency resources are needed to complement the foreign exchange financing for projects and in their absence the total development effort of the country is seriously impaired. As far as the threat to domestic mobilisation of resources is concerned, it will be taken care of by urging the least-developed member countries to improve their capacity to mobilise additional savings and to control as far as possible their administrative and non-developmental expenditures.

It follows, therefore, that in considering requests for local cost financing a case by case approach will have to be adopted and a comprehensive examination of the mobilisation effort of each country will have to be carried out so as to determine whether or not additional local currency resources can be raised without placing excessive strain on the economy. The Bank will have to satisfy itself that the country concerned is making a reasonable development effort and taking adequate steps for mobilisation of domestic resources and that the available resources are being allocated properly for the development programme of the country. At the same time, it will have to be established that the financial requirements of the development programme of the country exceed the limits of domestic savings so much so that it is prevented from fully utilising the foreign exchange offers available to it. If the IDB decides to embark upon local cost financing, it would be desirable that instead of considering local cost financing in general terms and for purchases of all types, preference may be given to projects which have a relatively low foreign exchange component but relatively high economic and social benefits. As observed earlier, it would be proper to adopt a case by case approach giving special attention to the needs of the least-developed member countries and with due regard to high social and economic benefit projects with low foreign exchange costs, particularly projects which are socially oriented, which are likely to generate substantial employment opportunities, which would involve capital-saving technology and which are expected to promote better use of local resources. Needless to say, in case the Bank decides to undertake local cost financing, it will be desirable to fix a limit both in terms of its overall financing and also in terms of the local cost element of an individual project. As a rule of thumb, the poorer the country the greater the proportion of the local cost which the IDB may finance. At the same time, in the interests of a cautious and gradual start, the Bank may make a beginning by providing a part of the local cost financing if it is not allowed any share in meeting the foreign exchange cost of the project.

5. Programme loans and sector lending

It may be useful to study the possibility of programme lending especially in relation to the least-developed member countries and for the purpose of effecting a quick transfer of resources. It is well known that there are certain difficulties in implementing this type of lending. However, it has its advantages insofar as it makes possible the provision of financial resources to certain countries which have a broad programme of economic and social development but not a sufficient number of well-prepared projects. As project lending cannot adjust to rapidly changing conditions, the IDB may resort to programme lending in special cases whenever a quick transfer of resources is required so as to prevent a severe interruption in a country's development programme and to overcome unforeseen temporary difficulties. The main criteria, therefore, is that the country has an immediate need for foreign exchange to meet temporary payments difficulties and that it would be in a position over a period to resume normal development activity without special assistance in the form of programme lending. Such cases may cover:

(i) Reconstruction or rehabilitation of the economy after a war or serious national calamity;

(ii) A sudden fall in export earnings where the economy is critically dependent on a single item;
(iii) A sharp deterioration of the terms of trade as a result of a rapid rise in import prices;
(iv) Structural constraints or capacity under-utilisation.

Such lending has been strongly commended by the Brandt Commission, which investigated the urgent problems of inequality in the world and the failure of its economic system.

6. Combination of operations

The IDB's Articles of Agreement discourage the combining of loan and equity. In a way this is justified for the reason that if loan financing is confined to infrastructure projects, opportunities and scope for equity financing in combination with loans are necessarily limited. However, there may be a strong case for combining equity and leasing by the Bank. This will enable the Bank to have sufficient exposure to the project, providing resources in reasonably large amounts thereby raising the average level of financing and at the same time obtaining a secure return from the project.

7. Time limits

It is worthwhile considering whether the IDB should have an agreement to terminate the agreement declared effective by a set date, say 60 days from the date of the agreement or, like the World Bank, the loan agreement should provide that if the conditions established for the effectiveness are not fulfilled by a specific date, the agreement will be cancelled automatically unless the period is extended. At any rate, it is necessary in each case that the IDB makes a realistic estimate of the time necessary to satisfy the conditions of effectiveness and specifies an appropriate date on that basis. The IDB should also consider and decide whether it will be useful to specify time limits for agreements to be effective and also for operations and withdrawals and disbursements to be completed within a specified period. This would have the effect of expediting the utilisation of the Bank's funds and avoid funds being sought and then not utilised for a long period, particularly in the case of foreign trade financing operations.

Chapter 15

The Least-Developed Member Countries

For a long time in the past, the problem of economic development used to be discussed in general terms applied to all developing countries. In recent years, largely as a result of work undertaken in forums such as the UNCTAD, the conviction has grown that within a wider strategy for development, special attention needs to be directed to the least-developed among the developing countries. This feeling is based on the recognition that developmental problems in these countries are particularly acute and the constraints on economic development are particularly serious. In the context of the special need for assisting the weakest developing countries, international development institutions and regional development banks have been urged to direct special attention to the least-developed countries in their membership.

It is noteworthy that Article 16(3) of the Agreement establishing the Islamic Development Bank unequivocally lays down that in conducting its operations, the Bank shall pay due regard to the needs of the relatively less-developed countries. This is obviously in line with the developmental character of the institution and also with the requirement that it should operate on the basis of Islamic principles. It is needless to emphasise that Islam ordains maximum compassion and assistance to the weakest and poorest. This emphasis is well reflected in the fact that more than one-third of the IDB's total membership consists of least-developed countries. In fact, since its inception the number of least-developed member countries has increased with the accession of some new members. That the IDB has been very keen to render service to these least-developed countries is borne out by the fact that there has invariably been a very short interval between the country becoming a member and the commencement of the Bank's operations in it. Almost in every case, the President of the Bank has lost no time in visiting the least-developed member country concerned personally for the purpose of holding discussions with the concerned authorities followed by a Bank mission to prepare for the first operation.

It is significant that during the first ten years of the Bank's operations nearly a half of the total number of project financing operations have been for the benefit of its least-developed members. As for the total amount, it works out to about one-third of the total project financing undertaken by the Bank during the first ten years. This is attributable largely to the fact that usually the projects in the least-developed countries are relatively smaller in size, which makes the average level of financing somewhat lower. In the case of foreign trade financing operations for the past ten years, nearly half were for the least-developed member countries though the amount involved has been in the region of 33 per cent of the total foreign trade financing by the Bank. All this is undoubtedly a measure of the importance which the IDB attaches to assisting its least-developed members by making the largest possible allocation to them backed by a suitable project pipeline in an attempt to carry out a substantial transfer of resources to them. It very definitely follows a low income or poor country emphasis in planning its operations, particularly when its annual operational programme is drawn up. In this regard, attention may be invited to certain other features of the Bank's policy in relation to the least-developed member countries. Firstly, it seeks to accord, as far as possible, priority to its least-developed members in respect of loan financing, which, by virtue of the fact that it is interest free and is conducted on the basis of a service fee to cover only the cost of operations, is deemed the most concessional mode of financing. It is focused on the infrastructural projects which are known to be a vital need of the least-developed member countries. Secondly, the Bank has by no means denied the least-developed members a considerable share in its equity financing operations despite the known shortage of suitable equity projects amongst least-developed countries. Thirdly, anxious as it is to promote equity financing in least-developed member countries, the Bank has granted lines of equity to certain national development banks in its least-developed member countries, which serve as a vehicle for transferring investment funds to the smaller industrial projects. This in the long run would prove highly beneficial to the national development banks by way of providing valuable experience and exposure in this field. Fourthly, the Bank has also undertaken leasing operations for the least-developed member countries.

In making the investments in its least-developed countries consistent with the soundness of the projects, the Bank has adopted a developmental approach rather than the narrow commercial considerations associated with traditional equity financing. Within the framework of its policies it has truly sought to play the role of a catalyst. Perhaps nothing could illustrate the concern of the IDB for its least-developed members better than the foreign trade financing operations it has carried out for their benefit. These operations are of a short-term nature taking the character of the placement of funds based on the criteria of safety, liquidity and high return. However, in the interest of providing a measure of balance of payments support and with a view to enabling them to import significant development inputs, the IDB has invested a substantial part of its short-term funds with the least-developed member countries which are known to suffer from deteriorating terms of trade, increased cost of imports, stagnation in export earnings and growing external indebtedness. Through these unique placement operations the Bank has not only helped them in improving the quality of import procurement, but also in promoting trade amongst them. Realising that a crucial element in the situation is to enhance the absorptive capacity of the least-developed member countries in order to develop and promote a suitable pipeline of projects, the Bank attaches the highest significance to the provision of technical assistance to its least-developed member countries. In fact, after the experience of the past years, it now seems set upon liberalising the technical assistance facility which would lead to a more active project identification and development. It may not be out of place to mention that its Articles of Agreement envisage the establishment of a special technical assistance fund which will not only enable the Bank to expand its operations in its least-developed member countries and improve their quality, but also generally increase their absorptive capacity by developing projects fully qualified for financing from other sources.

During the ten years since its inception, the Bank has made available to its least-developed members, financing of the order of US$1,544.27 million, comprising US$455.07 million worth of project financing and US$1,092.37 million of foreign trade financing. As far as types of financing are concerned, it is significant that about 51 per cent of loan financing, over 80 per cent of technical assistance, 25 per cent of equity financing, about 23 per cent of lease financing and more than 33 per cent of foreign trade financing has been directed to the least-developed member countries. In terms of geographical distribution, the main beneficiaries have been Bangladesh, Sudan, Yemen AR, Yemen PDR, Niger and Senegal.

During 1984, the Bank approved US$50 million for a Special Programme of Emergency Aid for the Sahelian member countries to assist them in tackling problems caused by persistent drought. The programme was directed towards the agricultural sector and included the provision of vaccines, animal feed, agricultural inputs, pumps for irrigation and boreholes and funds for water resource studies. The programme which was financed out of the Special Assistance Account, was composed of US$20 million or 40 per cent of the amounts as grants and US$30 million or 60 per cent as loans. Having regard to the fact that the least-developed member countries are susceptible to major national disasters such as drought, floods, cyclones and earthquakes, it is obvious that the IDB in helping these countries should make more active use of its Special Assistance Account.

In formulating a strategy and in developing an assistance programme for its least-developed member countries, the IDB would do well to bear in mind their main structural characteristics. These are: a very low per capita income, unduly large subsistence sector, high population pressure, very low agricultural productivity, extremely low level of natural resources exploitation, lack of even cottage industries, high rate of unemployment, acute scarcity of skills and very weak institutional and physical infrastructure. At the same time, the Bank should take into account the main constraints and difficulties to be overcome, such as the limited project pipeline, shortage of even local currency resources, lack of administrative and executive ability, inadequate support facilities, lack of data and poor communication links. What is suggested is that the IDB should consider each country individually and work out a plan of action. This is for the reason that though there are some common factors, such as the low GDP as an indicator of poverty, there are several other considerations to be borne in mind, such as the natural resource base, climate, institutional sophistication, extent of infrastructure. Countries differ in several respects: Bangladesh, for example, has a very high population density, which makes the development of an infrastructure by way of roads, irrigation, agricultural product markets, a very complex problem. Constraints to the development of the least-developed countries differ from case to case and factors such as location, natural resources, demographic and ethnic structures, social and political systems play varying roles. Therefore, the Bank instead of developing a global strategy, should seek to formulate a tailor-made programme for its various least-developed members. What seems to be required is that the IDB should develop an assistance strategy through a continuous dialogue with the recipient countries. It should adopt a country by country approach recognising that the process of economic development is unique to each country.

One of the obvious things is that bearing in mind the structure of production, the emphasis or thrust of the programme should be on the agricultural sector. The Bank should try to promote rural productivity as many of these countries are basically short of food. Attention should also be directed to their pricing policies, particularly in respect of cash crops and agricultural crops generally whose prices have been held down to protect the cost of living in urban areas. In other words, the rural–urban terms of trade must be changed and the first priority should be accorded to the food and agricultural sectors. This is for the reason that almost 80 per cent of the people in these countries derive their livelihood from this source and nearly half the gross domestic product originates from it. In this area, projects for improving the productivity of land through irrigation, fertilizers, and seeds deserve special attention. At the same time, areas such as rural roads and communications, storage facilities, institutional arrangements for rural credit and marketing should also be considered. Another major area of attention would be forestry, fish resources and livestock. Simultaneously, with these sectors, the IDB should explore the possibilities of generating projects in the area of human resources and social development, such as education and training. At the same time, communication and transportation must also receive the IDB's attention as they constitute a major bottleneck in some of the least-developed countries.

It needs to be emphasised that local cost financing and programme lending have great urgency in the context of assistance to the least-developed member countries. Similarly, there is need to diversify the assistance by extending it to housing, tourism and general education. Moreover, there is need for an integrated development as a whole, instead of undertaking single projects. Needless to say, technical assistance is another important area where the least-developed members are in dire need of assistance. Apart from providing funds for undertaking pre-feasibility and feasibility studies the Bank should also consider providing experts and also assistance under recently formulated technical co-operation programmes. The Bank should try to assist also in the setting up of project preparation units. Similarly, a concerted effort may be required to determine what special assistance can be provided through programme-lending designed to finance a general import programme. One way of according priority to the needs of the least-developed countries could be the establishment of a special fund or a notional earmarking of resources for the least-developed members to match the flow of resources to other developing member countries. Greater attention may have to be directed to the identification and preparation of pre-investment surveys in the least-developed countries. The Bank may also accord priority to the recruitment of such experts in the Bank as have a special knowledge of the problems of the least-developed amongst its members.

Basically the Bank should seek to increase its allocations to its least-developed member countries especially in respect of loans and grants. In fact loan financing by the IDB should be undertaken exclusively for the benefit of its least-developed member countries. Moreover, the Bank should be somewhat more flexible in respect of the financial return expected from a project and should accord greater weight to the social rate of return. Generally speaking, the IDB should maintain a poor country emphasis in its operations and, in making a choice of projects, should attach high importance to those having a special significance for the poor. A programme designed to help the least-developed countries will involve in relative terms not only a larger flow of technical and financial assistance for the least-developed countries, but also the application of comparatively more flexible norms and easier conditions. Not only may the financial criteria have to be somewhat relaxed in regard to the minimum rate of return, but greater attention may have to be directed to providing assistance not only for immediately productive investment, but for education, health and the social infrastructure. The attitude towards local currency financing may also have to be modified. Similarly, the Bank may have to develop an extra sympathetic attitude in regard to recurring and maintenance costs of on-going projects. In evaluating projects due account should also be taken of development potential and secondary benefits in addition to direct benefits, that is, the long-term social rate of return from development projects.

Another possibility that is worth exploring relates to the need for aid co-ordination. It is well known that the World Bank undertakes this function for the larger countries. However, in the case of the smaller least-developed Islamic countries, which have been receiving aid from a number of sources, there is also a need to bring about better co-ordination in the field of aid. The IDB might consider assuming this role in the case of some of its least-developed member countries.

Another area of major importance deserving attention on the part of the IDB relates to the need for assistance designed to improve the quality of economic management in the least-developed member countries. This would call for action in two main directions. Firstly, assistance would be provided to these countries for the purpose of enlarging the availability of statistics and data and especially for improving their quality. Secondly, short-term advisory services would be provided to these countries in important fields of policy making and economic management and control. Attention also needs to be directed to the development of the necessary institutional infrastructure for the purpose of promoting economic and social growth. This calls for a human resource development strategy also and emphasis on training at all levels. The problem which is beyond the IDB's control is the need for strengthening national sovereignty over natural resources. Nevertheless, the Bank can play a useful and constructive role by ensuring that the growing awareness of national governments in this area is translated into articulate action by offering them professional advice and support.

Another element which relates to the provision of special assistance to the least-developed member countries is the Bank's attitude towards local cost financing. It is well known that the least-developed member countries are not only acutely short of foreign exchange resources but are also unable to mobilise adequate domestic resources for financing their development programme. In the circumstances, many offers of foreign assistance remain unutilised because of the lack of local currency. In this perspective, perhaps, the IDB should adopt a more flexible attitude in agreeing to provide local cost financing to the least-developed member countries.

Experience has clearly shown that the foreign trade financing facility provided by the Bank under present terms and conditions does not suit the needs of the least-developed member countries. As a matter of fact, in some cases it has done more harm than good when, on account of the delay or default in repayment of an amount obtained as short-term foreign trade financing, much against its wishes, the Bank has also had to stop providing ordinary project financing to the country. It would, therefore, be in the fitness of things to devise a special Balance of Payments Facility for the exclusive use of the least-developed member countries which will enable them to obtain financing for essential imports for longer periods and a much lower mark-up. Perhaps a good percentage of resources from the Special Fund built up of interest earnings could be earmarked for this. In the case of this Special Foreign Trade Financing Facility, even items such as food and essential consumption items could be made eligible for financing.

Finally, in order to highlight the importance which the IDB attaches to assisting its least-developed members, one of the parameters that it should use for its Annual Operational Plan should directly relate to the least-developed member countries. What is proposed is that just as performance is measured and targets are set in respect of various types of financing and sectors as also the overall level of financing, a conscious effort may be made to prescribe quantitative targets in respect of the least-developed member countries every time an operational plan is formulated. Later, a critical review should be conducted to determine how far the targets in respect of the least-developed member countries were actually achieved.

Chapter 16

Relations with Other Institutions

1. International and Regional Organisations

The charter of the Islamic Development Bank clearly lays down that it should co-operate with all bodies, institutions and organisations having similar purposes in pursuance of international economic co-operation. The Bank has, therefore, from its inception endeavoured to establish close relations with other institutions. Representatives from international as well as regional development institutions were invited to the Inaugural Meeting of the Board of Governors in 1975. As a matter of fact, the meeting passed a special resolution urging the IDB to seek close collaboration with similar organisations. Soon after the inauguration, the Bank sent missions composed of some of its executive directors to the Asian Development Bank, African Development Bank, Inter-American Development Bank and the World Bank. The object was to become acquainted with their working and to survey possibilities of co-operation. These visits proved very useful in planning the organisational structure of the Bank and in the framing of its policies. What is more, a groundwork for co-financing was established, apart from the fact that the IDB was able to secure some short-term help from some of these institutions by way of a few professionals on loan until such time as the Bank recruited its permanent staff.

Over the years, the relationship with other institutions in the field has been strengthened in several other ways. The President of the IDB and other officials of the Bank have visited these institutions many times. In turn the heads and high officials of other organisations have made visits to the IDB. The annual meetings also provide an opportunity of close contact. In some cases special co-ordination meetings are held at regular intervals. With some of the institutions the Bank has entered into a formal agreement of co-operation. This includes UNESCO, UNIDO, FAO, IFAD and WHO. The Bank has observer status in the Development Committee of the World Bank and also in the UNCTAD. The Bank also maintains a close liaison with the EEC and OECD. In forging a close relationship with other institutions, it may be desirable to bear in mind two problems. Firstly, in co-operating, the older institutions should take care not to highlight their own role and contribution so as to eclipse the part played by the IDB; they should allow it proper recognition. Secondly, it may be desirable that the co-operating institution makes a tangible contribution financially to the development project, at least in the identification, management and supervision of the project. In some cases the latter condition is difficult to satisfy as they may not be financing institutions and may need to charge for the service they render such as an executing agency.

While the IDB is an independent institution, it maintains a close dialogue with the General Secretariat of the Organisation of the Islamic Conference. It also co-operates with the specialised agencies and institutions set up in the framework of the Islamic Conference, such as the Statistical, Economic and Social Research and Training Centre for Islamic Countries at Ankara, the Islamic Chamber of Commerce, Industry and Commodity Exchange at Karachi, the Islamic Centre for Development of Trade at Casablanca, the Islamic Foundation for Science, Technology and Development at Jeddah and the Islamic Centre for Technical, Vocational Training and Research at Dhaka. At the same time there is great need for closer relations between the IDB and these institutions. This would not only prevent the possibility of duplication but would enable the IDB to utilise the assistance of these institutions in its own work. The Bank should also consider helping these institutions financially, thereby acquiring a larger role in controlling them. There are also other development financing institutions which extend financial assistance to member countries. They are either national organisations, such as the Abu Dhabi Fund for Arab Economic Development (ADFD), the Saudi Fund for Development (SFD), the Iraqi Fund for External Development (IFED), the Kuwait Fund for Arab Economic Development (KFD) and the Libyan Arab Foreign Bank (AFB), or inter-governmental organisations such as the Arab Fund for Economic and Social Development (AFD) and the Arab Bank for Economic Development in Africa (BADEA) and the OPEC Fund for International Development (OPECID). The IDB has developed close ties with these institutions and regularly participates in the co-ordination meetings involving these institutions both at the level of directors of operations and also at the level of the heads of institutions.

2. National Development Banks

On its establishment, the IDB directed urgent attention to the promotion of close co-operation with the national development banks in its member countries. Development finance companies are financial intermediary institutions whose principal purpose is to provide medium- and long-term finance to productive enterprises. A good many development finance companies have come into existence in the past three decades in a number of member countries. International development banks have not only provided liberal finance to them but have also in many cases assisted in their establishment by participating in their equity. They have also provided lines of credit to these institutions from time to time. In the case of the IDB this was not possible as this would have involved interest. Against this background, the IDB sought to establish a relationship with them as a medium or vehicle for reaching the smaller enterprises in the member countries. Having regard to its own limited organisational strength and, even more, to the fact that considering the size of investments to be made in small enterprises, it would be uneconomic for it to undertake the identification and appraisal exercise, the IDB decided to entrust this work to the national development banks. For this purpose, it devised a special agreement which came to be known as the "line of equity facility". Under this arrangement, the IDB carries out an appraisal in order to satisfy itself that the bank concerned has the necessary expertise and experience and there is sufficient scope for equity investment in the country. National development banks which meet the criteria are allowed a line of equity. The IDB has granted as many as 15 lines of equity totalling US$101.26 million. In 1983, a similar arrangement was devised known as the line of leasing facility under which national development banks are invited to identify, appraise and forward relatively small projects for lease financing and line of instalment sale.

At the same time, the IDB has endeavoured to assist the national development banks through the provision of training facilities for their professional staff. It arranged a training programme in collaboration with the Industrial Development Bank of Turkey for the training of the technical staff members of the National Development Finance Institutions in Istanbul in April, 1983. The course covered various topics such as project preparation, project appraisal, group dynamics and export marketing strategy. The participants in the programme were national development banks from Indonesia, Senegal, Morocco, Malaysia, Pakistan, Jordan, Somalia and Bangladesh. That there is need for providing training facilities to national development banks is obvious. A number of development banks in the member countries are newly established and lack the technical expertise and experience required for undertaking development banking, especially in areas of project identification, appraisal and follow-up and project monitoring as well as loan administration and other operational activities. There is definite need for providing technical assistance to such banks for the purpose of institution building. The IDB can play an important role in this respect in co-operation with some of the well-established development banks of the member countries. Such assistance could be provided by organising special courses, deputing staff members of the newly set up banks for on-the-job training to the relatively well-established development banks and through the secondment of staff from experienced institutions to banks requiring help and consultancy support. Besides improving the working of these institutions, such training would be in the interest of the IDB as a significant number of its equity operations are conducted through line of equity arrangements. The Islamic Research and Training Institute (IRTI) could also assist in imparting training to the staff of the national development banks needing it.

Over the years, co-operation with national development financing institutions has grown. By the end of 1987, the Bank approved 13 lines of equity for 20 institutions in 16 member countries, 5 lines of leasing and 7 lines of equity/leasing/instalment sale amounting to US$84.08 million, US$47.20 million and US$58.92 million respectively. The total amount stands at US$190.26 million.

The IDB has, since 1980, made active efforts to promote the formation of an association of the national development banks operating in its member countries. The Association of National Development Financing Institutions in member countries of the IDB was formally established in 1986. It is composed of the General Assembly, a Management Committee and a General Secretariat and has the following objectives:

(1) To promote co-operation in all aspects and activities of development financing;
(2) To conduct and encourage research and studies for the purpose of developing ideas, techniques and methodology for development banking and financing in accordance with Islamic principles;
(3) To develop joint resources and set up facilities for training and improvement of principal human resources;
(4) To promote the establishment of joint venture projects with a view to accelerating the process of economic integration among member countries.

Based in Istanbul, it is expected to undertake various activities such as organising meetings, courses, seminars and conferences, arranging exchanges of staff and information and conducting training courses. It is also exploring other ways of enlarging co-operation with the national development banks. These relate to a number of areas such as collection of economic data about member countries, project identification and appraisal, and recruitment of professional staff for the IDB.

Since 1980, the Bank has held a meeting with the national development banks every year to discuss ways of promoting co-operation and questions of mutual interest.

The IDB has been the prime mover in the recent formation of a Federation of Heads of Consulting Firms from Islamic countries. The Federation which is located in Istanbul is designed to assist in:

(1) Development of consultancy services;
(2) Promotion of co-operation among its members by establishing a mechanism for systematic exchange of information, technology and expertise;
(3) Informing its members about consultancy assignments and possibilities of participation in various projects and programmes financed by the IDB and the national development banks.

3. Islamic banks

It has been the aim of the IDB to develop a close relationship with the growing number of Islamic banks. With this end in view, it has held extensive discussions with them. Apart from ad-hoc contacts, since 1980 the IDB has been organising a special meeting every year to coincide with its annual meeting to which the Islamic banks are invited for the purpose of discussing their problems and ways of co-operaton. The Bank has also mounted several special missions to the Islamic banks with a view to gaining acquaintance with their situation and identifying possibilities of bilateral co-operation. It has also sought to promote the establishment of Islamic banks by contribution to their equity. It has in operation an Investment Deposit Scheme under which the Islamic banks are enabled to place their surplus funds in the foreign trade financing operations of the Bank in accordance with the principles of Shariah. It has also undertaken some co-financing operations with Islamic banks. Finally, it has offered them training facilities through the Islamic Research and Training Institute.

The Bank is also engaged in setting up new procedures for co-financing arrangements with Islamic banks and for development of a trade portfolio.* The trade portfolio is expected to be established in the form of an autonomous fund. Though the participating Islamic banks will be involved in policy formulation and decision making, the resources will be mobilised through the issuing of certificates which will be negotiable and tradeable among Islamic banks at a later stage. These certificates may be floated for subscription by the general public in member countries.

The Islamic banks for their part have very high expectations of the IDB and expect it to play something of a parental role. They expect the IDB to

* Eleventh Annual Report (1985–1986), page 45.

plead their cause with the governments and central banks of member countries and use the leverage it may have with them for the purpose of helping the Islamic banks. Though the deposits they receive are mainly for a short term, they have a large capital structure and their deposits are generally on the increase, which opens up the possibility of using them for a longer period. Financing of Auqaf may be a specially suitable avenue for the Islamic banks. Such operations can be conducted on the basis of co-financing with the IDB. To start with, Islamic banks could participate directly in joint financing with the IDB in the field of foreign trade financing. The IDB could liaise and identify opportunities for such financing and promote the direct relationship of Islamic banks with the concerned institutions or the Islamic banks could place their money in the IDB's Investment Deposit Scheme for utilisation in the foreign trade financing operations. The Islamic banks could also assist the IDB in enlarging its scope of foreign trade financing by locating suitable opportunities for investment in foreign trade financing operations in the private sector in capital-surplus member countries which do not have balance of payments problems.

Another way of co-operation with Islamic banks would be for the IDB to use them as correspondent banks in appropriate cases. In order to tackle the problem of placements and surplus liquidity, the Islamic banks are known to have been pursuing the idea of a special institution. However, progress has been slow and no concrete results have emerged so far. Perhaps the right approach for the Islamic banks would be to try to bring pressure to bear upon their central banks to adopt a specially helpful policy towards them as regards credit control policies, as also in respect of providing financing to them when they need it and also to afford special opportunities for the placement of their surplus funds in conformity with Shariah. At the same time, the central banks may adopt special deposit protection measures in the case of Islamic banks so as to strengthen the confidence of depositors in these banks. It seems that the Islamic banks are not sufficiently united and close to each other. They meet often but fail to agree on issues. There is great scope for the banks to come closer to each other, share their experience and seek to find common solutions. In particular, the possibilities of inter-bank transactions and co-operation must be fully explored.

In recent years the Islamic banks have evinced growing interest in using the IDB's Investment Deposit Scheme for the placement of their surplus funds. This is the result of several factors. First, there has been a larger inflow of deposits into these banks as they have become established and confidence in them has grown. Secondly, the return which the Islamic banks offer to the depositor has become especially attractive as deposit rates have generally fallen in the international money market. Thirdly, in a situation characterised by recession and slack business conditions, the credit demand has not sufficiently increased, with the result that the Islamic banks have experienced increasing difficulty in marketing their resources. Fourthly, the return allowed by the IDB under its Investment Deposit Scheme has become much more attractive as interest rates available from traditional banks have declined. All these factors have led to a situation where Islamic banks are eager to make larger deposits with the IDB. This should be regarded as a favourable development, viewed in the context of resource mobilisation and the popularisation of the IDB's Investment Deposit Scheme. At the same time, these developments have led to something of a dilemma for the IDB. This is for the reason that unless it can enlarge the market for its foreign trade financing accepting large deposits from Islamic banks would have the effect of displacing some of its own surplus funds presently being employed in foreign trade financing and reducing its "halal" income, i.e. income earned in accordance with the rules set out by Shariah. On the other hand, widening the net for foreign trade financing increases the risk element, which the Bank can ill afford in the light of its past experience of payments defaults. In order to tackle this problem, action seems to be required in two main directions. First, there is a case for lowering the mark-up on foreign trade financing. This would enable the Bank to increase foreign trade financing to countries with a relatively safe payments situation and at the same time curb the excessive enthusiasm on the part of the Islamic banks to place their funds with the IDB. Secondly, the Islamic banks must be made to share the risk involved in foreign trade financing by linking their deposits with individual operations. This sharing of risk will make it possible for the IDB to enlarge the scale of its foreign trade financing, thereby investing the additional funds from the Islamic banks without having to pull out its own funds and avoid loss of "halal" income. Another useful step for receiving funds from Islamic banks would be to enlarge the Investment Deposit Scheme so as to allow deposits for the medium term to be utilised in leasing operations. This would spare the Islamic banks the effect involved in lease financing on a co-financing basis. Consideration may be accorded to the possibilities of financing collaboration also. For example, the IDB may in appropriate cases use the local Islamic banks on a selective basis and on a modest scale for placement of some short-term funds in some of their short-term activities conducted in conformity with Shariah. At the same time, it may look into the possibility of receiving some surplus funds from the local Islamic banks for investment in its foreign trade financing scheme while allowing greater flexibility to these banks in respect of deposit and withdrawal.

The problem of training in the field of Islamic banking is rendered difficult by the dearth of an adequate body of systematic knowledge pertaining to Islamic banking. Thus, any effort in this direction has to fall into two parts, namely: (i) development of the course content; and (ii) the establishment of an apparatus and organisation for imparting this knowledge through the provision of training facilities. Broadly speaking, there are two major and basic prerequisites involved, namely: (i) the development and evolution of a body of knowledge in regard to Islamic banking; and (ii) after the course content or the body of knowledge has been evolved, an effort has to be mounted to disseminate this knowledge through adequate training facilities. The first prerequisite, the development of the training content, involves a research effort as also actual Ijtehad which would reveal new information and knowledge. The second prerequisite presupposes the establishment of an adequate training apparatus and organisation in the field. This brings into sharp focus the inter-dependence which exists between research and training in the field of Islamic banking. While research and Ijtehad will help to develop the content of training during the actual process of disseminating knowledge and information, new ideas may develop which would be of interest and use in the field of research. True, there are a number of Islamic banks functioning at present, but their future development depends very heavily on the development and evolution of Islamic banking practices and policies and on the availability of adequate personnel and manpower well-versed and fully trained in Islamic banking. The problem of training in Islamic banking would call for a great deal of collaboration and co-operation among the various institutions involved, such as the need for decentralising the training structure in the long run so that the various Islamic banks may have their own training facilities supported and assisted by central machinery. However, in the short run the effort will have to be centralised and the ideal arrangement would be for the various Islamic banks to recruit staff and to assign them for training centrally. It may also be worthwhile for the IDB to try to serve as a kind of a bridge between the scholars engaged in work on Islamic banking and the Islamic banks which are in the field. In other words, the IDB may seek to provide the scholars and research workers with basic inputs and feedback from the practical working of Islamic banks and, on the other hand, it should assist in the utilisation of academic work in the operation of the Islamic banks.

It is the opinion of some people that the present "cosmetically different" modes of financing being practiced by Islamic banks are, in fact, a backdoor for interest and traditional banking with its attendant evil effects and with none of the advantages and benefits claimed for Islamic banking. According to them, the "mark-up", "service fee" and "management fee" charged by Islamic banks are just another name and form of interest. They argue that so far Islamic banking is almost wholly confined to Murabeha financing or the system of advance sales. This, it is contended, is simply because the Murabeha form of financing retains all the essential features of traditional banking, namely, a guaranteed repayment on a specific date and a fixed return linked to time. The only difference is the non-existence of the application of a penal interest rate in the case of default.

As far as lease financing is concerned, it is argued that though Islamic banks justify the leasing fee they charge on the ground that it represents the price for the use of assets financed by them, the condition that during the period of the lease, the ownership remains with the lessor, is no more than a pretext for charging a leasing fee. Their argument is that this situation is totally different from the one in which the lessee is charged a fee for the use of the assets unaccompanied by any obligation to acquire its ownership. It is also alleged that Islamic banks do not concern themselves with the crucial issue as to who their financing benefits and many a time divert and place substantial resources into the hands of traditional Riba (interest) banks. It is claimed that the Islamic banking system is entirely equity based, but the critics argue that almost all modes of financing practised by Islamic banks such as Murabeha, leasing, hire-purchase, mark down in price and rent-sharing are said to fail to meet this test as in every case the return is pre-determined.

Broadly speaking, there can be two distinctive approaches to Islamic banking. The first is to adjust and modify the practices followed by traditional banks so that Riba or interest is apparently eliminated. In sharp contrast to this would be the real concept of Islamic banking, namely, the establishment of an institution which links the providers and users of financial resources on the basis of profit and loss sharing and other financial practices permitted by Islam for assisting in the realisation of the socio-economic goals and the value system prescribed by Islam. The general view is that progress by way of a fundamental breakthrough or a real transformation of banking in line with the dictates of Islam is yet to come. Interest has so far concentrated on developing modes of financing which technically, or on the face of it, do not involve interest. There is little appreciation and understanding of the wider concept and objectives of Islam. Instead of treating profit as the sole objective, Islamic banks must blend it with the needs of Islamic society.

Financing based on the sharing of profit and loss is the real crux, core, essence and heart of Islamic banking. Therefore, instead of continuing to place reliance on the so-called second best methods of financing, Islamic banks must embark upon and enlarge their operations on the basis of profit and loss sharing with at least two parties maintaining proper accounts audited by chartered accountants. If abolition of interest is desired, a real beginning by way of a real change must be made. Instead of placing exclusive reliance on security, Islamic banks must develop a capacity for a comprehensive appraisal and evaluation of credit proposals and clients backed by an effective system of credit supervision, at the same time avoiding excessive exposure to any one party, sector or type of financing activity and maintaining a well diversified portfolio.

The evil effects of Riba banking are well recognised and the merits of Islamic banking are undeniable. Much discussion has taken place and a good deal of material has appeared to justify the prohibition of interest in Islam and on the conceptual aspects of Islamic banking. In this situation, attention and effort have to concentrate on how to employ and expand Islamic banking in its comprehensive and real sense.

It is with this paramount objective in view that it is proposed that a comprehensive and critical survey of the actual practical working of Islamic banks, which are already on the ground, be undertaken. The aim should be to analyse their actual operations, business conducted by them, policies which they pursue, problems which they face and their appropriate solutions. Information about individual banks may not be disclosed or divulged. Instead, an effort should be made to follow a cumulative approach and to present a general but well integrated overall picture of Islamic banking as it is being actually practised. In other words, by studying individual institutions closely, a general model of Islamic banking should appear.

Simultaneously with the study of individual Islamic banks, a comprehensive and critical study should be undertaken of those countries which claim to be operating an Islamic banking system on a national basis. The aim must be to carry out a critical and candid examination of how far the system is contributing to the goals set by Islam and the advantages of Islamic banking, such as priority to the financing of essential items, better and more efficient allocation of resources, socio-economic justice, mitigation of wide disparities of wealth and income and concentration of economic power, financing of medium and small entrepreneurs, and encouragement of talented borrowers lacking security. The effort should be to determine how far the nature, outlook and operations of banks operating in these countries have undergone a transformation? How far are they serving public interest rather than individual or group interest? How far are they helping in realising the socio-economic goals of Islam? Are they responsive to the needs of Islamic society or are they playing a merely profit-maximising role? How far have they acquired a multipurpose character from being mere commercial banks and how far are they making a more careful evaluation of credit proposals instead of depending solely on the security offered? How far is the banking system according a priority to fulfilling the needs of society so that food, clothing, housing, medical facilities and education receive abundant financing before credit resources are directed to the production of goods and services which are less essential from the Islamic standpoint? How far have the large volume of funds which had remained idle because of the aversion to Riba become available for productive investment? How far has the system succeeded in enlarging its financing of medium and small enterprises? How far are credit resources now gravitating towards skilled and talented entrepreneurs who have ability and sound enterprise but lack security? How far has it brought out the large fund of entrepreneurial skills which had remained dormant? How far is the system guided by the nature and quality of credit proposals rather than by the security or financial guarantees offered by the party? If answers to the foregoing questions are not positive then there is no escape from the conclusion that the Islamic banking system which has been devised is not truly Islamic. This must make us ponder how to evolve and develop methods of financing and practices which are fundamentally different and not superficially different from the interest-based operations of Riba banks.

One of the major requirements of Islamic banks is to evolve and develop a set of criteria for evaluating their performance which is distinct and different from that in use by traditional banks. Traditional banks judge their success in terms of volume of deposits, advances and profits. Islamic banks must enlarge the criteria by taking into account many other factors related to their modes of financing and utilisation of the savings of the Ummah in furtherance of the socio-economic objectives set by Islam. In the case of Islamic banks, success has to be measured in terms of how far they have been able to introduce and popularise Islamic banking and move away from traditional banking practices. The prohibition and abolition of interest is really a policy instrument and not a policy objective. It is a means and not an ultimate end. The Islamic banks must therefore bear in mind the impact of what they do.

It must be realised that the challenge of Islamic banking is two-fold. It is both quantitative and qualitative. The increase in the Islamic banks in recent years, and the fact that new Islamic banks continue to be established is, no doubt, satisfying. However, what is equally, if not more, important is to develop the art of Islamic banking. This is by no means an easy task and calls for sustained efforts and Ijtehad. That Ijtehad must be undertaken in a cautious manner without endangering the safety of Islamic banks is self-evident and most important for the reason that any weakening of the strength and solvency of Islamic banks would do serious damage to the cause by undermining confidence in Islamic banking.

Chapter 17

Economic Co-operation among Member Countries

Perhaps no single objective is highlighted so much in the charter of the Islamic Development Bank as the promotion of economic co-operation among its member countries. The Preamble states that the objectives of fostering the well-being of the peoples of the Muslim countries and achieving a balanced and harmonious development of these countries on the basis of Islamic principles and ideals could be best advanced through mutual financial and economic co-operation among the Muslim states. It emphasises the need for promoting and strengthening co-operation among member states in economic, social and other fields of activity. Article 16 of the Agreement lays down that in conducting its operations, the Bank shall pay due regard to the objective of promoting complementarity in the economies of member countries. The objective of co-operation has also been given prominence in the policy document of the Bank which underlines the need for financing regional and sub-regional projects and for according priority to projects and enterprises which promote co-operation among member countries taking into account the availability of raw materials, technology, financial resources, management and institutional capacity as also marketing arrangements.

The problem of economic co-operation and the role of the IDB in promoting it has to be viewed against the general background of the efforts made and progress achieved in this field in recent years. In this regard it may be noted that besides the establishment of the IDB as an independent international institution in 1975, several other organisations have come into existence under the auspices of the OIC. These are the Statistical, Economic and Social Research and Training Centre of the Islamic Countries (SESRTCIC) in Ankara, the Islamic Foundation of Science, Technology and Development (IFSTAD) in Jeddah, the Islamic Chamber of Commerce, Industry and Commodity Exchange (ICCICE) in Karachi, the Islamic Centre for Development of Trade (ICDT) at Casablanca and the Islamic Centre for Technical, Vocational Training and Research (ICTVTR) in Dhaka.

In addition to institution building, two agreements have been approved by the Islamic Foreign Ministers Conference. The first is entitled "General Co-operation Among Member States of the OIC" and the second is called "Agreement for Promotion, Protection and Guarantee of Investment Among Member States of the OIC". While the former agreement has been ratified by the required number of member states for implementation, the second has been ratified by only six member countries which falls short of the number required to bring the agreement into force.

The General Agreement covers broad areas for co-operation, namely (a) economic co-operation, including the transfer of capital and investment among member countries, the encouragement of joint projects which will promote complementarities among the national economies of member countries, and co-operation in the field of meeting food requirements from within the Islamic world; (b) technical co-operation, which includes the exchange of expertise and technical capacities available in member states and the establishment of an Islamic Foundation for advanced science and technology; (c) commercial co-operation which includes, among other things, the application of equal and non-discriminatory commercial treatment among member states, enlarging and developing trade exchange through, inter alia, trade liberalisation by reducing or removing customs and other restrictions, and giving consideration to the special circumstances of the least-developed member countries.

The second agreement lays down the basic principles for promoting the transfer of capital among member countries. It is also meant to protect the interests of investors against possible non-commercial risks in the host country. It also guarantees the transfer of capital and its net proceeds in cash, without the investor being subjected to any discriminatory treatment. The agreement also proposes the establishment of an Islamic institution for the insurance of properties within the territories of the participating countries.

In 1981 at the Third Islamic Summit held in Mecca a "Plan of Action to strengthen economic co-operation among the Islamic countries" covering ten broad areas was approved. The implementation programme for this plan was prepared by a meeting of senior inter-governmental experts and approved by the 13th Islamic Foreign Ministers Conference held in Niamey in August

1982. The General Secretariat of the OIC and the committees set up by the First Ministerial Conference on agriculture and industry were made responsible for follow-up. Realising that progress was halting and slow, the Fourth Islamic Summit held in Casablanca in 1984 decided that of the ten areas identified for co-operation in 1981, six may be accorded priority. These are (1) Food, Food Security and Agricultural Development; (2) Industry; (3) Science and Technology; (4) Trade Exchange; (5) Transportation and Communication; and (6) Energy.

Since its inception the IDB has endeavoured to fulfil its mandate in regard to the promotion of economic co-operation among its member countries. In the first place, by providing large amounts of foreign trade financing and insisting that, as far as possible, imports should be made from member countries, the bank has sought to promote co-operation in the field of trade. A concerted attempt has been made to establish new trading relationships and to introduce new trade items. Secondly, the IDB has accorded priority to the financing of regional and joint projects. The OMVS Manantali Dam Project financing in 1981 involving Mali, Mauritania and Senegal is a good example of this. Thirdly, the Bank has introduced a Programme of Technical Co-operation designed to promote co-operation among member countries in the technical field. Fourthly, it has constantly tried to encourage the use of consultants from member countries. More recently, it has been directing attention to the promotion of joint ventures and the establishment of a clearing group for its member countries. Additionally, it has striven to promote closer co-operation among economic institutions in member countries also. Its efforts to have an association of national development banks bear testimony to this. As far as joint ventures are concerned, in July 1983 the IDB organised a workshop in which experts and businessmen from Muslim countries participated. The workshop identified several impediments to joint ventures such as lack of skills for organising such ventures, administrative bottlenecks, inadequacy of capital resources, lack of marketing information, foreign exchange restrictions and the absence of a central point of contact in member countries. The workshop suggested the establishment of a central unit in the Bank for the promotion of joint ventures. Recently, the Bank has initiated action in this field by offering to assist some joint ventures in Pakistan.

Perhaps for joint ventures general macro-level studies are not so important. What is required is the identification and then the preparation of project profiles and the bringing of the parties together. Instead of conceiving a plan of action, the objective should be to develop as many specific projects as possible. The effort should be to try to encourage the flow of investments from capital rich and oil exporting countries to the oil importing countries with the help of partners from the industrialised countries.

Taking trade as a measure of economic co-operation and complementarity, it may be observed that, according to an estimate, the total imports of Muslim countries from other Muslim countries comprise even less than 10 per cent of their total imports, whereas the exports of Muslim countries to other Muslim countries are hardly 5 per cent of their total export trade. This is a measure of the vast scope for trade promotion. This task, in fact, embraces many things. The ultimate objective should be the development of a comprehensive system of preferences amongst member countries as a whole. This is for the reason that self-reliance presupposes mutual trade and the granting of preferences in favour of all member countries. This should result in a pyramid of sub-regional, regional and global arrangements. As the various member countries are at different levels of development, such a scheme has to take this fact into account by way of including exports of primary commodities, processed agricultural products and a number of simple industrial products also in the scheme of preferences. In addition to the preferences, and the removal of tariff and non-tariff barriers, promotional measures are also needed through the utilisation of the existing state trading mechanisms for promoting imports from member countries. There are various possibilities to be explored such as a free trade area, a customs union, a common market, and an economic union. In the case of the free trade area, the main aim is to expand trade among members through abolition of tariffs in respect of products they produce themselves. In a customs union, in addition to this, there is a common external tariff. In the case of a common market, there is a free flow of commodities as well as factors such as labour, capital, enterprise and technology. In addition, there is a common tariff policy. In an economic union there is the fullest integration.

A clearing union could be established by the central banks and other monetary authorities of the members of the IDB. It would be designed to establish a system for clearing payments among the participating countries on a multilateral basis. The main purposes of such a union would be as follows:

(i) to provide a facility to settle on a multilateral basis payment for current international transactions among the territories of participants;
(ii) to promote the use of participants' currencies in current transactions between them and thus to effect economies in the use of the participants' foreign exchange reserves;
(iii) to promote trade and economic activity among the member countries through the provision of credit backing;
(iv) to promote monetary co-operation among the participating countries and closer relations among their banking systems.

Membership of such a union would be open to the central banks or monetary authorities of each of the member countries of the IDB. Participation in another clearing group or arrangement should not preclude participation in an Islamic Clearing Union. Those central banks or monetary authorities which sign the Agreement not later than three months from the date the Agreement has been signed by six such central banks or monetary authorities would be deemed to be founder members. Subsequently, other central banks or monetary authorities that are eligible to participate may become members of the Islamic Clearing Union by signing the Agreement and accepting the Rules and Regulations and decisions of the Board of Directors. The accounts of the Islamic Clearing Union could be kept in a common unit of account known as the Islamic Dinar, the value of which shall be equivalent to one Special Drawing Right of the International Monetary Fund. The participants may have the right to exclude certain payments for specified transactions as eligible for channelling through the clearing facility. Otherwise all payments for current international transactions as defined by the Articles of Agreement of the International Monetary Fund and from a resident in the territory of one participant to a resident in the territory of another participant may be deemed to be eligible payments. In order to promote the use of the clearing facility participants may adopt measures designed to provide incentives to make payment for individual transactions through the clearing facility. Settlement may be made of net positions at the end of each three-month period. The accounting period could be four weeks. If a participant's net credit position at the end of an accounting period exceeds the limit of 1/12th of its visible exports to the other participants, the participant may have the right to an immediate settlement of the amount of the excess. If a participant's net debit position at the end of an accounting period exceeds the limit of 1/24th of its visible imports, it could pay the excess to the participant with net creditor position in proportion to the absolute net creditor position of each. Each member may be notified of the amount it shall pay to or receive from each other participant at the end of each accounting and settlement period. Each debitor participant may make the payment in convertible foreign exchange specified for the purpose within two days of receiving the notice. In the event of a default by any participant, the Union may have the right to suspend it and impose a fine on it. The Islamic Clearing Union may have its own Board of Directors and also a General Manager and staff. The Board of Directors may make arrangements with a central bank or monetary authority of a member to provide the necessary services and facilities for the operation of the clearing facility. The Board of Directors may approve the Annual Budget of the Union and determine the formula under which expenses shall be apportioned among members. Members may have the right to withdraw from the Union after giving adequate notice. However, such a member could remain liable for meeting all its obligations to other participants until the final settlement of accounts takes place. It is important to realise that the success of the clearing union would depend greatly on the credit backing that it would enjoy.*

* The IDB is reported to be studying the possibility of establishing a multilateral

A concerted effort should also be made to encourage regional and joint projects. There is special need for it in strategic areas such as food production. It may be worthwhile in the context of the IDB to try to encourage the financing of joint projects by excluding such projects from national allocations of resources by the IDB. There has to be a separate provision for such projects in the annual financing plan of the Bank.

What appears to be required is a comprehensive survey for identifying tangible possibilities of economic co-operation among our member countries. What is more, it would be necessary also to determine the steps required to bring about such co-operation. The aim should be to protect the national interest of each country and provide an equitable sharing of the cost and benefits. It should be remembered that the edifice of economic co-operation among Muslim countries has to be built not only on their political will, but on a realisation that it would help to foster individual national economic interest also. What would need to be studied, would not only be their existing economic structure, but also the economic potential and their production and development plans. Insofar as the study helps to identify possibilities of joint ventures and specific projects, it would have the additional benefit of enlarging opportunities of financing by the IDB. The study should also seek to focus on the factors leading to the lack of trade such as the absence of suitable payment arrangements, non-availability of shipping and insurance facilities and double taxation etc. It could well lead to a well-conceived proposal for the establishment of a payments union, a joint shipping arrangement, a treaty for the avoidance of double taxation and a corporation for joint insurance and re-insurance facilities. It should pay special attention to the possibilities for the transfer of financial resources as also the transfer of technology and skills among member countries.

There is also great need for making an effort for promoting co-operation in the field of the capital goods industry. In this connection, the first task is to survey the engineering industries in the Islamic countries, then procedures have to be devised and steps taken to facilitate trade of capital goods among Islamic countries. Finally, there is need for consultation and co-operation among Islamic countries in the development of certain strategic capital goods. The aim should be to achieve the minimum economically viable production level in respect of certain types of capital goods by means of a regional aggregation of demand. The benefits to be gained from the development of the capital goods and industrial machinery sector should be maximised through promoting and strengthening links amongst the member countries of the IDB. This in turn calls for the pooling of their research and development efforts, exchange of capital goods specialists and also a training programme in manufacturing and design technology.

---

clearing facility at the instance of the Standing Committee for Economic and Commercial Co-operation.

It may also be worthwhile for the IDB to undertake a comprehensive economic survey of Muslim countries to determine the prospects for development and economic co-operation amongst them. The effort should be not only to discover possibilities of co-operation at the national level but also to take into account the possibilities of institutional co-operation, that is co-operation among the economic institutions existing in Muslim countries.

Finally, it has to be realised that economic co-operation cannot be promoted through an emotional appeal in the name of Islam. Areas of co-operation have to be identified and suitable forms in which co-operation can take place have to be designed. This should be such that the costs and benefits both direct and indirect, tangible and intangible, are shared equally amongst the participating countries. Such opportunities can be identified through in-depth studies of the economies of Muslim countries comprising an examination of their present economic situation and future development prospects and plans. In particular the future development plans have to be clearly and comprehensively studied. From such a study rough estimates of the goods to be imported in the future by various Muslim countries can be prepared. The possibilities of the procurement and the production of some of these goods by the other Muslim countries on the basis of their resources and endowment and geographical location can be determined. These possibilities may include national projects as also joint ventures. The IDB may finance the preparation of such studies. What the Bank should realise is that political solidarity is not always long lasting as it changes with governments. However, if the solidarity is based on economic factors, it will have a much more solid foundation and prove to be long lasting. The IDB must aspire to become the premier institution for bringing the Islamic countries together for economic development and co-operation, leaving the Organisation for Islamic Conference to concentrate on political matters. This is a task which requires more technical expertise, organisational skill, strategic planning, initiative and intellectual leadership than financial resources.

Chapter 18

Assistance to Muslim Communities

The Islamic Development Bank was conceived as an institution that would render service to the entire Muslim Ummah. The very first article of the Bank's charter stated that the purpose of the Bank shall be to foster the economic development and social progress of member countries and Muslim communities individually as well as jointly in accordance with the principles of Shariah. The second article relating to the functions and powers of the Bank envisaged the establishment of a Special Fund to give assistance to Muslim communities in non-member countries.

In January 1977 the management of the Bank prepared a broad proposal for the establishment of the Fund for Muslim communities in non-member countries which was the subject of a long discussion by the Board of Executive Directors. The consensus which emerged was that the matter was so complicated as to require much more study and deliberation before any specific proposal could be approved for setting up the Fund. The Board, however, felt that, in view of its importance, the matter should be submitted to the Board of Governors for eliciting their views at their annual meeting the same year. Two basic points seemed to emerge in the course of discussions by the governors: first, that the IDB should develop adequate professional and administrative strength before taking on new tasks and, second, that it would not be realistic or fair so soon after the large subscriptions made by the members to the capital of the Bank to approach them for contributions for a Special Fund. This was particularly so as the Bank had available large resources not immediately needed in its operations.

Thus the matter remained under study until the third meeting of the Board of Governors in Kampala in 1979 when a special resolution was passed that the Special Account of the Bank representing the interest proceeds of deposits with foreign banks should, among other things, also be utilised for assistance and relief to Muslim communities. Since then until 1988, the IDB has undertaken 100 operations covering 349 projects totalling US$168 million to help the Muslim communities in non-member countries. This effort has embraced the Muslim communities in Asia, Africa, Europe, Australia, and the Pacific and North America. In the field of refugee assistance, help has been extended to the Ugandan and Eritrean refugees in Sudan, Ogaden refugees in Somalia, Chadian refugees in Cameroun, Eritrean refugees in Djibouti and Afghan refugees in Pakistan. Relief has also been provided to member countries affected by natural disasters and calamities. Finally, financial support has been extended to Islamic centres and cultural activities.

While these efforts by the IDB are laudable, a great deal more needs to be done. In this connection it would be well to take note of three basic points. In the first place, as far as non-member countries are concerned, the status and economic and political circumstances of the Muslim communities differ greatly, which would clearly call for a case by case approach. Secondly, the Bank's assistance should solely focus on the economic uplift of the Muslim communities instead of any religious activities. Thirdly, the success of any effort or programme to help the Muslims in non-member countries greatly depends on the degree of their organisation. In cases where the Muslim community is not well organised it becomes very difficult to channel assistance to them from outside. As a start, the Bank should collect information in regard to the Muslim communities and their economic requirements as also the means of assisting them. It should devise the basis or criteria for determining the size of the Fund and the way it should be mobilised. It may study the problem in selected non-member countries on a sample survey basis. The IDB could, for example, look at the problem as it exists in the Philippines, India, Africa and the Western countries. The object should be to determine the special needs of the Muslim communities in these four cases and to identify and devise methods of channelling assistance to them. For this kind of work what seems necessary is first to make contact at the level of governments and enlist their support, so as to prevent any misgiving on their part and then to enlist expert local assistance to study the problem and find an appropriate solution.

Some of the basic questions to be explored are as follows:

(1) The areas where financial assistance and resources are most urgently required.

(2) The priorities in terms of sectors such as education, health, small business, cottage industries, etc.

(3) The appropriate forms of assistance:
   (a) loans
   (b) profit-sharing
   (c) leasing
   (d) equity participation;

(4) The broad terms of such assistance as required in terms of:
   (a) amount
   (b) period
   (c) cost;

(5) The basic requirements in relation to guarantees, transfer of capital and dividends;

(6) The best way to approach the beneficiaries, directly or through government;

(7) Approach and supervision of projects.

As soon as the study has been completed the Fund for Muslim communities should be set up. The purpose of the Fund shall be to enable the IDB more effectively to carry out its purpose of fostering economic development and social progress of Muslim communities and to serve as a practical expression of unity and solidarity of the Muslim Ummah, by providing financial assistance for the economic and social development of the Muslim communities in non-member countries, having due regard to the economic conditions of such communities and their needs as also the most suitable and desirable ways of helping them. The authority of the Board of Governors, the Board of Executive Directors, the President and the staff of the Bank shall extend to the operations of the Fund in the same manner as it applies to the ordinary operations of the Bank. The administration of the Fund will be governed by special regulations to be devised for the purpose. The Board of Executive Directors shall lay down and adopt guidelines and operating procedures for the efficient administration of the Fund. The resources of the Fund shall consist of (i) contributions from member countries in response to a resolution to be passed by the Board of Governors. The contributions may be paid in two equal instalments of 50 per cent each in freely convertible currency acceptable to the Bank. Each member making a contribution shall deposit an instrument of contribution specifying the amount of his contribution and the manner in which the payment thereof shall be made to the Bank. Contributors shall be free to increase the amount of their contribution at any time and at appropriate intervals the Board of Executive Directors will review the resource position of the Fund and make recommendations to the Board of Governors; (ii) resources set aside by the IDB under Article 42(i) of the Agreement, from its net income arising out of its ordinary operations; (iii) resources from any non-member government or from any national or international entity, public or private. The operations of the Fund shall be so designed as to assist the social and economic development of Muslim communities in non-member countries and will be channelled through the governments of those countries with special provisions for supervision. The resources of the Fund shall at all times and in all respects be held, used, committed, invested or otherwise disposed of entirely separately from the ordinary capital resource of the Bank. The IDB would be free to invest any resources of the Fund not immediately required for the conduct of the operations of the Fund. The administrative expenses relating directly to the operations of the Fund shall be charged to the Fund. The net income accruing to the Fund shall be retained in the Fund. The IDB will be responsible for maintaining accounts of the Fund, which shall be submitted to the Board of Executive Directors at the end of every quarter. The accounts of the Fund shall be audited at the close of each financial year by the External Auditors of the IDB and the audited financial statements of the Fund shall be submitted to the Board of Governors in terms of Section 13 of the Bye-Laws of the Bank. The Board of Executive Directors shall report on the resources of the Fund and its operations in its Annual Report to the Board of Governors.

As regards the resources, there are various options available: for example, after determining the size of the initial resources required, the amount could be distributed over the entire membership in proportion to their subscription. This will have the merit of providing for the largest participation in the important task of helping Muslim communities. The second alternative could be to fix the size of the Fund and distribute it among the four largest subscribers to the ordinary capital of the Bank. At the same time, the other members could be invited to contribute on a voluntary basis whatever they can to the Fund. The third alternative could be to fix the size of the Fund and to make an appeal for resources allowing any member to make a contribution. This arrangement would be purely voluntary and would depend entirely on the goodwill of various members.

Chapter 19

Mobilisation of Resources

The founders of the Islamic Development Bank realised that perhaps one of the most complex tasks that the Bank would face would relate to resource mobilisation. This feeling stemmed from the fact that owing to the Shariah requirement and the prohibition of interest, resort to the traditional modes of resource replenishment were clearly ruled out. In the circumstances, the IDB would have to devise and develop new methods of resource mobilisation. Against this background, in terms of Article 2(vi), the Bank was empowered to accept deposits and to "raise funds in any other manner". The latter part of the article was deliberately kept general and vague so as to allow maximum scope and freedom to the Bank in evolving new methods of mobilising resources. At the same time, the institution was launched with a very substantial resource base by way of its capital structure, so that it would not face any shortage of funds for quite a few years and so would have enough time and opportunity for designing new instruments of resource mobilisation.

The Bank started with an authorised capital of ID2 billion and a subscribed capital of ID750 million in a period of five years. Even more significant, however, was that member countries were required to pay the entire amount of capital in a freely convertible currency acceptable to the Bank. In other words, the entire amount had to be paid and there was no callable portion. Similarly, the entire payment was to be in foreign exchange as there was no provision for local currency payments. This provided a sharp contrast to the cases of other international development banks. In the case of the World Bank, for example, the member countries were required to pay only 2 per cent of their subscription in dollars and hard currencies and 18 per cent in the form of local currencies. The remaining 80 per cent of the capital represented the callable element or, so to speak, a guarantee against which the World Bank borrowed from the international capital market. This shows that the strain on the capital subscribers was much less compared with the case of the IDB.

It goes to the credit of the IDB that despite its initial comfortable resource position and large surplus funds, it did not become complacent about its task of resource mobilisation. As a matter of fact, realising that the worst time to look for resources was when they were actually needed and bearing in mind that in its case resort to conventional methods was not possible, the Bank directed attention to this problem fairly early. In 1978, it invited a group of experts under the chairmanship of Mr. Saeb Jaroudi to advise the Bank in the matter. The report presented by the group surveyed the various developmental problems facing the member countries and identified certain areas such as agriculture and rural development, industrial development, mining, infrastructure and social sectors where the Bank's contribution could be more effective. The Report attempted a broad estimate of the resources the IDB would require for its operations under various assumptions and came to the conclusion that the subscribed capital of the Bank, which at the time stood at ID790 million, should be increased to the level of the authorised capital, that is, ID2 billion. This, the Report observed, would be sufficient to finance the Bank's ordinary operations for the ensuing five years. The Report could not recommend alternative or new methods of mobilisation for the IDB in the short run and only observed that the Bank should continue to look for ways other than an increase in its capital for financing its activities. The Report was first placed before the Board of Executive Directors and was later circulated to the Governors of the Bank.

Realising that the only means of replenishing its resources in the immediate future was to strengthen its capital base, a comprehensive memorandum was submitted to the Board of Governors at the annual meeting in Khartoum in 1981 proposing an increase in the subscribed capital of the Bank. The case was based on the following factors:

(1) The IDB had already completed four years of its operations. During this period total approvals by the Bank including both project financing and foreign trade financing had totalled ID759.53 million (US$943.32 million) covering 114 operations in 30 member countries. As regards the tempo of acceleration, project financing had expanded from ID13.45 million in 1396H to ID119.25 million in 1399H. As regards foreign trade financing which was started in 1397H (1977), aggregating ID43.61 million in that year, the quantum had increased to ID262.43

million in 1399H. Apart from the quantitative increase, there had also been a very notable diversification in its operations. Starting with loan operations, the Bank was embarking on four other types of operation, namely, equity financing, leasing, profit sharing and financing foreign trade. The amount involved in technical assistance as also the number of projects in that field had also increased. What was more, the Bank had over the past years, developed a sizeable project pipeline and had also expanded its technical and organisational capability to serve the member countries. The Bank was faced with a situation that at the end of 1399H (1979) its uncommitted resources were equivalent to about two years' commitments at current level of ordinary operations. In fact, if account was taken of the foreign trade financing operations, the need for resource mobilisation became even more vital and urgent. Experience of other international institutions had shown that attention should be directed to the problem of resource mobilisation long before total commitments equal aggregate resources. This held particularly in the case of the IDB which could not have ready access to the international capital market and must devise other methods of mobilisation.

(2) In estimating its future resource needs, the Bank had generally taken into account the requirements of member countries in terms of their development programmes, aid flows and international developments having a bearing on the problem.

(3) The membership of the Bank and the number of recipient countries had increased substantially since the establishment of the Bank. It stood at 22 when the Bank was inaugurated but had grown to 36 with four others seeking membership which included some of the poorest Muslim countries.

(4) The cost escalation and the rising price level made it necessary to raise the quantum of financing in absolute terms.

(5) The Bank was required to direct special attention to the least-developed member countries which also had resource implications.

(6) In the interest of promoting co-operation, the Bank must direct greater attention to regional projects which were larger in size and required additional resources.

(7) A stage had been reached when the Bank must embark on country programming which was bound to enlarge the resource needs insofar as tentative allocations had to be made to meet the needs of a large number of countries. In this respect, account had also to be taken of the future international outlook. The world economy was characterised by the twin forces of inflation and recession. Inflation continued to increase the resource requirements for development through escalation of costs whereas recession affected the foreign exchange earnings of member countries as also the aid flows from industrialised countries.

On the one hand rising import prices and adverse movement of the terms of trade had exerted a serious strain on the external payment position of member countries and, on the other, as the developed economies slowed down, the export earnings and foreign exchange availability of member countries would be affected further.

(8) The need for balance of payment support and foreign trade financing was likely to grow further. The Bank must step up its foreign trade financing operations especially strengthening their developmental impact.

(9) In the case of the IDB, by virtue of the very nature of its operations, which required loan financing to be de-emphasised and priority accorded to equity, leasing, profit sharing and foreign trade financing, the tempo of disbursement was relatively faster.

(10) As for the supply aspect, sizeable financial resources were available in certain member countries which could be utilised for productive investment on an increasing scale in capital-scarce Muslim countries. This would be mutually beneficial, reducing the dependence on the traditional investment avenue and the commercial banking system of the West where investments were eroded by inflation.

(11) It was the endeavour of the Bank in drawing up an operational programme and in choosing the mix of various types of financing to achieve the maximum reverse flow and to generate additional resources reducing the dependence of the Bank on further capital increases.

(12) The Bank was determined to make every effort to move into a situation where the increase in capital did not remain the sole method of resource mobilisation and its future needs were met in as many different ways as possible. As a token of its earnestness and to do what it could on its own to augment its resources, it had already decided to introduce an Investment Deposit Scheme for meeting the growing needs of foreign trade financing.

The entire matter was considered and discussed by the Board of Governors and it was agreed to raise the subscribed capital of the Bank to the level of its authorised capital, that is, ID2 billion. At the close of 1405H (1985), the total capital resources* of the Bank stood at ID2,112 million, comprising ID1,645 million of ordinary capital resources and ID467 million of Special Fund resources.

In this context, it may be noted that the entire concept of obtaining deposits is somewhat foreign to the realm of international development banking and the provision in regard to deposit mobilisation constitutes a unique feature

* Capital resources of the Bank broadly consist of ordinary resources from capital subscribed by member countries, reserves and retained earnings and the special fund resources built out of interest proceeds from surplus funds placed with banks.

of the IDB as a kind of substitute to the traditional borrowing function resorted to by other international and regional development banks.

Besides the increase in its subscribed capital, the other means used by the IDB for augmenting its financial resources is the mobilisation of deposits.

Ever since the commencement of operations, the Bank had been approached by prospective depositors. The first in this regard was the Organisation of the Islamic Conference which actually made two deposits with the Bank. These deposits, however, were not in the nature of investment deposits insofar as the OIC did not expect any return on them. Subsequently, however, the Bank received several other inquiries in regard to the possibility of placing investment deposits with the Bank in accordance with Shariah which could yield a return to the depositor. True, the Bank did not face any serious resources constraint in the years immediately following its establishment. At the same time, it realised that it would be judicious to make a beginning in the field of deposit mobilisation. The Bank felt that regardless of the size of the deposits which the Bank would succeed in mobilising, it would greatly improve its image and strengthen its hand by demonstrating that it had already started enlarging and diversifying the sources and means for resource mobilisation. Besides being a mobilisation device, such a step would also demonstrate the Bank's interest in assisting other institutions in employing their surplus funds in accordance with Islamic principles.

It was in this context that the IDB introduced an Investment Deposit Scheme in September 1980. The Investment Deposit Scheme conforms to Shariah and at the same time provides a reasonable return to the investors. The funds generated through the Investment Deposit Scheme are utilised in the foreign trade financing operations of the Bank. The Bank accepts deposits from institutions as well as individuals. Amounts totalling a minimum of US$250,000 and not exceeding US$1 million equivalent, denominated in Islamic Dinars, can be deposited at any time, and amounts in excess of US$1 million are to be deposited following negotiations with the Bank. The earnings from the Scheme which are distributable to the depositors are directly linked to the activities and profitability of the foreign trade operations of the Bank. An account with a bank in one of the member countries specifically for the purpose of the Deposit Scheme, is denominated in Islamic Dinars and is operated strictly in accordance with the principles of Shariah. Some local Islamic banks have responded to IDB's invitation and have placed deposits under the Investment Deposit Scheme. The balance as at the end of the year 1407H (1987) stood at US$115.64 million. The Bank is now engaged in improving and modifying the Investment Deposit Scheme in order to make it more responsive to its needs and to ensure that the depositors truly share in the risk of default and delays associated with foreign trade financing operations. Each investment deposit would be matched against a specific transaction of the Foreign Trade Financing Scheme. The "matching" process would be entirely based on "First-in first-matched" concept. After the placement, the depositor would receive his funds and returns when the beneficiary had met his obligations to the Bank. As for matching the supply with demand the best and the surest way is to try to link it with each transaction as the Bank goes along. For example, after a project is approved by the Board, the IDB may issue a notification that it has approved a US$30 million project for a member country, that it is going to put up US$20 millions out of its own resources and that investors are invited to make up the remaining 10 millions.

The IDB has also been exploring possibilities of developing co-financing arrangements with the Islamic banks and has already made some progress in this direction. The most significant development in this regard is the establishment of the Islamic Banks' Portfolio which is already in operation. Its initial capital of US$65 million composed of share certificates having a par value of US$1,000 each has been subscribed by the Islamic banks which also, in turn, oversee its general policies. The IBP has been established as a special fund under the terms of Article 22 of the IDB Charter and has a Participants' Committee of 13 members. The IDB is expected to manage the operation as a Mudarib although the accounts of the Portfolio would be totally separate from those of the Bank's which would use its own manpower for managing the Portfolio. The Portfolio will be used mainly for financing trade among Islamic countries provided both importers and exporters come from member countries of the OIC. It may also use its resources to finance exports from member countries to non-member countries as well as imports to a member country from a non-member country provided the interest of the Islamic beneficiary country is served. It can also undertake leasing operations. The main beneficiary of the fund would be the private sector. Share certificates constituting the initial capital are negotiable and tradeable among Islamic banks. Based on the financial position of the fund, the IDB is responsible for announcing prices of certificates periodically. The net profit would be shared by the IDB (5 per cent) whereas 5 per cent would be held for supporting the official investment of the Portfolio and 90 per cent would be disbursed among the certificate holders in proportion to their shares. By the end of 1987, nine short-term trade financing operations covering 16 to 18 months and one leasing operation had been approved under the arrangement. This totalled US$23.5 million.

The Bank is also making active efforts to assist the development of new instruments of resource mobilisation. In this connection, it has provided financing for a comprehensive feasibility study on the subject of Muqaradah bonds. Muqaradah bonds resemble other conventional bonds with respect to the mode of issue, determination of value, name of beneficiary and their marketability. At the same time, they do not provide a fixed return to their holders in the form of interest but depend on the profits accruing to the project. They are limited fixed value documents and are issued against funds provided to the sponsors of a particular project. The project intended to be financed by means of Muqaradah bonds must be economically feasible, independent from other projects and must be managed as a separate unit so that at the end of the financial year profits can be earmarked for the redemption of bonds and for distribution among the bond holders.

The real emphasis and effort in the future has to be in the direction of devising and developing such instruments and methods as can enable the IDB to mobilise resources other than share capital. This should not be impossible having regard to the fact that the projects and enterprises and the various activities which the Bank finances are expected to be profitable and productive, yielding a good return. It is a question of managing the operations of the Bank in such a way that the Bank remains in a strong and sound financial position and is able to obtain a return which it can share with the providers of resources. It is understandable that a great deal depends on the confidence that the investors have in the Bank, but over a period of time the Bank has to project a certain image of financial strength and soundness which can generate sufficient confidence, inducing providers of capital to entrust their funds to it without endangering their safety and at the same time earning a reasonable return. True that in the beginning, it will not be possible for the Bank to offer competitive returns to the providers of resources compared to those they can obtain from the market by means of fixed investments. However, realising that there is a great moral satisfaction attached to providing resources for the IDB and faced with the alternative that they may be forced to provide further doses of capital to the Bank, which would not earn them any return, governments may be induced to place deposits with the Bank which will earn some return though it may not be as high as the interest earnings from foreign banks. The real effort should be to develop confidence and to devise a mobilisation instrument which would conform with the dictates of Shariah.

It cannot be over-emphasised that instead of adopting a global or overall approach to the problem of resource mobilisation, the Bank should follow a disaggregative approach. What is suggested is that it should take each type of operation separately and devise a different technique of resource mobilisation in each case. This may be illustrated with reference to the fact that broadly speaking the operations of the Bank fall into two distinct categories, namely, those which yield a high rate of financial return and those which do not. Leasing clearly falls in the first category whereas loans belong to the second category. Again, it would be proper to divide the operations from the standpoint of the term for which they are undertaken. Loans constitute long-term operations, leasing medium-term and foreign trade financing short-term operations. Techniques of resource mobilisation would have to be developed taking into account the characteristics of each type of operation. For operations with a high return, recourse can be had to the market whereas in the case of operations which are unremunerative, the Bank will have to resort to the establishment of special funds through contributions from the member countries and allocations from its own income. Indirectly, the ease or difficulty in mobilising resources would tend largely to determine the size and relative share of the different modes of financing and types of operations.

The IDB should also explore possibilities which might exist at the level of governments and institutional investors in the Muslim countries. Having regard to the fact that some of the international financial institutions have been able to mobilise enormous resources from some of the member countries with surplus capital, it would be worthwhile for it also to try to tap this source. While with the recent developments in the oil market, the situation has changed, it would be unwise altogether to discount such possibilities of resource mobilisation.

The idea of linking resource mobilisation to specific projects seems to be a highly promising one and could well be organised in the way that a central bank floats a tender for loans among banks and individuals who wish to invest their money. The problem of guarantees should not be too difficult in view of the belief that investments can be guaranteed provided the guarantor is not the institution directly receiving the funds but another agency like the central bank.

It is significant that the IDB has not been able even to realise the targets for financing proposed in the Jaroudi Report. Even taking the low growth target, the shortfall is very substantial. Furthermore, the growth in the IDB's operations in the first ten years compares unfavourably with that achieved by other international development banks in their initial years. The situation becomes all the more unpalatable when account is taken of the price level and the rate of inflation. All this clearly points to the fact that instead of being resigned to a 15 per cent acceleration annually in its operational performance in money terms, the Bank should attain a much higher cruising level. That this would require a massive effort of resource mobilisation can hardly be denied. For this purpose, the IDB must become better known in the market place and use its large seed capital as a base for developing a leverage and for mobilising resources from outside. Besides achieving a sizeable increase in its total resources, the Bank must strive hard to diversify its mobilisation devices. That after a decade of establishment over 95 per cent of its ordinary resources have come from capital increases clearly underlines this challenge.

Of late, the Bank has intensified its efforts at resource mobilisation.* In this connection, it is working towards the establishment of an Islamic fund to be known as the IDB Unit Trust. This is designed to help it gain experience in listing, introducing and marketing conventional instruments and in developing a secondary market. It will be an open-end mutual fund and will also be used to disinvest from the Bank's portfolio some mature profitable investments

* Eleventh Annual Report (1985–1986).

in equity and also some of the ship leasing investments. Shares will be offered to individual and institutional investors. The IDB would be the trustee and manager for the Unit Trust and the Board of Executive Directors would serve as the governing body. The purpose is to pool the savings of the investors and channel them to viable projects which attain a reasonable profit level. The sources of the funds for the Unit Trust will be the certificates issued in various denominations which will be negotiable and transferable.

The role of the Unit Trust as a means of mobilising resources for the Bank appears to be rather limited for a number of reasons. In the first place the limited availability of equity holding by the Bank which is yielding an attractive return would be a clear constraint. Secondly, if the Bank's intention is to disinvest its equity holdings which have become profit yielding after a long waiting period thereby denying itself the income, the alternative possibility of disinvestment at the national level is always available. Thirdly, if the Bank expects to use the funds mobilised through the Investment Trust for future equity financing operations, such an expectation may not materialise in the background of the past unhappy record of equity investment activity by the Bank. Finally, the open-ended Unit Trust will, by its nature, be subject to the threat of withdrawal of resources by the investors, thereby failing to provide a durable or stable resource base for the Bank.

This would, in turn, render it impossible for the resources covered through the Investment Trust to be invested in long-term and illiquid assets such as shares, leasing or instalment sale operations.

The establishment of an open-end unit trust for the mobilisation of resources is indeed a somewhat unusual and novel step. Unit trusts are used primarily to assist small investors, who are uninitiated in the complexities of share markets, in channelling their savings to profitable investments. As a matter of fact, it needs consideration whether it would not have been more productive and simpler to try to mobilise resources from the market within the framework of the investment deposit scheme by adopting a disaggregative approach taking each type of operation separately and seeking deposits for it bearing in mind the basic features and conditions or, alternatively, issue certificates revolving around these operations. As far as the durability of the resources is concerned, it could be achieved by making the deposit receipts or certificates negotiable and interchangeable so that a secondary market is created and the Bank is not required to cash them.

Following the basic Islamic principle of profit sharing, resources for the Bank may be mobilised through certificates or deposits revolving around the remuneration activities of the Bank. In view of the fact that loans are made on the basis of a service fee only designed to cover the administrative costs and that the equity financing undertaken by the Bank has not proved to be profit yielding, resources for these two types of activity will have to be raised through the injection of fresh capital, retaining earnings or the establishment of special funds.

The two modes of financing which are clearly marked out for resource mobilisation on a profit sharing basis through the acceptance of deposits or the issuing of investment certificates are foreign trade financing and leasing. Funds from instalment sales operations are released to be employed for operations which at present do not yield a profit.

Another way of easing the pressure on the Bank's resources is the introduction of back to back leasing arrangements whereby instead of purchasing plant or machinery for leasing, the Bank could itself lease them on a back to back basis.

It is time that the IDB considered a flotation of Mudarabah Certificates to attract funds for its operations. Based on the realisation that Islamic Shariah permits in principle the issuing and exchange of certificates, two types of certificate may be proposed: (1) investment certificates linked to a specific project or a group of projects; and (2) general certificates for raising funds to be used by the Bank in any area deemed appropriate. The development of a secondary market for these certificates will add to the durability and permanence of this mobilisation instrument.

One idea which could be mooted for consideration by the member countries in order to strengthen the resource position of the IDB is that they hold a percentage of their foreign exchange reserves in special profit sharing certificates to be issued by the IDB. Similarly, the Bank could explore the possibility of absorbing and diverting to itself some of the funds which are currently being made available by the capital rich member countries on a bilateral basis.

There can be little doubt that resource mobilisation is the key issue facing the Bank in the coming years. It is one which calls for concerted efforts by the IDB to raise additional resources from the financial markets by leveraging its present capital base. It has to have the outlook of a bank rather than a fund. The development of both a primary and a secondary market is essential for the efficient mobilisation of financial resources. While the existence of a primary market is needed for providing financial resources to those who can employ them productively, the existence of a secondary market is essential to help savers and investors liquify their investments whenever they feel the need to do so. One vital requirement for effective resource mobilisation seems to be to enlarge such activities of the Bank as yield a revenue. This would include equity financing, leasing, instalment sale and profit sharing operations. In the interest of a successful mobilisation of resources, it is also crucially important to resolve the problem of overdues.

In addressing itself to the task of resource mobilisation the IDB would do well to bear in mind that there is such a thing as a global or overall availability of resources. This underlines the need for adopting a cautious approach as far as the mobilisation effect of various purposes is concerned. In other words, resources raised for one purpose may reduce the scope for mobilising resources for another purpose which may be more crucial and important.

Chapter 20

Placement of Surplus Funds

Conventionally, the placement function is not mentioned explicitly in the Articles of Agreement spelling out the functions of the various international development banks. This is for the reason that a distinction is made between the original or primary functions of the bank and a consequential or secondary operation such as placement of surplus funds. However, in the case of the Islamic Development Bank, it was necessary to include the placement of funds in the list of the Bank's functions. This was for an important reason. The reason was that since the Bank was required to operate on the basis of Islamic principles and since it was precluded from receiving interest, in the absence of an explicit reference, those responsible for running the Bank could have interpreted the Charter as requiring them not to invest the funds which were not needed in operations. In order to avoid such a misunderstanding, it was decided to put the placement operation alongside the main functions which the Bank was expected to perform. At the same time, on account of the constraint relating to interest, the management of the Bank was given flexibility by providing that the placement of funds not needed in operations could be made "suitably". As a matter of fact, it is this flexibility which constitutes the challenge of finding new ways of placing the Bank's surplus funds.

One of the first problems which the IDB faced on its establishment related to the placement of its surplus funds. While under Article 6(4) of the

Agreement, the Saudi Arabian Monetary Agency had been nominated as the trustee and depository for the IDB, it required clear directions from the Bank as to the modes of placement to be followed. The Bank realised that it would be faced with large surplus funds, as on the demand side there were several factors militating against a rapid utilisation of its resources, such as the lack of organisational strength and the absence of a suitable pipeline of projects. Moreover, on the supply side, the members were committed to the payment of their subscriptions at regular intervals which would add to the Bank's liquid resources regardless of the tempo of utilisation. At the same time, the costs of operation for the IDB were likely to be high for several reasons. For one thing, the IDB did not have access to a rather inexpensive manpower as is the case with institutions like the Asian Development Bank. In fact, there was an acute labour shortage locally, requiring the Bank to tap alternative sources which had the effect of raising the costs. Again, the Bank had to spend large sums on the construction and renovation of the physical facilities. It had to furnish and renovate its temporary headquarters. It had to put up additional accommodation both by way of office space for its staff through the construction of an annexe building and also residential accommodation comprising a complex building as housing for the professional staff. Moreover, the bill for the services of professional staff was going to be high in the case of the IDB for several reasons. In order to cut down the gestation period and in the interest of making an early start, the Bank was on the look-out for experienced personnel who would obviously be more expensive. Moreover, the Bank had to resort to obtaining experienced staff from other international development banks on a secondment basis which was bound to add to the operational costs. Whereas the costs of operations were likely to be high, there were significant constraints operating on the income side. Investment in equity of new enterprises or financing of profit sharing schemes were likely to bring a return with a substantial lag. This meant that apart from the income which might flow from investments in on-going enterprises and projects, as far as its income in the immediate future was concerned, the Bank would be left only with the prospect of charging a service fee on the operations relating to infrastructure and social projects. All these factors, taken together, could create a serious "current income" problem for the Bank.

The foregoing factors underlined the need for the Bank to generate income from its surplus resources. As a matter of fact, as far as the objective of financial soundness, strength and viability was concerned, the IDB had to set its sights rather high. It was of the greatest importance to aim at a high degree of profitability. This was for the simple reason that it was unrealistic to assume that it would be possible for the Bank to augment its funds and mobilise new resources simply through a religious appeal. What seemed necessary was to obtain a high return from the Bank's resources which could be passed on to the provider of these funds. It was true that the Bank would not borrow from the capital market and that the resources that it would receive would not be entitled to interest payment. However, if the Bank was to mobilise adequate resources from its member countries on an interest-free basis, it would have to generate enough income and, after meeting its operational costs and consistent with the need for building up an adequate reserve, earmark a large portion of its income for distribution as profits to the providers of funds. The ability of the Bank to undertake concessional financing also depended directly upon its financial strength and profitability.

As the Bank lacked professional expertise, one of the Executive Directors, at the invitation of the President, undertook a study on the subject. After holding discussions in Basle, Frankfurt, Paris and London and following consultations in Cairo and Algiers, he submitted a study entitled "The Problem of the Investment of Funds not Needed in Operations" in May 1976 which was later placed before the Board of Executive Directors as a working paper. The Study* began with the statement of the problem and the identification of basic issues and considerations bearing on it. Based on the experience of other international development banks, it described the conventional ways of investing funds not needed in operations and proceeded to discuss the conditions on which the IDB was expected to function as far as the placement problem was concerned. Next an extensive survey was undertaken of the alternative investment opportunities in the field of the stock market, unit trusts, real estate, foreign trade and commodity markets and their principal features. Having completed this examination, the paper dealt with the possibilities for the placement of short-term funds at the level of member governments. It then set out the various options available to the Bank in case it could not discover and devise a method of placement of funds which, apart from providing safety, liquidity and a reasonable return, would truly satisfy the requirements of Shariah. The study was based on two cardinal convictions: first, that Islam prohibits interest in all its forms and ramifications and that the prohibition against interest was total, and rejects the view that the prohibition did not apply to the taking of interest from non-Muslims. In fact, this seemed to be a derivation from the Jews who are required by their religion not to take interest on financial dealings amongst themselves and overcome the difficulty simply by setting up an intermediary. The second conviction on which the study was based was that the IDB had to resist the temptation of overcoming its problems in conforming to Shariah by means of camouflage. Perhaps the greatest disservice which could be done was to create an impression that a mere change of terminology represented a complete solution to the problem. Camouflage of this kind, by disposing of the problem, took away the incentive and closed the door for further effort by way of scientific enquiry and practical experimentation for finding a genuine and really adequate solution to the problem.

* The Problem of the Investment of Funds not Needed in Operations by Dr. S. A. Meenai, Executive Director (May, 1976).

Before proceeding to determine the suitability of the available financial instruments for investment, the Study argued that the two crucial conditions to be satisfied were:

(i) the return on placement of funds should not be pre-determined or fixed in advance; and
(ii) the return instead of being derived from an interest rate or price of capital should be based on the return accruing from the actual utilisation of the funds. In other words, the return had to be related directly to efficiency of performance.

Besides the dual criteria emanating from Shariah set out above, three other attributes were to be sought, namely, safety, liquidity and adequate return. Attention had also to be directed to two important factors, namely: (1) the tax aspect; (2) the institutional effort that would be required by way of the in-house expertise for making the placements. The Study then proceeded to apply the conditions set out above to the various financial instruments available for the placement of funds so as to determine their suitability for the IDB. As observed earlier, there were two main categories of financial instrument which the international development banks used for the purpose of investing funds not required in operations: first, gilt-edged securities, and second, time-deposits and deposit certificates. As regards the gilt-edged market, it could again be broken into two parts: (i) fixed interest stocks; (ii) gilt-edged securities such as treasury bills issued at a discount on their face value. As for fixed interest stocks, interest was writ large on them. Of the gilt-edged securities, which were issued at a discount and appreciated in value, attaining their face value after a specified period, the treasury bill was a good example. While interest was not explicitly written on the instrument, it was evident that the value of these instruments was governed by interest. Interest also figured directly in the case of time deposits and deposit certificates.

Turning to the other avenues of investment, such as the stock market, the risk element was known to be high. In many cases the return on shares or dividend income was more than off set by the capital loss suffered through a lower price. In other words, the criterion of safety was not satisfied in the case of the share market. As for liquidity, while technically shares could be disposed of at any time, the important point was that at the time when the sales might be undertaken, the share values might be low, causing heavy capital losses to the institution. As a matter of fact, investments in stocks were not considered to be advisable for the short term. Barring speculative developments, the possibility of earning a high return, as also of making capital gains in the share market, was distinctly limited in the short run. There were better ways of earning profit as also capital gains in the long run. However, the problem of placement of funds not needed in operations was basically a short-term problem and an institution could be exposed to the risk of serious losses in case recourse was taken to placement in the stock and share market. An institution which decided to go into the stock market had to be prepared to operate for longer periods. As for going into defensive shares, such as utilities which did not fluctuate in value very much, the possibility of large capital gains was rather limited. As for placements through investment trusts, though they had the advantage of operating on a more diversified and specialised basis, basically they were subject to the same risks and problems which characterised stock market investment. Real estate was also unsuitable for short-term investments. The liquidity element was conspicuous by its absence in the case of real estate investment. Then there was the question of administering property which covered such items as the collection of rent, repairs, insurance, watching the dates of rent reviews and the payment of ground rent. To the initial cost of the property one had to add the surveyor's fees together with the solicitor's fees and outlays including stamp duty. Rent review possibilities and tax rates had a direct bearing on both the return and the value of the property. Another possibility of unconventional placement related to the commodity markets. Broadly speaking, there were two types of investment operation in the commodity markets: (1) purchase and sale of commodities with a view to making a profit from the price differential; and (2) transactions involving purchases at the spot rate and contracts to sell forward on a stipulated date. The first type of transaction was purely speculative in character and could well turn into a gambling game as price fluctuations in the world commodity markets were known to be large. As for the second type, it partook of the character of credit extension. The operation means that one set of people extend credit to the others who needed the commodities later and the return on such investments was the function of the three months treasury bill rate.

Having reached the conclusion that conventional modes of placement had to be ruled out, the Study argued that a systematic effort should be made to find new modes of placement in co-operation with the member governments. Any financial transaction involved at least two sides, namely, an investor and a recipient. It was obvious that the IDB could not resort to new methods of investment unless those methods were accepted by the potential recipients. Tangible possibilities of placement might exist in member countries which needed foreign exchange and resorted to short-term borrowing in the international money markets. Member governments could utilise the short-term foreign exchange resources from the IDB productively and provide a return to the Bank. The governments with whom the surplus funds would be placed could utilise them in foreign trade or for maximising industrial output through balancing and modernisation. The main requirement would be to work out a technique for relating the return to the use of funds or, so to speak, the performance of the users and above all to weigh the foreign exchange risk involved by evaluating the credit-worthiness of the member countries. Another possibility for short-term placement of funds at the national level seemed to stem from the fluctuations which characterised the export markets of some member countries. What was necessary was to explore the possibility of placing some short-term funds at the disposal of such member countries as faced depressed and unfavourable market conditions in the short run for their exports. The placement of funds by the IDB could have the effect of enhancing the holding capacity of the member countries enabling them to sell at a higher price eventually. The difference between the price at which they would have been obliged to sell, if the funds from the Bank had not been made available, and the price at which they finally disposed of their exports could be shared between the Bank and the member country. Similarly, it may be useful to explore the possibility of short-term placements based on the import of certain identifiable inputs for a short term, thus enabling members to make an economic gain which they should share with the IDB. The reaction of the Egyptian authorities was very warm to this proposal. In fact, the Minister of Economy declared that he was prepared to approve of the arrangements forthwith. However, it was pointed out that the matter needed to be studied and examined in the light of the prevailing economic situation in the country and in the framework of its policies and development priorities. It was, therefore, proposed that the idea be examined in detail and the reaction of the Egyptian authorities be set out in a paper indicating the size of the funds they wished to be placed with them, the period of such placement, the uses to which the funds would be put, the manner in which the return on the use of these funds would be determined and the institutional arrangements required to be made for supervising this operation. The idea was pursued further in Algeria, where it was found that, as a matter of policy, the government did not favour the participation of foreign capital and ownership, presumably as a result of the foreign domination of past years. It was pointed out that obviously a distinction had to be made between foreign capital as such and the funds which would be made available by the IDB of which the Algerian Democratic and Popular Republic was a member. Long discussions were held with the Finance Minister and also with the Governor of the Central Bank. The Finance Minister expressed sympathy for the idea and promised to have the matter examined in the light of their own policy and priorities and send the final reaction to the Bank.

The Study proposed action in two main directions. The first step was to take such action as would have the effect of reducing the size of the surplus funds, thereby making the problem of surplus funds more manageable. In this connection, the most important step was to intensify efforts to commence operations at the earliest. This in turn called for action in three directions. First, the administrative and technical machinery had to be built up as expeditiously as possible and then be set in motion as speedily as possible. For this purpose, (i) the work of recruitment of professional staff had to be speeded up, (ii) adequate professional assistance had to be obtained from other institutions, both international and national, on a secondment basis for giving an immediate push to the Bank's operations and later to train and guide the newly recruited staff. Secondly, it was suggested that immediate contact be established with other institutions inviting them to send specific proposals for co-financing arrangements and work started on them immediately. Thirdly, it was proposed that member countries be invited to send specific proposals and, in particular, the national development banks be approached to suggest specific possibilities of equity participation in on-going enterprises for expansion and modernisation so as to enable the IDB to market its resources and generate income in the short run. All these steps were expected to have the effect of reducing the size of the surplus and generating the income needed to meet the Bank's operational expenses.

The second direction in which action was called for was Ijtehad and evolution of new methods and financial instruments for the investment of the Bank's funds not needed in its operations which, while providing safety, liquidity and return to the Bank, would also conform to Shariah. For this purpose, priority should be given to seeking placement opportunities at the national level, that is with member governments. It could not be overemphasised that success would depend on enlisting their co-operation. It was unrealistic to expect this kind of co-operation from non-member governments and foreign institutions. It was only through co-operation with member governments that the IDB, which had been charged with the responsibility of conducting its operations in accordance with Shariah, could carry out its mandate in letter and spirit.

On the basis of the Study, the Board of Executive Directors held long discussions on the subject and at its seventh meeting in July 1976, took the following decisions:

(1) The Bank may continue to follow through SAMA the practice of placing its funds with foreign banks for the time being.
(2) A Special Account be opened to which revenues accruing from the above placements be credited until the Board of Governors' directives be obtained.
(3) A committee of five Executive Directors, chaired by the President, be entrusted with the task of preparing a study on modes of investing such funds for short and long terms which would meet the requirements of Shariah and combine the basic criteria of safety, liquidity and adequate return.
(4) The Bank should accelerate its operations and financing of viable projects.

The effort led to two main developments. In the first place, in line with the approach suggested in the study that a solution to the placement problem should be sought at the national level, a foreign trade financing operation was devised under which the IDB used some of its surplus funds for short-term financing of imports of developmental inputs required by member countries. In course of time, this operation has become by far the largest operation of the Bank and more than twice the size of its annual project financing. Secondly, a Special Fund came into being to which all interest earnings accruing on conventional placements with banks have been credited. As for the utilisation of the interest proceeds constituting the Special Fund, the Bank sought guidance from Islamic Ulema more than once. Some of them took the position that they would not be prepared to offer any suggestion in this regard until and unless the IDB gave up the practice of placing its surplus funds on interest altogether. Their line of reasoning was that any solution suggested by them would have the effect of perpetuating this practice directly involving interest. Others opined that the Special Fund could be used for financing Islamic causes other than those set out in the Bank's Articles of Agreement.

Subsequently, the Board of Governors passed a resolution that every year half of the interest earnings should be utilised to establish a Special Reserve as cover for exchange fluctuations and the other half be used for setting up a Special Assistance Account. The IDB has continued to follow this practice. At the same time, in order to systematise its placement of funds with banks, the IDB devised a set of guidelines for the purpose, emphasising the need for safety, liquidity and adequate return and stating that considerations of wide geographical coverage and equitable distribution of resources among member countries did not apply to these investments. The two other objectives were diversifications in terms of currencies, financial centres and countries and the need for linking the investments with the SDRs for the preservation of the value of the Bank's capital. Placements could be made in the form of deposits up to one year and current and call accounts with the leading banks having a presence in one of the major money centres with attention to their credit-worthiness and the terms which they offered. The guidelines laid down that preference would be accorded to banks in which member governments or financial institutions held equity provided the banks were sound and could offer competitive terms for placement of funds. This has led to placement with member country banks also.

The quest for finding new modes of placement which would conform to Shariah continues. In early 1984, the IDB embarked upon a new placement arrangement under which funds placed with selected banks are invested in commodity transactions through banks. Under the arrangement funds are placed with a bank in a Call Account on which it pays interest at two-day notice Call Account rates pending utilisation of funds. On utilisation of funds in commodity trading transactions under the arrangement, the Bank has the discretion to enter into commodity purchase and sale transactions at a mark-up on the basis of Morabah on condition that the return to the IDB shall not fall below one per cent of what the return could have been on the date of transaction of placement in fixed deposits of a similar time period based on rates paid by it on Euro-dollar deposits. Under the arrangements, all obligation of third parties are guaranteed by the concerned bank and the IDB does not carry any third party risks. The average profit from such commodity dealings for the year 1404H (1984) was 10 per cent while the profit from foreign trade financing operations was 8 per cent. The depositors' share of profit from foreign trade was 7.9 per cent. At the close of 1985, the total sum placed under this arrangement amounted to ID48.41 million. At the same time the placements with Islamic banks stood at ID5.10 million.

It is noteworthy that, as observed earlier, foreign trade financing, having become an integral and permanent part of the IDB's functions, cannot any longer be deemed to be a mechanism for dealing with the surplus funds not immediately required for project financing. This is for the reason that once invested in foreign trade financing, the surplus funds cannot be pulled out and diverted to project financing unless the scale of foreign trade financing be reduced.

Another possibility for placement may exist in the direction of undertaking a reverse operation of what the Bank is now doing in the field of trade financing. This could be based on the Bank acquiring ownership of the exportable surplus in a certain commodity and extending finance against it at a pre-determined price backed by an agreement that the country will undertake to export the commodity at higher prices when the market conditions improve and share the profit with the IDB. This will have two advantages. First, the country will obtain foreign exchange resources and also a holding capacity which might enable it to obtain a better price. Secondly, it will involve the Bank in buffer stock financing which is so much sought after in the context of developing countries.

The IDB should also endeavour to develop a capability for handling the placement function entirely on its own and relieve the Saudi Arabian Monetary Agency of this responsibility.

Placements by the Bank in arrangements in conformity with Shariah, namely instruments which are not interest bearing, and earning income on the basis of actual results stood at ID223.33 million or 18.14 per cent of total deposits at the end of 1407H (1987). It may be noted that such placements have more than trebled since 1406H (1986). It is expected that by the end of 1988 almost the entire liquid funds would have been placed in accordance with Shariah. At the same time, over 30 per cent of the total liquid funds were placed with banks wholly owned by member countries or in which member countries had a controlling interest.

Chapter 21

Financial Management

The need to build the Islamic Development Bank into a financially sound and strong institution cannot be over-emphasised. Financial strength and soundness should not be misconstrued as profit-making. What is required is that the institution should have the necessary strength and soundness to command and mobilise sufficient resources for the performance of its wide-ranging functions and the discharge of its onerous responsibilities. In other words, the financial strength and viability of the Bank is not in the interest of the providers of financial resources alone. It is, without doubt, in the interest of the recipients and the net users of resources too. This is for the simple reason that if the Bank is to accomplish its complex task and render service to its member countries, it must attract and obtain adequate financial resources on a continuous basis, apart from what it has or might get as capital. The larger the resources flowing to it the larger can be its role and contribution in promoting the economic development of its member countries. Not only the size or quantum of resources that it will offer, even the cost or price at which the financing will be provided would depend directly on the financial strength of the institution. To cite an example, its ability to provide larger concessional finance on the basis of a service fee would be governed by its overall financial strength so that it can absorb all indirect costs and for its loans charge a price confined to the direct costs.

It is satisfying to note that, leaving aside the paramount need for more financial resources and an efficient mechanism for mobilising them, after 12 years of working, the IDB is in a sound financial situation. At the end of the year 1407H (October 1987), the paid up capital of the Bank stood at US$2,062.23 million. The overdues in capital subscription stood at US$356.50 million. The deposits mobilised through the Investment Deposit Scheme amounted to US$115.64 million. The interest proceeds for the year aggregated to US$64.41 million. The Special Reserve Account stood at US$421.01 million and the Special Assistance Account at US$329.49 million. The total funds placed with banks were over US$1,584.71 million of which about 35 per cent was with banks wholly owned by or with a controlling interest held by member countries. As for reserves, the Capital Reserve stood at US$21.42 million, the Special Reserve at US$454.81 million, and the General Reserve at US$159.57 million. The gross income from operations amounted to US$77.13 million and total expenses to US$20.99 million. The net profit for the year 1407H (1987) amounted to US$48.59 million. Since 1403H (1983) the Bank has made a total provision of US$59.21 million for depreciation in the value of the equity investments of the Bank.

As far as the overall financial position of the IDB is concerned, an issue of major significance is that of overdues. It appears that some of the recipients of foreign trade financing have not been able to make repayments on time. In fact, in a few cases the problem has become chronic. This is by no means surprising. In the first place, several of the member countries have a very weak balance of payments. Their import needs are inflexible while, in several cases, they are dependent upon a few exports. Secondly, by its very nature, the financing which they receive from the IDB under its foreign trade financing, is of a short-term character. It is, therefore, very difficult for them to make timely repayments. In some degree, the problem has arisen as a result of the IDB's anxiety to help all its member countries and particularly those which are the most needy without paying too much attention to their credit-worthiness. The foreign trade financing scheme is designed to serve principally as a placement mechanism, so pre-supposes a high degree of safety and liquidity. What is all the more regrettable is that the defaults and persistent overdues have, much against its wishes, forced the Bank to suspend its project financing operations in the defaulting countries.

The situation seems to call for a two-fold approach. On the one hand, adopting a case by case approach, the situation of default should be corrected. Here, the Bank would necessarily have to be flexible and try to accommodate the countries in distress by accepting relatively easy payment plans and by trying to assist the default countries in their export effort through the foreign trade financing scheme, utilising the proceeds for discharging their debt to the Bank, and, in deserving cases, by agreeing to accept local currency payment in the short run while retaining the right of repatriation when the payments position of the country concerned improves. Furthermore, sympathetic consideration may be accorded to the conversion of the short-term foreign trade financing obligations into long-term investments in the form of leasing and equity. Once the position has been regularised, project financing in these countries may be resumed. This expedient should only be used to solve an intractable payments problem and should in no case be allowed to become normal or routine practice. Secondly, what is far more important is not to offer short-term foreign trade financing facilities to countries which clearly lack the capacity to make timely repayments.

Quite apart from the difficulties which the IDB has faced in receiving repayments on account of foreign trade financing provided to some member countries, there is a recognised and obvious need for making credit-worthiness analysis an integral and essential part of the Bank's overall country economic work. In this connection, it may be relevant to invite attention to Article 16 dealing with Considerations Relevant to Financing. Article 16(1)(ii) clearly lays down that "in conducting its operations the Bank shall pay due regard to the prospect that the recipient and its guarantor, if any, will be in a position to meet their obligations under the contract." It has to be realised that credit-worthiness analysis forms a vital part of country economic and sector work. As a matter of fact, all aspects of this work have implications for debt servicing capacity. Therefore, the ideal way of approaching this task is to establish arrangements for country economic and sector work. As far as the work on credit-worthiness itself is concerned, success will depend partly on evolving a comprehensive framework for the purpose and partly on ensuring that the data used for the purpose is of the requisite quality. Among the various factors to be taken into account in examining credit-worthiness, special attention has to be directed to the following:

(1) A critical evaluation of the quality of economic management in the country.
(2) An assessment of the outlook for the country's main exports.
(3) A projection of its important requirements.
(4) An analysis of the price trends of exports and imports.
(5) Likely availability of external capital both commercial and concessional.
(6) The current and future debt service liability.
(7) The liquidity position in terms of reserves and potential borrowing capacity.
(8) An assessment of the country's ability to make adjustments to unexpected adverse movement.
(9) The position in regard to the exchange rate and over-valued exchange rate as a major factor causing debt servicing problems.

As far as data is concerned, a concerted effort must be made to obtain the most reliable information both from country sources and also from the IMF and other institutions.

If past experience and future trends are any indications, the problem of overdues and timely repayment is likely to become even more serious in the future. The payments arrangement will work smoothly as long as the financing made available to member countries goes on increasing constantly. The real test will come when, as a result of the rapidly increasing needs of project financing, the IDB may decide to divert some of its resources presently in foreign trade financing away from it. Recipients would then find repayments difficult when faced with the prospect of having to repay more than they receive under the foreign trade financing facility.

As far as accounting, budgeting and auditing are concerned, some suggestions can be made. For instance, it may be useful, like other institutions, to establish a joint Audit Committee at the level of the Executive Directors with the following terms of reference:

(1) To consider the selection of a firm of auditors to conduct the audit of the books of the Bank.
(2) To discuss with the auditors the scope of their examination.
(3) To review the statements and auditors' opinion with the auditors after the audit has been completed.
(4) To invite the auditors' recommendation regarding internal financing controls and other matters.
(5) To satisfy itself that the Bank's internal audit and operations evaluations are efficient and adequate.
(6) To report to the Board of Executive Directors on its discussion with the auditors and on the results of its review on the internal audit and operations evaluations and to submit such conclusions and recommendations as the committee deems appropriate.

Secondly, in framing the administrative budget, it might be a good idea to give the central place to the operational programme of the Bank for the year. Thirdly, the need for developing proper systems and procedures for accounting and financial control for the Bank cannot be over-emphasised. This is a matter which requires early attention to ensure that the Bank has a fool-proof system of financial control. If systems and procedures are allowed to sprout without proper planning, it will cause a great deal of trouble later.

Apart from appointing a firm of auditors with an international reputation, the IDB must operate on the basis of a comprehensive set of financial projections relating to capital inflows, deposits, repayments of principal amounts and income receipts. The projections may include information on commitments and also an estimation of disbursements during a financial year. This will be necessary in order to give an idea of the liquidity or cash position of the Bank at the end of the year. Another major factor would relate to the reverse flow of principal and return on investment. Here the different implications of different types of operation would have to be borne in mind. Equity participation, profit sharing and infrastructure financing would have different implications viewed in the context of the reverse flow of principal and also the return. In the case of equity, the investment will remain absorbed until repatriated and the return in the form of dividend income would start flowing back after the gestation period. In the case of profit sharing the principal investment will be recouped in accordance with the repayment schedule and the return, as in the case of equity, will begin to be received after the enterprise starts making profits. In the case of social and physical infrastructure financing, the return would only be the service fee accruing to the Bank from the day of commitment of funds and the principal amount would be received back according to the amortisation terms. In any case, it would be necessary for the Bank to work out the income and cash flows on different assumptions. This will enable it to strike a balance and achieve a compromise in regard to the conflicting objectives of high profitability and concessionary financing of the social and physical infrastructural development. On the one hand, the financial capacity of the Bank to provide concessionary financing would grow as its non-concessionary operations bring in income after the end of the gestation period. On the other hand, it would be clearly wrong to be guided solely by motives of profitability and high financial return and to neglect or starve the financing of social and physical infrastructure schemes on this account.

Finally, in evaluating the performance of the IDB in respect of financial management, it is necessary to bear in mind that it has been the recipient of nearly US$2 billion as capital. These are resources which were entirely without cost. This is indeed a highly privileged situation for the IDB compared to other institutions which have to raise the major portion of their resources from the market by incurring a substantial cost for themselves.

Chapter 22

Organisational Problems and Improvements

It may be appropriate to begin with a word about the Board of Governors in which all the powers of the Bank are vested. In practice, however, most of the powers have been delegated to the Board of Executive Directors. The Board of Governors has retained only a few of the powers concerning matters such as the admission of new members, increasing or decreasing the capital of the Bank, election of the President and Executive Directors, approval of the balance sheet of the Bank and the amendment of the Agreement establishing the Bank. They meet once a year. In addition to this annual meeting, there are three other channels available to them for maintaining contact with the affairs of the Bank. These are the Executive Directors who represent them in the Bank, the visits which the President and other officials make to the member countries and also the occasional meetings which Governors hold with the management of the Bank when they are sometimes in Jeddah.

Considering the fact that the success of the Islamic Development Bank depends very greatly on the direction, guidance and support it receives from its member governments, it is very important to strengthen and vitalise the contact with the Governors. In this context, it should be ensured that the Executive Directors maintain the closest possible relationship with the governments they represent. This is by no means easy when the Executive Directors are non-resident and part-time, and presents a contrast to other institutions where the executive directors reside at the headquarters, so allowing them to maintain a constant watch over and contract with the affairs of the institution. Several of the Bank's Executive Directors represent an entire group of countries though they belong to only one of them. The general tendency isfor executive directors of international institutions to be preoccupied with matters which directly concern their constituents rather than taking an overall view. Apart from the Executive Directors, the senior management of the Bank should undertake briefing missions to the member countries from time to time and hold discussions with the Governors and other authorities which, far from being confined to bilateral matters such as financing for the country, must embrace policy issues, progress achieved by the Bank and problems and difficulties faced by it. The management of the Bank during these visits should hold a wide ranging dialogue with the authorities so as to inform them of the policies of the Bank and seek the reactions and directions of the Governors so as to help the Bank in policy making.

The objective should be to heighten the sense of accountability and to promote a feeling that the Bank is under constant surveillance and critical scrutiny. The annual meeting of the Bank, for example, should be devoted to a close and critical review of the institution's working, instead of showering polite praise and expressing general satisfaction. The occasion should be used for a candid and critical examination of the Bank's performance not so much from a national standpoint as in relation to the overall objectives and task assigned to it. If it is felt that a discussion of this kind in public or in an open meeting would not be in order, it might be useful to structure for this purpose a separate committee composed of Governors. This Committee of Governors should serve as a special forum for a critical evaluation of the Bank's performance and working every year and for a detailed discussion of sensitive issues. This special forum should consist of a group of Governors formed on the same basis as the Board of Executive Directors. In other words, the Governors of the same nationalities as comprise the Board of Executive Directors, should constitute the Committee of Governors. This group may meet in camera at the same time as the annual meeting is held.

This leads us to the Board of Executive Directors. In this regard, it may be appropriate to recall that the need for and the role of the Board of Executive Directors engaged a great deal of attention before the formulation of the Articles of Agreement establishing the IDB. After taking into consideration the various factors, it was proposed in the draft, which was placed before the Preparatory Committee Meeting in Jeddah in May 1974 that the Board of Executive Directors should consist of ten full-time members resident in Jeddah and that on the pattern of other international development banks, they should also have their alternates. When the draft was discussed and examined by the Preparatory Committee, it was decided that the Board of Executive Directors should be composed of ten full-time members resident in Jeddah but the idea of having Alternate Executive Directors be dropped in the interest of economy. It was realised at that time that the absence of Alternates could create some serious problems as the Executive Directors could obviously not be expected to be present at the headquarters continuously and throughout the year. Apart from annual leave and visits to their constituencies, they had to leave Jeddah on other official work. Furthermore, it was not possible to rule out situations such as illness, which might prevent an Executive Director from attending a Board meeting. Therefore, while no provision was made for Alternate Executive Directors, a clause was inserted in the Bye-Laws of the Bank, Section 6(a)(iii) to the effect that "when an Executive Director is unable to attend to the business of the Bank, he may designate a fellow Executive Director to represent him on the Board in his absence." Thus, the Articles of Agreement establishing the Bank clearly defined the role and requirements in regard to the Executive Directors. The Executive Directors who were made responsible for the direction of the general operations of the Bank and for the on the spot exercise of all the powers delegated to them by the Board of Governors, were required under Article 33 to function at the principal office of the Bank and to meet as often as the business of the Bank required. The Bye-Laws of the Bank reiterated that "each Executive Director shall devote to the activities of the Bank such time and attention as the interest of the institution requires and shall normally be available continuously at the Bank's principal office." The matter also came up for detailed and specific discussion at the Inaugural Meeting of the Board of Governors in 1975 and after debating and considering various issues, the Board of Governors unanimously decided that the Executive Directors should be resident in Jeddah and work in the Bank full-time. Thus, a final seal of approval was affixed on the arrangement.

In terms of the Articles of Agreement, the Board of Governors at its Inaugural Meeting elected six Executive Directors, while four Executive Directors were chosen by the four highest subscribing member countries. Of the six elected Executive Directors, five moved to Jeddah in order to take up residence. The sixth Executive Director, being his country's Ambassador to the Kingdom, was already living in Jeddah. The Executive Director nominated by Saudi Arabia, being an official of the Saudi Arabian Monetary Agency, was present in Jeddah too. However, the three Executive Directors nominated by Libya, the United Arab Emirates and Kuwait could not take up residence as required by the Articles and came to Jeddah to attend meetings of the Board whenever they were held. Subsequently, at the second annual meeting of the Board of Governors held in March 1978 in Kuala Lumpur, a special committee was appointed to study and submit recommendations on the reorganisation of the Board of Executive Directors, which met in Jeddah in August of the same year and recommended that the Board should be made non-resident and part-time. This recommendation was circulated to the Governors and was duly approved and the Board of Executive Directors has functioned on this basis ever since.

It may be worthwhile to review the matter in the light of the experience gained in the past ten years and the present stage of the Bank's development and the role it is expected to play in future. Other international financial institutions have full-time resident boards and perhaps for reasons which apply to the IDB with equal force. Even leaving aside general practice and precedents, the Executive Directors by virtue of the fact that they have to direct the operations of the Bank and keep a constant watch on its working on behalf of their Governors, have necessarily to be present continuously at the Headquarters. They are expected to keep their Governments fully informed about developments as they take place, which task they can perform only when they are in constant contact with the Bank and are present at the Headquarters. The presence of all the Executive Directors in Jeddah on a full-time basis could ensure more frequent and regular meetings with full attendance of Executive Directors and unhurried and relaxed decision making by the Board. The main idea is that as the Governments or Governors cannot be present, through appointment of resident Executive Directors they are enabled to exercise the necessary supervision and to influence and guide the Bank in its work. The Executive Directors also facilitate the operations of the Bank by conveying its thinking to their Governments and vice versa. There is a great deal for the Executive Directors to do and whether their job is a sinecure or arduous depends entirely on them. When they are not engaged in meetings and discussions, they have to study and contribute to making the operations of the Bank successful and to improving their own capacity to deal with the technical issues. By their continuous presence at the Headquarters, the Executive Directors can also serve as the main prop for the management of the Bank who can get the necessary support and guidance from them on a continuous basis.

It may be pointed out that the task of the IDB is perhaps more complex by virtue of the fact that the Bank has to operate on the basis of Shariah and that it needs no emphasis that the Executive Directors, if they are to do justice to their important task, should devote their entire attention to it in an uninterrupted manner and improve their ability to undertake it through extensive study and deliberations. It would be unrealistic to expect that what other international financial institutions try to achieve through a resident board of executive directors with a team of alternates, advisers and technical assistants, functioning on a full-time basis, it is possible for the IDB to accomplish through non-resident part-time Executive Directors. That making the Board of Executive Directors resident and full-time would involve a financial cost is undoubtedly true but, at their level, what is required is to exercise the maximum possible economy in the fixing of emoluments and benefits in the Bank by resisting the temptation of making them comparable with the levels obtaining in sister institutions and by practising the Islamic precepts of sacrifice in the service of the Ummah rather than by giving up or dispensing with something which is deemed to be in the interest of the Bank.

With almost ten years of working experience behind it, and recognising the task which lies ahead, it is vitally important for the Bank to consider as to what is required to be done in the field of organisation and administration with a view to improving the Bank's performance in the future. The task assigned to the Bank is so formidable and extensive as to call for assembling and preserving as much administrative and professional expertise and acumen as possible. There are many tasks which the Bank has yet to undertake calling for top-level talent for planning, executing, co-ordinating and supervising the efforts in each field. The style of management and the organisational structure should be such as to leave sufficient time at the top for larger issues of policy making, planning, high-level contacts, mobilising support from the governments and Board of Executive Directors for the right decisions, projecting the image of the Bank and providing overall direction to it in the years to come. The process of decentralisation should not remain confined to the management level alone but should embrace the entire organisational structure of the Bank.

The task of decision making has to be shared as widely as possible instead of remaining concentrated at any one point. It is necessary to establish a system whereby decisions of different types and varying degrees of importance are made at various levels. It is clearly not conducive to efficiency to concentrate decision making at one point in the organisation while other functionaries merely provide the input or act in an advisory capacity. If the task of decision making is distributed, it will not only lead to elimination of delays but would result in a marked improvement in the quality of the decisions themselves. The object of decentralisation should be to organise the Bank's work in such a way as to achieve maximum efficiency. This could be done by looking at its own situation as also the situation prevailing in other international financial institutions. There is need for defining in more precise terms the role of the various organs of the Bank and for determining what functions should and should not be performed at a particular level so that requisite capacity is created for carrying out those functions at lower levels. In order to have an effective system of decision making, clear cut functions with adequate authority need to be specified and it should be ensured that those given the authority have the capacity to carry them out properly. A particular job which could be carried out at a lower level should not be undertaken at higher levels in the Bank. Decentralisation of the Bank's work and the delegation of authority and responsibility presupposes the availability of sufficient guidance to those making the decisions. For this purpose, the Bank must step up its efforts to prepare comprehensive instructions, manuals, rules and regulations and guidelines so as to serve as a framework for decision making at various levels.

In a new institution which lacks adequate expertise and experience, there is generally a tendency to have frequent recourse to decision making through the establishment of committees. That there are obvious advantages in having matters discussed and resolved through exchange of views among the relevant officials cannot be denied. However, too frequent a resort to committees leads to a dilution of individual responsibility. Many a time, greater care is exercised if one has to take a specific decision rather than if one expresses a view which then gets mingled with the consensus reached by a group of people. A minor difficulty about committees is that they cannot be invested with powers of final decision making. The result, therefore, is that the real process of decision making actually starts after the committee comes up with some proposals and the time lag involved is often long.

There is active need to strengthen supervision in the Bank at all levels. Without this, it is not possible to utilise the organisational strength fully. There is also urgent need to introduce a degree of planning. This can be achieved not so much through the establishment of planning sections or manuals, but by means of developing an attitude of mind at all levels that activities have to be consciously planned. Not only the various departments but divisions, sections and even individual officers should have a plan of action and an effort has to be made from time to time to determine as to how far the targets are met and intentions and plans duly realised.

One of the basic problems confronting the IDB has been in the field of recruitment. The Bank must devise an effective machinery for recruiting the personnel it needs. In this connection, much closer liaison has to be established between the Bank and the member Governments and institutions by inviting them to bring to the notice of their employees the job opportunities and personnel requirements of the Bank. The Bank has to adopt a more active approach to employing staff by using probationary arrangements, which would enable it to try out a large number of people and then absorb only those who measure up to the requirement. While following the system of recruitment on geographical representation, care should be taken that it does not affect the quality of the staff and efficiency of the Bank and recourse may be had to recruit staff for fixed terms until such time as a substitute from the desired geographical area becomes available. It is also necessary to bear in mind the disparity existing in the manpower markets in the member countries and it should be possible to try to safeguard the interests of the institution and to make up for the inexperience in certain markets by the experience and expertise available in certain other manpower markets in member countries.

The importance of training in any organisation or institution is self-evident. It is particularly important for an institution like the IDB which is in the process of establishing itself and which has several special features. It may be recognised at the outset that there is a two-way relationship between the organisational strength of an institution and training. On the one hand, the institution can increase and expand its organisational strength by availing itself of training facilities and opportunities on an extensive scale and, on the other, it is only possible to avail itself actively of training facilities if the institution has the necessary staff strength, a part of which it can spare for training. This seems to indicate action in two directions. In the first place, the Bank should consciously build up what may be called a training reserve. This will enable it to use the training facilities and opportunities. Secondly, it should seek to meet its staff needs through recruitment of personnel who have the potential but who can only be put in actual jobs after a spell of training. The training needs of the Bank have to be appraised and determined carefully. This exercise has to be followed by an effort to identify the source or the means by which these needs can be met. As regards the types of training, there may be several, such as academic courses leading up to degrees and diplomas, practical and professional training programmes, seminars and workshops, on-the-job training and study visits. The Bank has to be fairly selective in the choice of training facilities. As staff strength is limited, it cannot afford to waste it on opportunities which are not relevant or useful for the Bank. It has to be extra careful in ensuring that the facility would be really useful and in no case should a training offer be availed of simply because some institution, for its own reasons, makes it. In choosing the trainees, due attention should be paid to their ability to gain from it and in no case should training be regarded as a spell of rest and recreation. In some cases, the Bank will have to devise its own training programme to meet its specific needs and sometimes even request institutions to tailor a programme to meet its special needs. Finally, it would be necessary to remember that the importance of training can be duly recognised only by relating it to promotion prospects. In no case should the training benefit be lost by imparting a certain kind of training to a certain individual who is then drafted to another job. Finally, a question which will have to be tackled would relate to the need for ensuring that the Bank would not be deprived of the benefit that should come to it by virtue of the training that it imparts to its employees.

Recognising that the IDB has to be sufficiently competitive, a conscious effort has to be made to devise a salary structure in relation to other international development banks and financial institutions rather than the United Nations which has hitherto been the case in devising salary scales. Attention should be directed to the conditions prevailing in Jeddah and those in other places where international development banks are located such as Washington, Manila and Abidjan. The basic aim should be to ensure that salary levels are fixed in proportion to the responsibility attached to a position. Basically, qualifications and experience should be the determining factor in deciding the position a staff member should occupy. However, once the staff member is deemed to be fit for performing a certain job, he has to be paid according to the responsibility he assumes. Finally, it deserves to be remembered that the objective of recruiting staff of the requisite standard and then retaining them cannot be achieved solely by offering an attractive salary scale. It has to be supplemented by other important factors, such as the working conditions, promotion policies and several other steps. For an institution like the IDB with the provision of three languages, it is vitally important that an active effort is given to building sufficient strength of interpreters and translators. Similarly, while avoiding over-staffing, it must be ensured that there is an adequate strength at the level of the supporting staff, particularly reporters, stenographers and typists for various languages, which will save the professionals much time and is bound to have a healthy effect on the general efficiency of the organisation.

The present organisation of the Bank consists of the following departments:

(1) Administration Department.
(2) Bank's Secretariat.
(3) Economic and Policy Planning Department.
(4) Legal Department.
(5) Operations and Projects Department – split into three departments on a linguistic basis: Arabic, English and French.
(6) Treasury and Finance Department.

Additionally, there are the offices of the Internal Auditor and Organisation and Methods. The Islamic Research and Training Institute also forms part of the organisation of the Bank. The Bank's staff strength exceeds 500 drawn from member countries and Muslim communities, including 132 professionals. The largest strength of professionals is concentrated in the Operations and Projects Departments. While recognising the need for geographical representation, it is by no means essential for every member country to be represented on its staff if it involves the lowering of standards. Furthermore, if IDB staff compensation levels are made equivalent to those prevailing in other international financial institutions, care must be taken to ensure that those who benefit from them have comparable qualifications, experience and ability. As far as the departmental organisation is concerned, the Bank would do well to be guided by its own special needs arising out of the functions assigned to it instead of the conventional organisational pattern in other international development banks. This may, for example, call for a separate Economic Co-operation Department, a Development Policy unit, a liaison office for Islamic banks and a unit for national development banks.

As far as the organisation of the Bank is concerned, like many other international development banks, there is specific provision in the Articles of Agreement for the setting up of branch offices and agencies. In this perspective, it may be appropriate to consider whether it would be desirable for the IDB to move in the direction of establishing a degree of local presence either through regional offices or resident representatives or by means of establishing liaison with other international agencies present on the spot. The basic objective of a regional office is to achieve relative proximity to the member countries with the object of improving efficiency of the Bank's operations and to assist in the implementation of Bank-assisted projects. It can also play a role in aid co-ordination and other operational activities. While a regional office can be structured to perform a wide variety of functions, ranging from project implementation, monitoring, project supervision, country programming, country economic and sector work and project identification and appraisal as well as participation in local aid co-ordination meetings, the basic requirement is that there should not be any duplication with the work done at the headquarters. Another way of ensuring local presence is through the establishment of resident offices in various countries. In this matter, one has to be guided partly by the interest expressed by the member country concerned and also by the size and complexity of the Bank's operations in that member country. There has to be the need for extensive and continued dialogue between the Bank and the country. Another factor may be the need for the Bank to engage in frequent aid consultation and local co-ordination with other donors. As far as the organisational structure of the office is concerned, it should depend largely on the type and functions of the office. The World Bank has as many as 30 field offices, which are of two types: (1) facilitating offices, which serve to expedite implementation, ensure follow-up of current issues and facilitate the work of the headquarters missions; and (2) operational offices, which perform in addition to the facilitating functions some of the operations normally carried out by the headquarters, such as country economic and sector work, country programming and project evaluation. Most of the field offices are facilitating offices. As far as the Inter-American Development Bank is concerned, it has offices in all its member countries. The Asian Development Bank has established only three resident offices and the African Development Bank has two offices so far.

In this connection, it would be relevant to recall that whereas in the case of almost all international development banks, a provision exists for branch offices and agencies outside the headquarters, they have all developed as highly centralised institutions. True, some of the international development banks, such as the Inter-American Development Bank and the World Bank, have established representative offices in their member countries. However, their progress in this direction has been slow. Until 1968, the World Bank's overseas establishment was very small. Since then, there has been considerable growth. However, it is noteworthy that most of these have a single professional staff member in the mission while several of the missions have less than three professionals. In this regard attention may be directed to provisions governing the location of office in the Articles of Agreement of the World Bank. Section 9(a) of the Articles provides that the principal office of the Bank shall be located in the territory of the member holding the greatest number of shares, while Section 9(b) lays down that the Bank may establish agencies or branch offices in the territories of any members of the Bank. What is really interesting is that in the case of the World Bank the Articles make a distinction between branch offices and regional offices which is not the case with other banks. Under Section 10, entitled Regional Offices and Councils, it is provided that the Bank may establish regional offices and determine the location of and the areas to be covered by each regional office. Section 10(b) states that each regional office shall be advised by a regional council representative of the entire area and selected in such manner as the Bank may decide. Despite these provisions and in spite of the fact that the way was clearly open for the Bank to develop as a decentralised agency, with lending operations concentrated in the various regions of the Bank, this path does not seem to have been followed by the World Bank. It seems to have developed as a highly centralised institution with all fundamental decisions being made in Washington. Another factor deserving attention is that the establishment of branches or regional missions has been undertaken some long time after the organisation and establishment of the head office. This would provide a contrast to the IDB's situation where the organisation at the headquarters has yet to be fully established. This seems to dictate caution in two directions. In the first place, the establishment of the regional offices should not in any way affect the development of the head office. Secondly, if and when regional offices are set up, every effort should be made to ensure that there is no duplication or overlapping of work between the head office and the regional offices. The role of the regional offices has to be spelt out in clear terms and their authority properly defined to ensure that they function as adjuncts and complements to the head office rather than in any way trying to compete with it.

Considering its wide ranging task and its limited organisational strength, the IDB would do well not to take on burdens which, however important in themselves, may not clearly belong to it. If for lack of another organisation and as an initiator it has to involve itself in any such task, it should gradually pull out of it by structuring and promoting the growth of an organisation specially designed to undertake it. This constitutes a heavy burden on the limited manpower in the Bank and uses up valuable management time. If causes like these must be supported, the best course is for the IDB to provide financing and let a specialised organisation take the administrative burden. This would relieve the Bank of work for which it has no special competence and enable it to use the time and effort so saved for the task for which it has been set up. At the same time, maximum use should be made of outside expertise for tackling complex problems such as the development of new modes of financing, placement of surplus funds and mobilisation of resources in accordance with Shariah.

Being regarded as the premier multilateral institution in the Islamic world, one problem that the IDB faces is the pressure from other quarters and organisations to assist in and take on tasks in which they are directly interested but which may not be deserving of the highest priority viewed in the context of the overall task assigned to the Bank. This underlines the need for developing a proper strategy and well thought out scheme of priorities by the Bank. Otherwise, instead of a conscious rationing and allocation of its financial resources and organisational strength in accordance with its own priorities, it will find itself engaged and involved in tasks and efforts which have been thrust upon it by others. Every request for assistance that it receives must be considered in the context of its own priorities. The Bank must seek to conserve its organisational strength and skills and must embark on new operations and initiatives after lining up the requisite staff and establishing an adequate organisational infrastructure by way of policies, systems and procedures.

Experience has shown that many institutions in their anxiety to expand their organisation rapidly end up with serious over-staffing problems and need a pruning exercise. In such situations, what is required is a comprehensive evaluation exercise designed to ensure that each incumbent of a professional position has the requisite academic qualifications and experience and the institution has the right professional strength in every critical area. The emphasis must be on quality rather than quantity. While it is desirable that recruitment takes place on a wide geographical basis, political and geographical considerations must never be allowed to affect efficiency and incentive. The benefits of a systems approach and organisation based on a clear definition of objectives and priorities supported by adequate planning can hardly be over-estimated. The future of the institution seems to depend heavily on the success it achieves in solving its organisational problems.

Chapter 23

Research and Training

A unique feature of the Islamic Development Bank is that under its Articles of Agreement, it has been entrusted with the task of undertaking research to enable the economic, financial and banking activities in Muslim countries to conform to Shariah. This is in addition to the Article which requires it to extend training facilities for personnel engaged in development activities in member countries. The training function is by no means unusual. The Economic Development Institute of the World Bank is the best example of this. Similarly, all international development banks undertake a great deal of economic research and policy planning work designed to assist and support their operations and activities. For this purpose the institutions maintain large departments for research and policy formulation. This applies to the IDB with equal force. However, what needs to be underlined is that the task assigned to the IDB, in terms of Article 2(xi) of the Agreement establishing it, is totally distinct and different in that it is designed to assist the Islamic countries to follow Shariah in their economic, financial and banking activities.

Though conscious of the importance of establishing an organisation for research and training, the Bank could not initiate any action in this direction, owing to its preoccupation with more urgent tasks related to its financing operations, until several years after its establishment. It was in 1979 at the annual meeting held that year in Kampala that the Board of Governors passed a resolution in regard to the establishment of an Institute in Jeddah.

The resolution said that each year the net proceeds accruing from the Bank's deposits in foreign banks, after writing off losses, if any, in the value of foreign assets, should be allocated, among other things, for the setting up of an Institute in Jeddah for training and research aimed at helping and guiding member countries to re-orient their economies, financial and banking activities in conformity with the Islamic Shariah. The management of the Bank engaged Professor Korkut Ozal from Turkey to prepare a detailed study on the subject. He submitted a "Study on the Establishment of an Islamic Research and Training Institute (IRTI) for the Islamic Development Bank" in May 1980. This report was examined by a group of experts along with the management of the Bank. As a result of the discussion, the recommendations contained in the Report were refined and revised. It was unanimously agreed that the Institute should be established as early as possible and that it should function as "an autonomous and scientifically independent entity". The areas to be covered by the Institute, as stated in IRTI's statute, would encompass research to enable the economic, financial and banking activities in Muslim countries to conform to Shariah, and to extend training facilities for personnel engaged in development activities in the Bank's member countries. As regards its activities, it was proposed that they be divided into three areas, namely, research, training, and information collection and dissemination. It was felt that in carrying out its activities the Institute must seek to achieve maximum co-ordination with the existing organisations in the field. In respect of the organisational arrangements, it was stipulated that the Institute be governed by a 15-member Board under the chairmanship of the President of the IDB. It was envisaged that the Institute should endeavour to build up a common pool where "the scholars of Shariah and scientists of social and engineering services will develop a common language and terminology, exchange views and information, analyse the issues, deliberate on new formulations and check and discuss conformity with Shariah."

The Statute of the Islamic Research and Training Institute was approved by the Board of Executive Directors of the IDB in April 1981. The Board also approved a budget for the Institute amounting to over ID4 million for the first year. With this, the process of recruitment of professional staff for the Institute started. However, the research activities of the Institute could not begin before February 1982. The work started with the preparation of an annual programme of research activities. Several short-term research projects, primarily in the areas of Islamic economics and co-operation among Muslim countries, were planned and assigned to outside research scholars and action was initiated to establish relations with other research organisations. As regards training, a number of short-term seminars were planned with priority to Auqaf activities and Islamic banking and finance.

The Islamic Research and Training Institute is composed of three technical divisions: Research, Training, and the Information Centre, supported by an Administration and Finance Division. The Research Division is composed of three sections: Internal Research, External Research, and Dissemination. Each section functions under the supervision of a co-ordinator under the overall direction and co-ordination of the Head of the Research Division. The Training Division is responsible for providing training facilities in Islamic economics to Shariah-observing agencies and for training personnel engaged in development activities in the Bank's member countries. The Administration and Finance Division conducts the administrative and financial affairs of the Institute. In June 1984 an Academic Committee to assist and advise the management in attempting to achieve the academic objectives of the Institute was established. The Committee is designed to evaluate and review the research programmes of the Institute, to evaluate and review research criteria to govern the research activities to be undertaken by IRTI and to advise on the academic issues of training activities. In 1988 the total number of professional staff working at IRTI was 22. Since 1984, the majority of research has been based on research capacity available within the Institute. It constitutes the core of the research programme focusing on the areas of Islamic Economics, Islamic Jurisprudence and Economic Co-operation between the OIC member countries. Since its inception, the following research projects have been published:

(1)	Economic Research Institutions of the Islamic World (E)	Dr. A. Gul and S. Doha
(2)	Islamic Economics: A bibliography (E)	Tariqullah Khan
(3)	Economic Co-operation among the Members of the League of Arab States (E)	Dr. M. A. Gulaid
(4)	La Co-operation Economique Entre les Pays du Maghreb (F)	Dr. R. Saadallah
(5)	Prospects for Co-operation through Trade among OIC Member Countries: A Commodity Level Analysis (E)	Kazim R. Awan
(6)	The Theory of Economic Integration and its Relevance to OIC Member Countries	Dr. A. Satiroglu
(7)	Development and Problems of Islamic Banks (E)	Dr. Ausaf Ahmad
(8)	The Economic Impact of Manpower Migration among Selected OIC Member Countries (E)	Dr. Emin Carikci
(9)	Economic Co-operation and Integration among Islamic Countries (E)	Dr. Volker Nienhaus

The Information Centre which constitutes a division of IRTI is designed to collect, systematise and disseminate information. Its main objectives are:

(1) To provide data on different aspects of the economic and social structure of member countries;
(2) To provide technical support and assistance in the field of information in member countries; and
(3) To disseminate information contained in these data bases to member countries.

While it is too early to judge the performance of the Institute, some general observations may be in order. Having regard to the fact that the two functions assigned to the Bank in relation to training and research are the subject of separate articles in the IDB charter and, more particularly, considering that providing training to personnel engaged in development activities and undertaking research to enable the economic, financial and banking activities in Muslim countries to conform to Shariah by no means form an integral whole, it might be asked whether it was proper to roll these two activities together and place them in one organisation. At the same time, this is likely to have at least one advantage in that the product of research could be utilised to serve as the content and subject matter of some of the training programme. If the task assigned to the IRTI is to be accomplished and the expectations associated with it are to be fulfilled, the proposal regarding the appointment of an Advisory Board should be implemented as soon as possible. The Committee should be so constituted as to have the capacity to give the proper direction to the activities of the IRTI. This is a role that the Board of Executive Directors, the management or any academic committee cannot be expected to perform effectively. In establishing the advisory committee and deciding as to who should serve on it, attention should be directed to the objectives and functions of the Institute. While the management and the Board of Directors may exercise overall control instead of exercising detailed supervision over the IRTI's affairs, they should leave it to function as an autonomous entity under its Director and Advisory Board. In other words, the Institute should be granted maximum freedom and autonomy in its working and bureaucratic procedures must be avoided as far as possible. Recognising that the success of the IRTI would depend crucially on the person who heads it, it must be ensured that its director should possess the necessary academic qualifications, experience, organising capacity, dedication and qualities of leadership. In manning the Institute and selecting the professional personnel for it, maximum care should be exercised to ensure that they are competent, suitably qualified and experienced. Often the specialisation of the professional staff conditions the activities of the Institute. In the case of senior appointments, the IRTI should follow the practice of identifying suitable persons and then inviting them to take up the position rather than the traditional method of recruitment through advertisement.

The IRTI would do well to consider carefully the gigantic task assigned to it. Broadly speaking it consists of several parts, such as determining what Shariah requires in respect of economic, financial and banking activities, how these requirements can be met, what are the difficulties and problems involved and how solutions can be found through sustained research and Ijtehad. The Institute will also have to establish close contacts with countries seeking to move towards Islamisation and also keep in touch with efforts which are being made in the field by institutions as also by individuals. It must concentrate on undertaking research on the whole economic model presented by Islam. It should not only study the various institutions such as Zakat, Ushur and Riba, but also investigate their interdependence and inter-relationship. As far as the overall task of conformity with Islamic principles is concerned, it should not confine itself to offering solutions which merely avoid apparent violation of Shariah, but must find propositions firmly based on the Islamic principles.

As far as the scope of assistance by the IRTI to the IDB is concerned, it should focus sharply and solely on work related to making the Bank's operations and policies conform to Shariah and on allied matters. This would warrant exercising care in two main directions. First, under no circumstances, should the IRTI be burdened with work which legitimately belongs to the Economic and Policy Planning Department of the Bank. Secondly, there is no need to create any capability in the E&PP Department for handling Shariah matters. All work related to Shariah must be concentrated in the IRTI regardless of whether it is designed to help the economic, banking and financial activities in the member countries or the operations of the IDB itself. It cannot be over-emphasised that in formulating its work programme and topics for research, the IRTI should bear in mind its basic purpose. Before fixing a priority and selecting a subject for research, it should invariably ask itself how far it would enable the economic, financial and banking activities in Muslim countries to conform to Shariah.

Finally, bearing in mind that many of the international and regional development banks hold training courses for personnel engaged in development work, the IDB, instead of competing with other institutions, may try to devise and develop training courses for personnel from the least-developed member countries, which are tailor-made, in the sense that they take fully into account the characteristics and conditions prevailing in the poorest countries and the challenge and difficulties they present to those undertaking development work. In designing its training courses and programme, the IRTI should accord special attention to the needs of national development banks and even more to those of the Islamic banks. As a matter of fact, it should seek to develop a two-way relationship with them. On the one hand, it should assemble the raw material by way of problems from the practical experience of institutions in the field and on the other, offer them, in return, the finished product emerging from its research effort for testing on the ground and facilitating actual operations.

Chapter 24

Conformity to Shariah

The first major area in which Shariah had to be applied related to the placement of liquid funds. Well before commencing operations, the Islamic Development Bank had to contend with the problem of placing the sizeable funds it had received as subscription from its members. The initial exploration which was undertaken clearly showed that there was no way of investing or placing these funds in the international money market or with conventional banks which would satisfy the requirements of Shariah. This led to an effort by the Bank to seek ways and means of placing them at a national level, that is with member countries. This, in turn, gave birth to what became known as the foreign trade financing operations of the IDB. Simultaneously, it was decided that the placement operations in the conventional manner with banks must continue until such time as alternative methods could be found. Nevertheless, it was resolved that the interest proceeds from these deposits should be held separately. This gave rise to the question as to how these massive funds built out of interest could be utilised. Consultations with the Ulema led to the conclusion that under the rule of "necessity" interest proceeds could be utilised for assistance to the poor in member and non-member countries and to assist Islamic communities in non-member countries to maintain their Islamic identity and legitimate rights. Subsequently, the matter was brought before the Board of Governors in the year 1979 and a resolution was passed that the interest proceeds be utilised half and half for establishing a Special Reserve to meet any losses resulting from fluctuations of currencies in which the Bank's deposits are held and for setting up a Special Assistance Account to be used for training and research and for providing assistance in cases of natural disasters and calamities. At the same time, apart from employing its liquid funds in foreign trade operations, the IDB has been placing part of its surplus funds with traditional banks for utilisation in commodity transactions.

Now turning to the application of Shariah to the financing operations of the IDB, it may be noted that the Bank charges a service fee on its loans to cover its costs. A fee ranging between 2 and 3 per cent per annum is charged. The poorer members are required to pay a service fee at the lower level and the middle income countries are charged at the upper level. The service fee becomes payable as soon as the loan becomes effective or 90 days after signing the loan agreement. In the loan agreement the service fee is expressed as a sum or amount of money rather than as a percentage charge. It may be asked why, if the intention is to recover the cost of loan administration and not the price for the use of the loan funds, the service fee is charged as a function of the amount of the loan and the term or period for which the loan is made instead of basing it on the actual costs. The answer is that if the total costs are to be shared by the totality of the borrowers, the most just method of apportioning the total cost among them is to take into consideration the amount of the loan each has received and the length of time the Bank has had to administer the loan. Even if the Bank were to make such an apportionment on the basis of a unit cost, that is the cost of each ID lent, here again the most relevant parameters would be the amount of the loan and the period of the loan. At any rate, it bears testimony to the Bank's anxiety to conform to Shariah that it decided to apply the new formula for determining the service fee with retrospective effect and to repay the borrower any amount which the Bank may have received in excess of what it was entitled to under the new formula.

As far as equity financing is concerned, which is an integral and distinctive feature of Islamic banking, no problems of clash with Shariah have arisen and one of the primary reasons for undertaking substantial equity financing operations in the past years despite the high degree of risk attached to them, was to popularise this highly preferred mode of Islamic financing as a vehicle for resource transfer.

As far as leasing is concerned, initially an effort seems to have been made by the Bank to impart an additional degree of acceptability to its leasing operations in two ways: first by ensuring that it was applied to high income yielding projects and secondly by fixing the quantum of the leasing fee in relation to the profitability factor and the cash flow. Lately, a new policy development seems to have taken place in that the leasing arrangement is being applied also to projects which do not themselves yield a revenue. This is on the ground that the leasing fee is just a price or charge for the use of the asset and no more.

More recently, a new mode of financing known as Instalment Sale has been introduced by the IDB. Although it may appear to resemble hire-purchase, in fact there is a basic difference between them. Under the former, ownership of the goods is transferred to the buyer on the conclusion of the contract, however under the latter, the hirer is given the option to purchase the goods which he can only exercise after payment of all instalments. In other words, the instalment sale system is a variant of Murabeha or the credit sale which the Fiqh Academy (the body of Islamic scholars responsible for correctly interpreting Shariah) has confirmed to be in conformity with Shariah.

As far as the foreign trade financing operations are concerned, they are conducted on the basis of Murabeha and a mark-up. Unlike a loan arrangement, where a penal rate of interest starts operating in the case of default, there is no additional charge or mark-up beyond the date when repayment of the entire amount becomes due.

The IDB has been utilising the Special Assistance Account for providing technical assistance on the ground that it does not generate a net income or return to the Bank.

As far as Shariah aspect is concerned, it would, perhaps, be appropriate to recognise that by voluntarily submitting its operations for review by the Fiqh Academy, the IDB has manifested a genuine concern for implementing the mandate of its founders.

It cannot be over-emphasised that the challenge of conforming to Shariah is by no means confined to modes of financing. On the contrary, it is much broader and extends to a much larger field. The IDB is clearly responsible and expected to build and incorporate the Islamic objectives and values into its overall policies, such as those governing the identification and selection of projects, their evaluation and appraisal, eligibility, terms and conditions for various types of operation, special attention to the least-developed members and the application of a basic needs approach as also compassion for those recipients who are, as a result of factors beyond their control, unable to honour and discharge their debt and obligations to the Bank. Under its mandate the IDB is expected to play a pioneering role in respect of Shariah, innovating all the way and designing a system of financing which could be followed by the entire Muslim world. Against this background, the Bank has to redouble its efforts to develop a system of financing comprehensive enough to provide a viable alternative to the interest-based system.

In conclusion, perhaps, it may be stated that in critically evaluating and judging how far the IDB has been able to meet the challenge of working on the basis of Shariah, it is by no means intended to under-estimate the complexities and difficulties which lie in its path. The real purpose is simply to point out that in its preoccupation with mounting financing operations, the paramount need for progressing towards the goal of making the IDB function in total conformity with Islamic principles, ideals, values and dictates should not be ignored or neglected. In this context, it ought to be remembered that the mandate which the IDB has received from its founders is indeed two-fold, that is, to establish itself and develop as an international development bank to foster the economic development and social progress of member countries and Muslim communities individually as well as jointly and at the same time to operate in accordance with the principles of Shariah. The question which the Bank must ask itself is whether, in the first 12 years of its life, it has made commensurate progress in both these directions and assuming that because progress in the second direction is more difficult than in the first, has the Bank directed, if not more, then at least equal, attention to the task it has been set in relation to Shariah compared to its efforts in stepping up its financial operations.

Chapter 25

Lessons from the Past and Outlook for the Future

We may now turn to some of the lessons emerging from the Islamic Development Bank's experience over the past 12 years since its inception in 1975. It may be observed at the outset that though loan financing was played down in the IDB charter, it has emerged as a major mode of the IDB's project financing over the years. Experience has shown that as the most concessional form of financing and having the needs of the least-developed member countries in view, together with their suitability for financing agricultural and economic and social infrastructural projects generally, loans on the basis of a service fee have to be maximised consistent with resource availability. There is need for the IDB to lengthen the period of its loans and also to adopt a system of graduation by establishing a GNP threshold for loan financing.

The IDB's experience has shown that as a development financing instrument, equity financing is a highly complex and difficult operation, particularly in public sector projects and unsupported by a loan. In view of its importance in Islamic banking, the IDB proceeded vigorously in the direction of providing equity financing for development projects. However, the experiment proved expensive and many of the projects ran into difficulty. Therefore, it has had to slow down this type of activity and is now engaged in devising corrective measures and safeguards and equipping itself better for undertaking equity financing by directing greater attention to the macro-economic conditions and policies affecting the project, stricter supervision and by trying to link disbursement to project implementation.

In the experience of the IDB, leasing and instalment sales have proved to be highly useful modes of financing remunerative projects, viewed both from the standpoint of risk and return.

Despite its intention to use profit sharing as a development financing instrument, the IDB has so far been able to make very little use of it.

Notwithstanding its best efforts and having diversified its mode of resource transfer, experience has shown that the overall level of project financing has not grown rapidly and remains rather low in relation to the needs of its member countries. The future of the IDB depends crucially on its ability to expand its operational effort rapidly. It is understandable that in view of its Islamic character, the Bank is viewed by its members with special understanding, in fact religious sympathy. However, as time goes by it is apt to be judged by more rigorous standards, such as the amount of resources the member countries have provided for it and the reverse flow of financing which they are receiving from it in comparison with other multilateral institutions like the World Bank. The stepping up of the operational programme is directly dependent upon a well-conceived and bold mobilisation effort hitched to various modes of financing and the building up of an adequate and efficient organisation.

Over the years, the average level of financing per project has not markedly increased, resulting in a mounting burden on the Bank's organisation. Experience has demonstrated that the overall operational effort cannot be expanded rapidly without raising the average level of financing.

While the IDB has resorted to co-financing as a means of marketing its resources, experience has shown that it has yet to make large scale use of the co-financing weapon for mobilising and attracting resources from other institutions for projects sponsored by it.

The IDB's experience has shown that despite its efforts to direct special attention to the needs of the least-developed member countries, which form the majority in its membership, only about one-third of its project financing has gone to them. In cases where the main bottleneck to the provision of financing is the lack of suitable projects, especially in the case of the least-developed member countries, a two-fold approach is indicated. On the one hand, the shortage of suitable projects may be overcome by a liberal provision of technical assistance and on the other, wherever possible, instead of becoming a prisoner of the project approach followed by traditional development banks, which adhere to the practice of packaging their financing into projects, under proper supervision and with adequate safeguards, the IDB may undertake to finance a part of their development programme and make finance available for general development and uplift purposes.

The IDB's experience has shown that one of the major complexities confronting Islamic development banking is that it has to strike a balance between need and credit-worthiness. This involves, so to speak, walking a tight-rope, as the two are not easy to reconcile. Initially, in respect of its foreign trade financing, the IDB was inclined to allow need to take precedence over the repayment capacity of the recipients. This, unfortunately, led to delays and defaults in repayments and the Bank, realising that such a situation led to the denial and loss of even project financing to the countries concerned, was forced to revise its attitude, thereby according greater importance to the credit-worthiness factor. It is not unreasonable to expect that member countries in meeting their obligations to multilateral institutions would accord an equal, if not preferential, treatment to the IDB as an Islamic institution instead of giving it a lower priority and expecting it to show greater patience in regard to overdues.

Though the IDB has been endeavouring to use other methods, such as an Investment Deposit Scheme, Islamic Banks Portfolio and a Unit Trust Scheme, so far it has had to depend heavily on capital increases as the primary source of resource mobilisation.

Experience has shown that the task of devising methods of resource mobilisation and replenishment, as also placement of short-term funds, in line with Islamic principles is even more difficult and complex than the marketing or provision of financing in ways which do not seem to violate Shariah. The success of the IDB depends crucially on the development of suitable techniques and modes of resource mobilisation free of Riba. Without a well-developed system of resource replenishment in line with Islamic principles, the resource needs of member countries cannot be met and an adequate programme of financing cannot be mounted. What is clearly warranted are not efforts to use the traditional method of mobilisation with marginal changes but the development of new Islamic financial instruments and the establishment of a secondary market.

An important feature of Islamic development financing is that instead of making it a global operation, resource mobilisation has to be conducted in a compartmental fashion linked to different modes of financing.

The IDB's experience has shown that as far as the organisational structure and management is concerned, having regard to its wider functions such as equity financing, it appears that Islamic international development banking must have a more decentralised organisational structure and a much stronger local presence than is the case with conventional multilateral institutions.

Experience has demonstrated that in Islamic development banking, there is much greater need for developing a capacity for project identification and generation in line with the socio-economic objectives laid down by Islam. It is only thus that projects which reflect Islamic priorities can be developed.

By virtue of its complex task, Islamic development banking needs a highly competent organisation and dedicated professional staff untarnished by political considerations and imbued with a burning desire to serve the Ummah.

Co-financing is undoubtedly a useful way of marketing resources and becoming operational quickly. At the same time, it needs to be realised that indirectly it tends to perpetuate traditional financing practices and policies and has the effect of retarding progress and relieving pressure for originality and innovation in line with Islam which alone can promote the development of a distinctive system of international development banking in conformity with Islamic principles, ideals and values.

While the IDB has made extensive use of its foreign trade financing operations for the placement of its surplus funds, they cannot be regarded as an ideal mechanism for the purpose as foreign trade financing has become an integral and permanent feature of the IDB's ordinary operation and, therefore, the surplus funds cannot be released from them unless substituted by an injection from outside.

Experience has shown that an important and vital challenge facing the IDB is the formulation and execution of a programme and action plan to assist the capital rich members, which do not need financing but are still in need of stepping up their economic development. Though these countries do not benefit by way of larger export earnings resulting from procurement flowing from IDB financing, they have made large contributions to the Bank's capital and it is towards these countries that the Bank will have to direct its resource mobilisation efforts in future.

Experience has shown that in Islamic international development banking, in view of its novel character, it is vitally important to develop a capability for evaluation so that the lessons which emerge can be built into subsequent operations. There has to be a premium on learning from mistakes so that they are not repeated.

Finally, an attempt may be made to lay down an agenda for the future development of the Bank.

It is important to realise that besides steering clear of interest, the IDB must have a moral dimension in its operations and policies in that it must operate in consonance with the value system of Islam and in furtherance of the socio-economic goals prescribed by it, such as the welfare of the people and relief of their hardships. Financing has to focus on agriculture, low-cost housing, food, clothing, medical facilities and education. Projects designed to meet the essential needs of the community have to be financed to the exclusion of luxury and non-essential items. In project identification, there has to be much greater application of social analysis which deals with the impact of projects on people. One of the important requirements is the preparation of a manual of project evaluation in line with Islamic principles.

In an Islamic perspective, the Bank has to follow a basic needs approach and a policy of non-involvement in prestigious projects not likely to benefit the masses. There has to be greater emphasis on social development, equality, Islamic values of co-operation and solidarity and a low income poor country approach so that even in absolute terms the largest resources are directed to poverty alleviation and social development in the least-developed member countries. Islamic development financing requires emphasis on building infrastructure and basic services.

As far as policy objectives are concerned, the raising of national income, improving its distribution, increasing employment, reducing dependence upon external assistance and the achievement of self-sufficiency must enjoy priority in Islamic development banking also. At the same time, it seems that in Islamic international development banking, it is more appropriate to aim at devising a policy framework which would provide incentives for desired behaviour from private entrepreneurs and an overall programme for the public sector instead of a highly elaborate plan for the whole economy with excessive reliance on physical controls. The real effort must be to design a long-term strategy for the realisation of the basic goals of the Islamic economy based on a partnership between the public and the private sectors.

It is well known that one of the principal threats to a country's development is its inability to adjust its development programme, particularly in the public sector, in accordance with the availability of resources. This threatens growth, leads to inflation and causes a balance of payments crisis. In an Islamic context the Bank would be rendering a real service, especially in the case of the least-developed member countries with a weak policy apparatus, by placing stress on the gathering of basic data and effective policy co-ordination.

One of the dilemmas faced by Islamic development banking is that based as it is on the urgency of need rather than the credit-worthiness and financial strength of the borrower, the risk of default is greater. On the other hand, in the interest of resource mobilisation at a reasonable cost, a good financial track record is vital. The only feasible alternative, therefore, is to strike a mean between these two conflicting factors by taking into account the quality of economic management and willingness to pursue appropriate policies for poverty alleviation as factors which tend to affect their low credit-worthiness.

As far as decision making is concerned, having regard to the Islamic principles and value system, Islamic international development banking has to be based on a well-balanced system of voting power. If the voting power cannot be distributed equally, in the interest of broad based decision making the proportion of the basic votes accorded to each member has to be substantially raised. In this regard, it is interesting to note that in the case of the World Bank the trend has been against concentration of voting power. Over the years, US voting power has been almost halved from 37.5 per cent to 19.5 per cent and it is not infrequently outvoted in Board meetings.

As for the capital structure, it is worthy of consideration whether the Bank may not also adopt the option of callable capital. It will have a two-fold advantage. First, the member countries will not have to hand over the callable capital and to this extent the burden on them will be less. Secondly, the callable capital backing would certainly strengthen the safety or credit-worthiness aspect for those investing in its operations. Initially, it was understandable that callable capital was avoided and the entire subscribed capital had to be paid up so as to provide an adequate resource base for the Bank's operations. However, the situation has changed over the years in that the member countries have already handed over considerable capital to the Bank and, in view of recent developments in the oil market, their capacity to contribute more cash to the Bank by way of capital has been impaired. In such a situation, it would not be out of place to consider introducing a callable capital element in Islamic development banking. The World Bank has a subscribed capital of US$85 billion of which only 8 per cent is paid up.

The Bank is expected to play an aggressive and highly active role in the spread of Islamic banking. On the one hand, it has to take a leading part in designing a banking model for the entire Muslim world to follow and which is not merely free of interest in the legal and formal sense but totally and really removed in spirit from the traditional banking system. On the other hand, it has to use its resources, expertise and leverage for promoting the establishment and growth of Islamic banks. Islamic development banking means that the Bank must try to advise and influence member countries in policy matters and the evolution of an economy in accordance with Islamic principles and objectives for which it must try to develop sufficient leverage. Far from being value-neutral and pragmatic, it has to seek to help the growth and welfare of the member countries in an Islamic framework. An effort should be made to provide financing tied to policy changes and to emphasise the need for a bias in favour of Islamic objectives and values.

It is expected of the IDB that it should encourage recipients to adopt Islamic modes of financing. So far profit sharing operations in international development banking have not expanded, largely because member countries do not offer such projects.

In an Islamic perspective the Bank must play an active advisory role in relation to its member countries. Besides offering traditional advice for establishing a macro-economic policy framework composed of a realistic exchange rate policy, a low rate of effective protection for industry, a realistic agricultural pricing policy, application of cost recovery principle in pricing public utilities and infrastructural services and controlling inflation and avoiding real wage increases unsupported by increased productivity, it must urge its member countries to pursue the socio-economic objectives and values prescribed by Islam. The Islamic concept of growth is extremely comprehensive, embracing as it does the moral, spiritual and material aspects of human life. Its sole objective is not the maximisation of growth of national income per se, irrespective of its effects on income distribution and social welfare. It is the duty of the Bank in an Islamic framework to sell this philosophy to its member countries as a policy reformer.

To sum up, the prospects for the IDB depend greatly on its success in achieving a substantial expansion in the volume of project financing, formulation of a programme for assisting capital rich member countries, development of equity financing as a means of transferring development resources, playing a catalytic and really active role in the promotion of Islamic banking, an effective policy role in urging member countries to help their growth and social welfare in an Islamic framework, assisting member countries in designing projects, building institutions and developing policies in conformity with Islam, evolving effective methods of resource mobilisation and placement of short-term surplus funds which do not violate Shariah, creating new financial instruments which accord with Shariah and the creation of a secondary market for them, greater use of profit sharing arrangements for development financing, formulating Islamic guidelines for the identification and appraisal of projects, evolving innovative approaches in an Islamic perspective and last but not least providing a forum in which Muslim countries meet to discuss their economic problems and social issues with a view to promoting maximum co-operation in tackling them.

Appendix 1: Selected Basic Indicators

Country**	Area (Thousands of sq. km.)	Total Population (million) (Mid-1986)	Population Density (Persons per sq. km.) 1986	Average Annual Growth of Population (%) 1980–85	Average* Annual Growth of Agricultural Production (%) 1980–85	Average* Annual Growth of Food (%) 1980–85	Life Expectancy at Birth (Years) 1985	GNP Per Capita (US$) 1985	Exchange Rate (National Currency Per US$) August 28, 1987
Afghanistan	648	18.61	35	2.6	0.8	0.9	—	—	50.60
Algeria	2,382	22.50	9	3.3	3.7	3.4	61	2,550	4.67
Bahrain	0.620	0.41	661	3.3	—	—	67	9,420	0.3769
Bangladesh	144	100.62	1	2.6	3.5	3.1	55	150	31.00
Benin	133	4.04	33	3.1	9.6	8.8	49	260	305.175
Brunei	6	0.23	26	3.0	—	—	74	17.57	2.107
Burkina Faso	274	6.75	41	2.6	9.2	6.4	45	150	305.175
Cameroon	475	10.45	45	3.2	1.5	1.9	55	810	305.175
Chad	1,284	5.08	4	2.3	3.6	3.1	45	—	305.175
Comoros	2	0.48	4	2.9	—	—	55	240	305.175
Djibouti	22	0.46	48	6.8	—	—	48	—	177.721
Egypt	1,001	48.50	50	2.8	3.3	4.7	61	610	0.70[b] 2.1827[c]
Gabon	268	1.15	233	1.3	1.3	2.2	51	3,670	305.175
Gambia	11	0.72	15	3.1	5.2	5.2	43	230	7.44
Guinea	246	5.75	43	2.4	0.4	−0.5	40	320	340.00 300.00[d]
Guinea Bissau	36	0.98	37	3.2	8.4	8.4	39	180	650.00[d]
Indonesia	1,905	162.90	88	2.1	6.5	6.7	61	530	1,638.00
Iraq	435	16.31	27	3.6	5.8	5.6	61	—	0.3109
Jordan	98	3.92	25	3.7	2.6	2.6	65	1,560	0.344
Kuwait	18	1.71	11	4.5	—	—	72	14,480	0.2816
Lebanon	10	2.34	234	—	2.3	2.5	—	—	268.00
Libya	1,760	3.92	2	3.9	14.6	14.7	60	7,170	0.2987
Malaysia	330	15.68	21	2.5	3.5	4.6	68	2,000	2.5215
Maldives	0.300	0.19	633	2.5	—	—	61	290	10.10
Mali	1,240	8.44	7	2.3	3.1	3.0	46	150	305.175

Mauritania	1,031	1.89	2	2.1	−1.7	−1.7	47	420	74.80
Morocco	447	22.10	20	2.5	2.9	2.8	59	560	8.35
Niger	1,267	6.33	5	3.0	−1.4	−1.4	44	250	305.175
Oman	212	1.29	164	4.8	—	—	54	6,730	0.385
Pakistan	804	97.73	8	3.1	4.9	4.1	59	380	17.564
Qatar	11	0.37	30	5.1	—	—	72	16.270	3.641
Saudi Arabia	2,150	11.98	6	4.2	26.6	26.9	62	8,850	3.751
Senegal	196	6.76	29	2.9	4.2	3.9	56[a]	370	305.175
Sierra Leone	72	4.00	18	2.2	0.1	0.5	40	350	22.80
Somalia	638	5.48	116	2.9	0.4	0.4	46	280	132.60[c]
Sudan	2,506	22.28	9	2.7	2.4	1.2	48	300	2.93[f]
									4.00[g]
Syria	185	10.27	18	3.6	0.0	−0.7	64	1,570	3.925[b]
Tunisia	164	7.26	23	2.3	5.5	5.5	66	1,190	0.8325
Turkey	785	50.30	16	2.5	2.1	2.2	64	1.080	892.33
Uganda	241	15.08	16	3.0	7.0	6.6	49	—	59.63[h]
UA Emirates	84	1.31	64	6.2	—	—	63	19.270	3.673
Yemen AR	195	6.80	29	2.5	4.1	4.2	45	550	10.00
Yemen PDR	333	2.36	141	2.6	1.1	0.5	46	530	0.343

* Exponential growth rates from figures in FAO, Monthly Bulletin of Statistics, April 1987.
** The member country Palestine is omitted as no figures can be given for it due to its occupation.

[a] Refers to 1984 [b] Official rate [c] Freemarket
[d] Public transactions rate [h] new shilling [f] Agricultural products
[g] Financial rate

Sources:
1. Country Reports.
2. *Financial Times*, August, 1987 (exchange rates only)
3. Monthly Bulletin of Statistics, July 1987, United Nations
4. World Development Report 1986, World Bank

Appendix 2: The Record for the First Twelve Years
1396–1407H (1976–1987)

(Amount in ID Million)

Particulars	*1396H* No.	*1396H* Amount	*1397H* No.	*1397H* Amount	*1389H* No.	*1389H* Amount	*1399H* No.	*1399H* Amount	*1400H* No.	*1400H* Amount	*1401H* No.	*1401H* Amount
Ordinary operations												
Projects												
Loan	1	6.00	11	55.41	5	25.46	6	33.74	9	52.68	5	31.11
Equity	1	7.45	8[bc]	35.73	5[bc]	26.86	8	39.79	10[bc]	37.04	10[b]	45.98
Leasing	—	—	2[bc]	7.72	2[bc]	12.50	2	16.25	6[bc]	38.47	3	30.69
Instalment sale	—	—	—	—	—	—	—	—	—	—	—	—
Profit sharing	—	—	—	—	1	4.27	—	—	—	—	—	—
Technical assistance	—	—	3	0.84	3	0.82	5	1.37	3	3.38	10	6.83
Total projects	2	13.54	23	99.70	15	69.91	21	91.15	27	131.57	28	114.61
Foreign trade financing	—	—	5	43.60	14	127.45	25	262.46	32	350.75	31	367.89
Total ordinary operations	2	13.45	28	143.30	29	197.36	46	353.61	59	482.32	59	482.50
Special operations	—	—	—	—	—	—	1	0.71	6	7.68	9	5.99
Grand total	2	13.45	28	143.30	29	197.36	47	354.32	65	490.00	68	487.88
Cancelled/withdrawn	—	—	1	0.05	4	21.38	4	23.11	6	19.57	4	24.51
Disbursements	—	—	—	12.73	—	92.94	—	212.86	—	362.78	—	479.79
Gross income	—	—	—	—	—	2.97	—	9.75	—	19.65	—	26.13
Net profit	—	—	—	—	—	(−2.19)	—	2.28	—	10.14		14.72
Reserves:												
Capital	—	—	—	16.64	—	16.64	—	16.64	—	16.64	—	16.64
Special	—	—	—	—	—	—	—	—	—	90.53	—	129.78
General	—	—	—	—	—	—	—	—	—		—	10.23
Balance on investment deposit scheme	—	—	—	—	—	—	—	—	—	—	—	43.81
Capital subscription	—	750.00	—	765.00	—	767.50	—	680.00	—	790.00	—	1,820.17[d]
Number of countries (at end)	—	26	—	32	—	34	—	36	—	40	—	41

— Nil or not applicable

[a] Totals may not add due to rounding

[b] [illegible]

1402H No.	1402H Amount	1403H No.	1403H Amount	1404H No.	1404H Amount	1405H No.	1405H Amount	1406H No.	1406H Amount	1407H No.	1407H Amount	Total Since 1396H No.	Total Since 1396H Amount
8	45.03	11	73.45	12	71.46	15	98.62	7	28.27	11	36.07	101	557.32
8[b]	28.72	5[bc]	15.61	1	6.00	3	8.73	2[bc]	10.00	2[bc]	5.75	63[bc]	267.66
7	57.99	8[bc]	75.00	11	120.47	9	92.10	8[bc]	62.54	1[c]	5.00	59[bc]	518.73
—	—	—	—	—	—	6	53.00	8	76.49	11	81.34	25	210.83
—	—	1	3.06	—	—	—	—	—	—	—	—	2	7.33
8	4.44	12	5.99	7	2.96	14	6.18	13	2.41	24	6.00	102	41.20
31	136.18	36	173.11	31	200.89	47	258.63	35	179.71	48	134.17	344	1,603.7
28	377.55	27	460.46	42	671.61	30	667.27	66	572.84	53	453.15	353	4,355.07
59	513.73	63	633.57	73	872.50	77	925.90	101	752.55	101	587.32	697	5,958.14
7	5.99	8	10.92	22	62.20	13	64.81	10	10.54	12	9.12	88	177.34
66	519.72	71	644.48	95	934.70	90	990.71	111	763.09	113	596.44	785	6,135.48
9	76.28	4	33.83	5	47.52	2	1.60	2	5.16	—	—	41	253.01
—	391.28	—	487.35	—	722.81	—	731.83	—	557.16	—	523.92		
—	30.23	—	26.18	—	34.83	—	62.69	—	74.13	—	60.00	—	—
—	16.93	—	2.45	—	18.37	—	43.61	—	42.66	—	—	—	—
—	16.64	—	16.64	—	16.64	—	16.64	—	16.64	—	16.64	—	—
—	166.67	—	200.66	—	235.55	—	264.28	—	326.51	—	327.08	—	—
—	24.96	—	41.88	—	44.33	—	52.70	—	81.31	—	119.64	—	—
—	50.04	—	155.39	—	77.10	—	67.70	—	87.27	—	89.84	—	—
—	1,822.67	—	1,822.67	—	1,850.17	—	1,952.27	—	1,958.37	—	1,958.37	—	—
—	42	—	42	—	43	—	43	—	44	—	44	—	—

Appendix 3: Member Countries' Subscriptions and Voting Rights as at 30.12.1407H (1987)

(million Islamic Dinars)

Member country	*Initial subscription*	*Increase in subscription*	*Total subscription*	*Votes*
1. Republic of Afghanistan	2.5	—	2.5	750
2. Democratic & Popular Republic of Algeria	25.0	38.1	63.1	6,810
3. State of Bahrain	5.0	2.0	7.0	1,200
4. People's Republic of Bangladesh	10.0	15.0	25.0	3,000
5. People's Republic of Benin	2.5	—	2.5	750
6. Negara Brunei Darussalam	6.3	—	6.3	1,130
7. Burkina Faso	2.5	3.8	6.3	1,130
8. Republic of Cameroon	2.5	3.8	6.3	1,130
9. Republic of Chad	2.5	—	2.5	750
10. Federal Islamic Republic of Comoro Islands	2.5	—	2.5	750
11. Republic of Djibouti	2.5	—	2.5	750
12. Arab Republic of Egypt	25.0	—	25.0	3,000
13. Republic of Gabon	3.0	4.5	7.5	1,250
14. Republic of Gambia	2.5	—	2.5	750
15. Republic of Guinea	2.5	3.8	6.3	1,130
16. Republic of Guinea Bissau	2.5	3.8	6.3	750
17. Republic of Indonesia	25.0	38.1	63.1	6,810
18. Republic of Iraq	10.0	15.2	25.2	3,020
19. Hashemite Kingdom of Jordan	4.0	6.1	10.1	1,510
20. State of Kuwait	100.0	152.2	252.2	25,720

21. Republic of Lebanon	2.5	—	2.5	750
22. Socialist People's Libyan Arab Jamahiriyah	125.0	190.3	315.3	13,000
23. Malaysia	16.0	24.4	40.4	4,540
24. Republic of Maldives	2.5	—	2.5	750
25. Republic of Mali	2.5	—	2.5	750
26. Islamic Republic of Mauritania	2.5	—	2.5	750
27. Kingdom of Morocco	5.0	7.6	12.6	1,760
28. Republic of Niger	2.5	3.8	6.3	1,130
29. Sultanate of Oman	5.0	2.0	7.0	1,200
30. Islamic Republic of Pakistan	25.0	38.1	63.1	6,810
31. Palestine	2.5	2.5	5.0	1,000
32. State of Qatar	25.0	25.0	50.0	3,000
33. Kingdom of Saudi Arabia	200.0	306.37	506.37	51,137
34. Republic of Senegal	2.5	3.8	6.3	1,130
35. Republic of Sierra Leone	2.5	—	2.5	750
36. Somali Democratic Republic	2.5	—	2.5	750
37. Republic of Sudan	10.0	15.2	25.2	1,500
38. Syrian Arab Republic	2.5	—	2.5	750
39. Republic of Tunisia	2.5	2.5	5.0	1,000
40. Republic of Turkey	10.0	150.0	160.0	16,500
41. Republic of Uganda	2.5	3.8	6.3	1,130
42. United Arab Emirates	110.0	84.7	194.7	19,970
43. Yemen Arab Republic	2.5	3.8	6.3	1,130
44. People's Democratic Republic of Yemen	2.5	3.8	6.3	1,130
Total	804.3	1,154.07	1,958.37	194,407

Appendix 4: Projects Approved by Country and by Type of Financing During the First Twelve Years 1396–1407H (1976–1987)

(ID million)

	Projects						
Country	*Loan*	*Equity*[a]	*Leasing*[b]	*Instalment*[c] *sale*	*Profit sharing*	*Technical assistance*	*Total*
Algeria	23.64	—	—	17.43	—	—	41.07
Bahrain	4.44	3.05	15.29	—	—	—	22.78
Bangladesh	33.60	5.25	37.78	—	—	—	76.63
Benin	8.30	—	—	—	—	2.32	10.62
Burkina Faso	9.89	5.42	3.51	—	—	4.04	22.86
Cameroon	19.85	13.76	—	7.30	—	1.38	42.29
Chad	13.85	—	—	—	—	0.24	14.09
Comoros	7.71	—	—	—	—	1.41	9.12
Djibouti	4.90	—	—	—	—	0.65	5.55
Egypt	10.30	5.00	5.00	—	—	—	20.30
Gabon	5.00	—	—	12.70	—	0.25	17.95
Gambia	2.99	—	—	—	—	0.73	3.72
Guinea	23.00	4.07	6.15	—	—	1.24	34.46
Guinea Bissau	—	—	—	—	—	0.46	0.46
Indonesia	15.00	16.84	8.56	3.12	—	—	43.52
Iraq	19.71	—	—	10.87	—	—	30.58
Jordan	19.00	29.38	52.69	27.37	—	0.53	128.97
Lebanon	7.44	—	—	—	—	0.33	7.77
Libya	—	—	26.05	32.72	—	—	58.78
Malaysia	23.64	8.30	12.50	4.47	—	—	48.91
Maldives	3.05	—	5.34	—	—	0.24	8.63
Mali	27.41	2.66	—	—	—	2.87	32.94
Mauritania	27.63	7.67	18.89	—	—	1.84	56.01

Morocco	23.34	36.08	3.53	5.60	3.06	0.23	71.84
Niger	22.90	9.22	—	—	—	4.52	36.64
Oman	14.55	7.01	28.66	19.61	—	0.24	70.06
Pakistan	18.35	25.16	75.83	20.05	—	—	139.39
Palestine	—	—	—	—	—	2.07	2.07
Senegal	25.85	15.33	9.30	—	—	3.11	53.59
Sierra Leone	6.00	—	—	—	—	2.44	8.44
Somalia	13.00	2.00	2.00	—	—	1.39	18.39
Sudan	13.00	6.10	—	—	—	0.29	19.39
Syria	14.65	—	32.00	—	—	—	46.65
Tunisia	33.67	20.61	23.39	10.43	—	—	87.99
Turkey	9.08	25.52	121.63	39.16	—	3.05	198.45
Uganda	8.76	—	6.00	—	—	1.76	16.51
UA Emirates	—	17.52	5.00	—	4.27	—	26.79
Yemen AR	26.51	1.70	19.73	—	—	2.85	50.79
Yemen PDR	17.30	—	—	—	—	0.72	18.03
Total:	557.32	267.66	518.73	210.83	7.33	41.3	1,603.07

— Nil   [a] Includes line of equity.   [b] Includes line of leasing   [c] Commenced in 1405H

Note: (1) Totals may not add due to rounding.
(2) For joint equity/leasing projects, figures are divided on a 50:50 basis.

Index